ARIZONA
Humoresque

ARIZONA
Humoresque
A Century of Arizona Humor

Edited by
C. L. Sonnichsen

PELICAN PUBLISHING COMPANY
Gretna 1992

The word "pelican" and the depiction of a pelican are trademarks of
Pelican Publishing Company, Inc., and are registered in the U.S.
Patent and Trademark Office.

Library of Congress Cataloging-in-Publication Data

Arizona humoresque : a century of Arizona humor / edited
by C. L. Sonnichsen.
    p. cm.
    ISBN 0-88289-869-8. — ISBN 0-88289-900-7 (pbk.)
    1. Humorous stories, American—Arizona. 2. American
wit and humor—Arizona. 3. Arizona—Fiction. 4. Arizona
—Humor. 5. Tales—Arizona. I. Sonnichsen, C. L. (Charles
Leland), 1901–
PS571.A6A7 1992
813'.010832791—dc20
                                       91-29733
                                        CIP

Illustrations by Jim Willoughby

Manufactured in the United States of America

Published by Pelican Publishing Company, Inc.
1101 Monroe Street, Gretna, Louisiana 70053

CONTENTS

IN SEARCH OF THE HO-HO-HO

There can be no doubt that the sense of humor—the ability to laugh at the mistakes and foibles of ourselves and others is one of the most useful and precious gifts the Creator has bestowed on his human children.

Introduction: In Search of the Ho-Ho-Ho

SINCE ARIZONA HAS EVERYTHING but an ocean view, it follows that it must have its share of the nation's humor. One object of this collection is to show that this view is correct. The problem in dealing with the subject is that no two people agree about what humor really is or how it works.

One writer believes that it is rooted in anger—that we disapprove of something in human conduct and react with sarcastic laughter. Back in the seventeenth century, philosopher Thomas Hobbes declared that we laugh because we feel superior. We are amused by other people's mistakes and misfortunes because they are not ours. In our time one thing we seem to agree on is that humor has to be hilarious. If there is no guffaw, there is no humor.

I learned about this in 1988 when an anthology of mine called *The Laughing West* fell into the hands of the reviewers. The headline attached to an evaluation which appeared in *Texas Books in Review* asked: WHERE IS THE HO-HO-HO?

From this experience and a few others like it I learned (a) that reviewers do not always read introductions, and (b) that in the minds of most of us, humor is not humor unless it tickles the ribs. Humorous and funny are the same.

As a matter of fact, much humor is not funny in that sense at all. Sick jokes may produce an embarrassed grin. Black humor and gallows humor do not provoke healthy laughter. And at the opposite end of the scale, the odd behavior of a parent or a child may cause chuckles and smiles, but not a ho-ho-ho.

Besides, people have different ideas about what is amusing. Many a man has told a joke that he thought was irresistible, only to be met with stony silence at the end.

Then too, there is the fact that tastes in humor change. Blackface

11

humor, acceptable in the days of the minstrel show, is no longer tolerable. The "western" dialect of the old cattleman in Alfred Henry Lewis's *Wolfville* (see "The Stinging Lizard" in this volume) was amusing and refreshing in 1897, but readers today, especially young people, find it difficult and boring.

For all these reasons, readers and reviewers are likely to disagree with the anthologist about what ought to go into this book and what ought to be said about it. To come a little closer to an understanding of these matters, it may help to return to the original meaning of the word "humor." Seven or eight centuries ago, everybody knew that the humors were the four body fluids recognized by medieval doctors: blood, yellow bile, black bile, and phlegm. These fluids provided a key to human personality and to human health. If you were full-blooded-sanguine—you were energetic, aggressive, cheerful, hearty—and perhaps a candidate for apoplexy. If your yellow bile was predominant, you were bilious, irritable and hard to live with. Too much black bile made you melancholy; too much phlegm made you phlegmatic. The words retain much of their original significance, but the medical implications were lost long ago.

In Shakespeare's time the basic idea gave rise to a spate of plays with titles like *Every Man in His Humor* and interest in human aberrations and eccentricities remains a stable part of our culture. A fascination with "characters" has been with us at least since Aristotle, but the English have shown a special enjoyment of their oddballs, and the colonists carried this special interest with them to the New World. Examples come readily to hand: Ichabod Crane, Simon Suggs, Davy Crockett, Jim Bridger, Huckleberry Finn, Elmer Gantry—and we might add Pecos Bill and Paul Bunyan.

These special individuals amuse us because they are different. We assume that our ways and our ideas are the right ones, and people who dance to a different tune are laughable. Philosophers have asked for two thousand years why this should be so. We could pity or despise the oddballs, and sometimes we do, but the ability to laugh at them, and at ourselves when *we* are ridiculous, is part of our standard equipment. We laugh because we laugh.

Not all queer ducks are amusing, of course. People who are

dangerous or disgusting are not funny. Benedict Arnold and Jack the Ripper tickled no one.

Unusual individuals may have first claim on the humorist's attention, but ordinary characters in unusual situations are just as interesting to him. Otherwise there would be no situation comedies. Rosemary Taylor's father in *Chicken Every Sunday* was a fairly typical businessman, but when his wife took in too many boarders any semblance of normalcy went out the window.

At his best the humorist is a social critic. As he makes fun of anti-social or irregular conduct, he is telling us how we *ought* to live. Humor is the best weapon we have for putting down hypocrisy, loose living, and double dealing. Political cartoonists—humorists all—are especially good at disclosure and exposure, and they can strip an unwary congressman of the last shred of respectability. Morris Udall, a great political humorist himself, points out in *Too Funny to Be President* that even in political humor "There must be a little love." The humorist, a human being himself, realizes that everybody is vulnerable and he does not cut too deep.

As a social critic, the humorist is likely to have done some serious thinking before he sat down to write. Oliver LaFarge, for example, comments on the deep gulf of misunderstanding between red men and white in "Dangerous Man." Since the white anthropologist pays for his error with his life, the humor of the situation is hardly obvious, but LaFarge finds grim amusement in the situation as the outsider and his Navajo hosts misread each other's minds. Likewise, Byrd Baylor in *Yes Is Better Than No*, comments with more obvious humor on the failure of city-dwelling Papagos and representatives of the Tucson welfare agencies to bridge a similar ethnic gap.

There can be no doubt that the sense of humor, unique to human beings, is one of the most valuable of the gifts the Creator has given his children. It helps us to bear our tribulations. It sweetens our social intercourse. It puts the fear of ridicule into the murky hearts of potential crooks, double dealers, and loose livers. It never stops working to keep society healthy, and it helps us to get at the truth—to assess people and things for what they really are. True, we sometimes make fun of the wrong things, but humanity would be diminished without it. It offers us something much more substantial than a ho-ho-ho.

ARIZONA
Humoresque

WILD TIMES IN THE TERRITORY

A deck of cards can preach a lesson to the worst sinner.

The way to California lay through the torrid deserts of southern Arizona, and outsiders pictured the Territory as a desolate landscape of vast distances, insupportable climate, and mortal peril from poisonous snakes, ferocious Mexican bandits, savage Indians, and blood-hungry desperadoes. It was "The Southwest Corner of Hell." The picture was darkened by the press and the public which loved to shudder at conditions supposed to exist in the Wild, Wild West. It was considered to be so bad that with very little exaggeration it became humorous, in a gruesome sort of way. In its progress toward civilization, the Territory had to overcome this stereotype, along with the other drawbacks.

ARIZONA—THE WAY IT WAS

ARIZONA IS A FINE PLACE to live—with air conditioning—but a century ago it was considered by everyone but the resident Indians and Hispanics as the jumping-off place of the universe. It was not just a matter of climate either. The Apaches lived by raiding and were good at their job. Mexican bandits plied their trade on both sides of the border and white desperadoes drank and fought in the cantinas and saloons, imperiling the lives of peaceful citizens. The distances were enormous; it took weeks and weeks to get to Arizona and weeks and weeks to get out of it. Every traveler reached for superlatives when he tried to describe the place. Mina Oury, who arrived in Tucson when it was still a mud village, called it "the most desolate, God-forsaken place on earth," and J. Ross Brown added in 1864 that Tucson was "literally a paradise of devils." Alfred Henry Lewis, who observed Wolfville/Tombstone in its heyday, noted that time was calculated from "first-drink time in the morning," and the law was in the hands of a vigilante group called "The Stranglers."

As one might expect, a major by-product of this fearsome ambience was humor. It flourished in two areas. On the one hand, by exaggerating just a little, outsiders saw the primitive customs of frontier Arizonans as ridiculous and laughable, though a few shudders were mingled with the amusement. On the other hand, the more-or-less permanent Anglo residents often found themselves in such dire straits that their only recourse was a round of rueful laughter. On both sides the cause of laughter was the same: the perception that something or somebody was so far out of line as to be ridiculous ("ridiculous," it is worth noting, means "laugh producing").

Behind all this is some human history. The word "humor" itself has deep roots, going all the way back to the Middle Ages.

19

Medieval doctors were convinced that human personality and sometimes human health were strongly influenced by the four body fluids: blood, yellow bile, black bile and phlegm—the "humors." We still use the term but "humorous" has changed considerably. We use it interchangeably with other words which mean "funny," but it still refers to human behavior, usually eccentric or peculiar.

A humorist, who specializes in offbeat individuals, is, or can be, a social critic. Like the cartoonist he penetrates disguises, catches wrong-doers in the act, and laughs at them. Since nobody likes to be ridiculous, he may deter some public figures from making bigger fools of themselves.

All nations since the Greeks have been fascinated by these "characters," but the English have been particularly fond of them. Since Chaucer all the great story-tellers have been character-mongers. In the eighteenth century the name for a particularly rugged individualist was "original genius," "original" for short. The English colonists brought their fondness for oddballs to the New World, and they found examples all the way to the Pacific Coast—Simon Suggs, Davy Crockett, Jim Bridger, Cherokee Sal, Mike Fink and Paul Bunyan, to name a few. The western world still enjoys them. They are at home in the early sections of this book.

As the population increased, however, and Tucson and Phoenix became cities, the quality of life and humor changed with the times. The action shifted to places like Mrs. Drachman's boarding house in Tucson. Indian country saw the biggest change of all. From Alfred Henry Lewis's seedy Apaches around Tombstone, the humorist turns to the Zapi reservation where educated tribesmen play golf on the country-club course and have to rent horses and costumes when they need to repel an invasion of white road builders. The humorist's stock in trade, however is the same as always—offbeat human beings in offbeat situations, still good for a chuckle as they have been for the last two thousand years.

THE STINGING LIZARD

Alfred Henry Lewis

ALFRED HENRY LEWIS. Born in Cleveland, came west to Tombstone in the 1880s and never completely recovered. *Wolfville* was a publishing phenomenon in 1897 and was followed by four other volumes in the Wolfville series. The Old Cattleman, the narrator, may have been Uncle Jim Wolf, a ranchman living in the area, but according to saloon keeper Billy King, the real provider of tales was Uncle Billy Plasters, another local cowman. Lewis chose to call his town Wolfville for obvious reasons. Mention of local features like the Bird Cage Theatre and the presence of identifiable local characters offer evidence that Wolfville is Tombstone.

The time is B.C. (Before Civilization). Homicides are frequent and expected, and justice is in the hands of a vigilance Committee ("Jack Moore does the rope work for stranglers"). The hour is identified as "first drink time in the morning, second drink time in the afternoon," and so on. It was the Wild West as people back East visualized it. The view is humorous and the emphasis is on bizarre situations and strange quirks of character. Lewis's comedy has lost some of its savor, but his stories are basic documents for any study of Arizona humor.

"THAR'S no sorter doubt to it," said the Old Cattleman after a long pause devoted to meditation, and finally to the refilling of his cob pipe, "thar ain't the slightest room for cavil but them ceremonies over Jack King, deceased, is the most satisfactory pageant Wolfville ever promotes."

It was at this point I proved my cunning by saying nothing. I

From *Wolfville*, by Alfred Henry Lewis. New York: Frederock A. Stokes. 1907, pp. 9–25.

was pleased to hear the old man talk, and rightly theorized that the better method of invoking his reminiscences just at this time was to say never a word.

"However," he continued, "I don't reckon it's many weeks after we follows Jack to the tomb, when we comes a heap near schedoolin' another funeral, with the general public a-contributin' of the corpse. To be speecific, I refers to a occasion when we-alls comes powerful close to lynchin' Cherokee Hall.

"I don't mind onbosomin' myse'f about it. It's all a misonderstandin'; the same bein' Cherokee's fault complete. We don't know him more'n to merely drink with at that eepock, an' he's that sly an' furtive in his plays, an' covers his trails so speshul, he nacherally breeds sech suspicions that when the stage begins to be stood up reg'lar once a week, an' all onaccountable, Cherokee comes mighty close to culminatin' in a rope. Which goes to show that you can't be too open an' free in your game, an' Cherokee would tell you so himse'f.

"This yere tangle I'm thinkin' of ain't more'n a month after Cherokee takes to residin' in Wolfville. He comes trailin' in one evenin' from Tucson, an' onfolds a layout an' goes to turnin' faro-bank in the Red Light. No one remarks this partic'lar, which said spectacles is frequent. The general idee is that Cherokee's on the squar' an' his game is straight, an' of course public interest don't delve no further into his affairs.

"Cherokee, himse'f, is one of these yere slim, silent people who ain't talkin' much, an' his eye for color is one of them raw grays, like a new bowie.

"It's perhaps the third day when Cherokee begins to struggle into public notice. Thar's a felon whose name is Boone, but who calls himse'f the 'Stingin' Lizard,' an' who's been pesterin' 'round Wolfville, mebby, it's a month. This yere Stingin' Lizard is thar when Cherokee comes into camp; an' it looks like the Stingin' Lizard takes a notion ag'in Cherokee from the jump.

"Not that this yere Lizard is likely to control public feelin' in the matter; none whatever. He's some onpop'lar himse'f. He's too toomultuous for one thing, an' he has a habit of molestin' towerists an' folks he don't know at all, which palls on disinterested people who has dooties to perform. About once a week this Lizard man goes an' gets the treemers, an' then the camp has to set up with him till his visions subsides. Fact is, he's what you-alls East calls 'a disturbin' element,' an' we makes ready to hang him once or twice, but somethin' comes up an' puts it off, an' we sorter neglects it.

"But as I says, he takes a notion ag'in Cherokee. It's the third night after Cherokee gets in, an' he's ca'mly behind his box at the Red Light, when in peramb'lates this Lizard. Seems like Cherokee, bein' one of them quiet wolves, fools up the Lizard a lot. This Lizard's been hostile an' blood-hungry all day, an' I reckons he all at once recalls Cherokee; an', deemin' of him easy, he allows he'll go an' chew his mane some for relaxation.

"If I was low an' ornery like this Lizard, I ain't none shore but I'd be fooled them days on Cherokee myse'f. He's been fretful about his whiskey, Cherokee has,—puttin' it up she don't taste right, which not onlikely it don't; but beyond pickin' flaws in his nose-paint thar ain't much to take hold on about him. He's so slim an' noiseless besides, thar ain't none of us but figgers this yere Stingin' Lizard's due to stampede him if he tries; which makes what follows all the more impressive.

"So the Lizard projects along into the Red Light, whoopin' an' carryin' on by himse'f. Straightway he goes up ag'inst Cherokee's layout.

"'I don't buy no chips,' says the Lizard to Cherokee, as he gets in opposite. 'I puts money in play; an' when I wins I wants money sim'lar. Thar's fifty dollars on the king coppered; an' fifty dollars on the eight open. Turn your kyards, an' turn 'em squar'. If you don't, I'll peel the ha'r an' hide plumb off the top of your head.'

"Cherokee looks at the Lizard sorter soopercillus an' indifferent; but he don't say nothin'. He goes on with the deal, an', the kyards comin' that a-way, he takes in the Lizard's two bets.

"Durin' the next deal the Lizard ain't sayin' much direct, but keeps cussin' an' wranglin' to himse'f. But he's gettin' his money up all the time; an' with the fifty dollars he lose on the turn, he's shy mebby four hundred an' fifty at the close.

"'Bein' in the hole about five hundred dollars,' says the Lizard, in a manner which is a heap onrespectful, 'an' so that a wayfarin' gent may not be misled to rooin utter, I now rises to ask what for a limit do you put on this deadfall anyhow?'

"'The bridle's plumb off to you, *amigo*,' says Cherokee, an' his tones is some hard. I notices it all right enough, 'cause I'm doin' business at the table myse'f at the time, an' keepin' likewise case on the game. 'The bridle's plumb off for you,' says Cherokee, 'so any notion you entertains in favor of bankruptin' of yourse'f quick may riot right along.'

" 'You're dead shore of that?' says the Lizard with a sneer. 'Now I reckons a thousand-dollar bet would scare this puerile game you deals a-screechin' up a tree or into a hole, too easy.'

" 'I never likes to see no gent strugglin' in the coils of error,' says Cherokee, with a sneer a size larger than the Lizard's; 'I don't know what wads of wealth them pore old clothes of yours conceals, but jest the same I tells you what I'll do. Climb right onto the layout, body, soul, an' roll, an' put a figger on your worthless se'f, an' I'll turn you for the whole shootin'-match. You're in yere to make things interestin', I sees that, an' I'll voylate my business principles an' take a night off to entertain you.' An' yere Cherokee lugs out a roll of bills big enough to choke a cow.

" 'I goes you if I lose,' says the Stingin' Lizard. Then assoomin' a sooperior air, he remarks: 'Mebby it's a drink back on the trail when I has misgivin's as to the rectitood of this yere brace you're dealin'. Bein' public-sperited that a-way, in my first frenzy I allows I'll take my gun an' abate it a whole lot. But a ca'mer mood comes on, an' I decides, as not bein' so likely to disturb a peace-lovin' camp, I removes this trap for the onwary by merely bustin' the bank. Thar,' goes on the Stingin' Lizard, at the same time dumpin' a large wad on the layout, 'thar's even four thousand dollars. Roll your game for that jest as it lays.'

" 'Straighten up your dust,' says Cherokee, his eyes gettin' a kind of gleam into 'em, 'straighten up your stuff an' get it some'ers. Don't leave it all spraddled over the scene. I turns for it ready enough, but we ain't goin' to argue none as to where it lays after the kyard falls.

"The rest of us who's been buckin' the game moderate an' right cashes in at this, an' leaves an onobstructed cloth to the Stingin' Lizard. This yere's more caution than good nacher. As long as folks is bettin' along in limits, say onder fifty dollars, thar ain't no shootin' likely to ensoo. But whenever a game gets immoderate that a-way, an' the limit's off, an' things is goin' that locoed they begins to play a thousand an' over on a kyard an' scream for action, gents of experience stand ready to go to duckin' lead an' dodgin' bullets instanter.

"But to resoome: The Stingin' Lizard lines up his stuff, an' the deal begins. It ain't thirty seconds till the bank wins, an' the Stingin' Lizard is the wrong side of the layout from his money. He takes it onusual ugly, only he ain't sayin' much. He sa'nters over to the bar, an' gets a big drink. Cherokee is rifflin' the deck, but I notes he's got his gray eye on the Stingin' Lizard, an' my respect for him increases rapid. I sees he ain't goin' to get the worst of no deal, an' is organized to protect his game plumb through if this Lizard makes a break.

" 'Do you-all know where I hails from?' asks the Stingin' Lizard, comin' back to Cherokee after he's done hid his drink.

" 'Which I shorely don't,' says Cherokee. 'I has from time to time much worthless information thrust upon me, but so far I escapes all news of you complete.'

" 'Where I comes from, which is Texas,' says the Lizard, ignorin' of Cherokee's manner, the same bein' some insultin', 'they teaches the babies two things, —never eat your own beef, an' never let no kyard-thief down you."

" 'Which is highly thrillin',' says Cherokee, 'as reminiscences of your youth, but where does you-all get action on 'em in Arizona?'

" 'Where I gets action won't be no question long,' says the Lizard, mighty truculent. 'I now announces that this yere game is a skin an' a brace. Tharfore I returns for my money; an', to be frank, I returns a-shootin'.'

"It's at this p'int we-alls who represents the public kicks back our chairs an' stampedes outen range. As the Lizard makes his bluff his hand goes to his artillery like a flash.

"The Lizard's some quick, but Cherokee's too soon for him. With the first move of the Lizard's hand, he searches out a bowie from som'ers back of his neck. I'm some employed placin' myse'f at the time, an' don't decern it none till Cherokee brings it over his shoulder like a stream of white light.

"It's shore great knife-work. Cherokee gives the Lizard aige an p'int, an' all in one motion. Before the Lizard more'n lifts his weapon, Cherokee half slashes his gun-hand off at the wrist; an' then, jest as the Lizard begins to wonder at it, he gets the nine-inch blade plumb through his neck. He's let out right thar.

" 'It looks like I has more of this thing to do,' says Cherokee, an' his tone shows he's half-way mournin' over it, 'than any sport in the Territory. I tries to keep outen this, but that Lizard gent would have it."

"After the killin', Enright an' Doc Peets, with Boggs, Tutt, an' Jack Moore, sorter talks it over quiet, an' allows it's all right.

"'This Stingin' Lizard gent,' says Enright, 'has been projectin' 'round lustin' for trouble now, mebby it's six weeks. It's amazin' to me he lasts as long as he does, an' it speaks volumes for the forbearin', law-abidin' temper of the Wolfville public. This Lizard's a mighty oppressive person, an' a heap obnoxious; an' while I don't like a knife none myse'f as a trail out, an' inclines to distrust a gent who does, I s'pose it's after all a heap a matter of taste an' the way your folks brings you up. I leans to the view, gents, that this yere corpse is constructed on the squar'. What do you-all think, Peets?'

"'I entertains idees sim'lar,' says Doc Peets. 'Of course I takes it this kyard-sharp, Cherokee, aims to bury his dead. He nacherally ain't lookin' for the camp to go 'round cleanin' up after him none.'

"That's about how it stands. Nobody finds fault with Cherokee, an' as he ups and' plants the Stingin' Lizard's remainder the next day, makin' the deal with a stained box, crape, an' the full regalia, it all leaves the camp with a mighty decent impression. By first-drink time in the evenin' of the second day, we ain't thinkin' no more about it.

"Now you-all begins to marvel where do we get to the hangin' of Cherokee Hall? We're workin' in towards it now.

"You sees, followin' the Stingin' Lizard's jump into the misty beyond—which it's that sudden I offers two to one them angels notes a look of s'prise on the Stingin' Lizard's face as to how he comes to make the trip—Cherokee goes on dealin' faro same as usual. As I says before, he ain't no talker, nohow; now he says less than ever.

"But what strikes us as onusual is, he saddles up a *pinto* pony he's got over to the corral, an' jumps off every now an' then for two an' three days at a clatter. No one knows where he p'ints to, more'n he says he's due over in Tucson. These yere vacations of Cherokee's is all in the month after the Stingin' Lizard gets downed.

"It's about this time, too, the stage gets held up sech a scand'lous number of times it gives people a tired feelin'. All by one party, too. He merely prances out in onexpected places with a Winchester; stands up the stage in an onconcerned way, an' then goes through everythin' an' everybody, from mail-bags to passengers, like the grace of heaven through a camp-meetin'. Nacheral, it all creates a heap of disgust.

"'If this yere industrious hold-up keeps up his lick,' says Texas Thompson about the third time the stage gets rustled, 'an' heads off a few more letters of mine, all I has to say is my wife back in Laredo ain't goin' to onderstand it none. She ain't lottin' much on me nohow, an' if the correspondence between us gets much more fitful, she's goin' p'intin' out for a divorce. This deal's liable to turn a split for me in my domestic affairs.'

"An' that's the way we-alls feels. This stage agent is shorely in disrepoot some in Wolfville. If he'd been shakin' up Red Dog's letter-bags, we wouldn't have minded so much.

"I never does know who's the first to think of Cherokee Hall, but all at once it's all over camp. Talkin' it over, it's noticed mighty soon that, come right to cases, no one knows his record, where he's been or why he's yere. Then his stampedin' out of camp like he's been doin' for a month is too many for us.

"'I puts no trust in them Tucson lies he tells, neither,' says Doc Peets. 'Whatever would he be shakin' up over in Tucson? His game's yere, an' this theery that he's got to go scatterin' over thar once a week is some gauzy.'

"'That's whatever,' says Dan Bogs, who allers trails in after Doc Peets, an' plays the same system emphatic. An' I says myse'f, not findin' no fault with Boggs tharfor, that this yere Peets is the finest-eddicated an' levelest-headed sharp in Arizona.

"'Well,' says Jack Moore, who as I says before does the rope work for the Stranglers, 'if you-alls gets it settled that this faro gent's turnin' them tricks with the stage an' mail-bags, the sooner he's swingin' to the windmill, the sooner we hears from our loved ones at home. What do you say, Enright?'

"'Why,' says Enright, all thoughtful, 'I reckons it's a case. S'pose you caper over where he feeds at the O.K. House an' bring him to us. The signs an' signal-smokes shorely p'ints to this yere Chero-kee as our meat; but these things has to be done in order. Bring him in, Jack, an', to save another trip, s'pose you bring a lariat from the corral at the same time.'

"It don't take Moore no time to throw a gun on Cherokee where he's consoomin' flapjacks at the O.K. House, an' tell him the committee needs him at the New York Store. Cherokee don't buck none, but comes along, passive as a tabby cat.

"'Whatever's the hock kyard to all this?' he says to Jack Moore. 'Is it this Stingin' Lizard play a month ago?'

"'No,' says Moore, "t'ain't quite sech ancient hist'ry. It's stage coaches. Thar's a passel of people down yere as allows you've been rustlin' the mails.'

"Old Man Rucker, who keeps the O.K. House, is away when Moore rounds up his party. But Missis Rucker's thar, an' the way that old lady talks to Enright an' the committee is a shame. She comes over to the store, too, along of Moore an' Cherokee, an' prances in an' comes mighty near stampedin' the whole outfit.

"'See yere, Sam Enright,' she shouts, wipin' her hands on her bib, 'what be you-alls aimin' for to do? Linin' up, I s'pose, to hang the only decent man in town?'

"'Ma'am,' says Enright, 'this yere sharp is 'cused of standin' up the stage them times recent over by Tucson. Do you know anythin' about it?'

"'No; I don't,' says Missis Rucker. 'You don't reckon, now, I did it none, do you? I says this, though; it's a heap sight more likely some drunkard a-settin' right yere on this committee stops them stages than Cherokee Hall.'

"'Woman's nacher's that emotional,' says Enright to the rest of us, 'she's oncapable of doin' right. While she's the loveliest of created things, still sech is the infirmities of her intellects, that gov'ment would bog down in its most important functions, if left to woman.'

"'Bog down or not,' says Missis Rucker, gettin' red an' heated, 'you fools settin' up thar like a band of prairie-dogs don't hang this yere Cherokee Hall. 'Nother thing, you ain't goin' to hang nobody to the windmill ag'in nohow. I has my work to do, an' thar's enough on my hands, feedin' sech swine as you-alls three times a day, without havin' to cut down dead folks outen my way every time I goes for a bucket of water. You-alls takes notice now;

you don't hang nothin' to the windmill no more. As for this yere Cherokee, he ain't stopped no more stages than I be.'

" 'But you sees yourse'f, ma'am, you hasn't the slightest evidence tharof,' says Enright, tryin' to soothe her down.

" 'I has, however, what's a mighty sight better than evidence,' says Missis Rucker, 'an' that's my firm convictions.'

" 'Well, see yere,' says Cherokee, who's been listenin' all peaceful, 'let me in on this. What be you-alls doin' this on? I reckons I'm entitled to a look at your hand for my money.'

"Enright goes on an' lays it off for Cherokee; how he's outen camp every time the stage is robbed, an' the idee is abroad he does it.

" 'As the kyards lay in the box,' says Cherokee, 'I don't reckon thar's much doubt but you-alls will wind up the deal by hangin' me?'

" 'It's shorely five to one that a-way,' says Enright. 'Although I'm bound to say it ain't none decisive as yet.'

" 'The trooth is,' says Cherokee, sorter thoughtful, 'I wasn't aimin' to be hung none this autumn. I ain't got time, gents, for one thing, an' has arranged a heap diff'rent. In the next place, I never stands up no stage.'

" 'That's what they all says,' puts in Boggs, who's a mighty impatient man. 'I shorely notes no reason why we-alls can't proceed with this yere lynchin' at once. S'pose this Cherokee ain't stood up no stage; he's done plenty of other things as merits death. It strikes me thar's a sight of onnecessary talk yere.'

" 'If you ain't out workin' the road,' says Doc Peets to Cherokee, no heedin' of Boggs petulance, 'them stage-robbin' times, s'pose you onfolds where you was at?'

"Well, son, not to string this yere story out longer'n three drinks, yere is how it is: This Cherokee it looks like is soft-hearted that a-way,—what you calls romantic. An' it seems likewise that shovin' the Stingin' Lizard from shore that time sorter takes advantage an' feeds on him. So he goes browsin' 'round the postmaster all casooal, an' puts questions. Cherokee gets a p'inter about some yearlin' or other in Tucson this Stingin' Lizard sends money to an' makes good for, which he finds the same fact on caperin' over. It's a nephy or some sech play. An' the Stingin'

Lizard has the young one staked out over thar, an' is puttin' up for his raiment an' grub all reg'lar enough.

"'Which I yereafter backs this infant's play myse'f,' says Cherokee to the barkeep of the Oriental Saloon over in Tucson, which is the party the Stingin' Lizard pastures the young one on. 'You're all right, Bill,' goes on this Cherokee to the barkeep, 'but now I goes back of the box for this infant boy, I reckons I'll saw him off onto a preacher, or some sharp sim'lar, where he gets a Christian example. Whatever do you think?'

"The barkeep says himse'f he allows it's the play to make. So he an' Cherokee goes surgin' 'round, an' at last they camps the boy—who's seven years comin' grass—on the only pulpit-sharp in Tucson. This gospel-spreader says he'll feed an' bed down the boy for some sum; which was shore a giant one, but the figgers I now forgets.

"Cherokee gives him a stack of blues to start his game, an' is now pesterin' 'round in a co't tryin' to get the young one counter-branded from the Stingin' Lizard's outfit into his, an' given the name of Cherokee Hall. That's what takes him over to Tucson them times, an' not stage-robbin'.

"Two days later, in fact, to make shore all doubts is over, Cherokee even rings in said divine on us; which the divine tells the same story. I don't reckon now he's much of a preacher neither; for he gives Wolfville one whirl for luck over in the warehouse back of the New York Store, an' I shore hears 'em as makes a mighty sight more noise, an' bangs the Bible twice as hard, back in the States. I says so to Cherokee; but he puts it up he don't bank none on his preachin'.

"'What I aims at,' says Cherokee, 'is some one who rides herd on the boy all right, an' don't let him stampede off none into vicious ways.'

"'Why don't you keep the camp informed of this yere orphan an' the play you makes?' says Enright, at the time it's explained to the committee,—the time they trees Cherokee about them stages.

"'It's that benev'lent an' mushy,' says Cherokee, 'I'm plumb ashamed of the deal, an' don't allow to go postin' no notices tharof. But along comes this yere hold-up business, an', all inadvertent, tips my hand; which the same I stands, however, jest the same.'

"'It's all right,' says Enright, some disgusted though; 'but the next time you makes them foundlin' asylum trips, don't walk in the water so much. Leave your trail so Wolfville sees it, an' then folks ain't so likely to jump your camp in the dark an' take to shootin' you up for Injuns an' sim'lar hostiles.'

" 'But one thing more,' continues Enright, 'an' then we orders the drinks. Jack Moore is yereby instructed to present the compliments of the committee to Rucker, when he trails in from Tucson; which he also notifies him to hobble his wife yereafter durin' sessions of this body. She's not to go draggin' her lariat 'round loose no more, settin' law an' order at defiance durin' sech hours as is given to business by the Stranglers.' "

SURVIVAL AT CALABAZAS

James Cabell Brown

INFORMATION ABOUT JAMES CABELL BROWN is scarce. George Chambers, who republished *Calabazas* in 1961, found that he was a native Californian with friends and business connections in San Francisco, where his book was published. He came to Calabazas in the Santa Cruz Valley north of Nogales on business of some sort, possibly connected with the land speculation that was going on in anticipation of the arrival of a railroad from Tucson to Nogales. The story is "admittedly fiction," says Chambers, but the village is obviously painted from life, with Col. C. F. Sykes's ramshackle hotel in the middle, and "none of the chapters are exaggerations of the time and place." Brown gets a good deal of amusement out of a rowdy and unhurried way of life.

If a person seeking valuable and interesting information will take a map and pass his finger down the center of Arizona until at a point where the boundary line dividing the United States from Mexico diverges from an east and west direction, to one running northwesterly until it meets the Colorado River, he will see near the diverging point a dot marked, Calabazas [English gourds or squashes.] This dot is the location, and Calabazas is the name of the town; a town with a short history, it is true; a history not widely known, but none the less interesting and eventful. By seeking further he will see that it lies at the junction of two railroads—on the map—that it is on the banks of the Santa Cruz River, and the astonishing additional fact, that the said river has neither source nor outlet.

From *Calabazas*, San Francisco: San Francisco News Company, 1891. Reprinted by Arizona Silhouettes, George W. Chambers, ed. Tucson, 1961, pp. 13–19, 23–28, 35–37.

Calabazas is, what is left of it, near the head of the Santa Cruz Valley. At this point the river carried no water excepting after heavy storms. It was just as well, for the Calabazans, present or prospective, never bathed, and, without exception, were total abstainers—from water.

The valley at Calabazas was about a quarter of a mile wide. Opposite the town site a small valley, or canon debouched, down whose rocky bottom a railroad was being built. To the southwest were seen the mountains forming the boundary between Mexico and the United States, between which and the town laid extensive "mesas," or elevated table-lands, that ended in low bluffs overlooking the dry river bed. Half a mile south of the town a small ridge jutted out from the mesas, almost entirely closing the valley. At the point of this ridge was a dense, green patch of small Cotton-wood trees. Thence to the boundary line ten miles distant, called, through this region, "The Line," are a series of low hills and small valleys.

The land upon which Calabazas stood was the property of the Calabazas Land and Mining Company, the town being a newly born child of the same Company. The C. L. & M. Company claimed all the earth from the Mexican boundary to as far north, east, and west as they conveniently or safely could. Unless some one found a mine or spring, there was none to dispute their title, for the land was valueless except in proximity to water. A railroad was projected to run from Tucson down the valley. It is still projected.

Calabazas had for neighbors, Tubac, an ancient aboriginal and Mexican village of not more than thirty people, about twenty miles north, with whom it had a feud, and Nogales, situated just over the line, consisting of a highly esteemed mescal distillery, and the Mexican Custom House buildings.

I hope it will not be assumed that Calabazas was an aggregation of iron and stone warehouses filled with luxuries for its inhabitants, or that the hum of its crowded streets was to be heard for miles away, or that the residence streets were lined with shade trees, or that the mansions of the aristocracy were embowered in tropical flowers, or that its society was divided into 'four hundreds.' Such would be doomed to poignant disappointment.

Calabazas City, as I found it, consisted of the foundation of a prospective hotel which was known sarcastically, as the "Hotel Futurity." A small frame building used as a country store and post office, with that wonderful assortment of cheap and varied wares never seen but in country stores, and a small brick house of two stories, one room to each story, the lower floor of which was used as a saloon, the upper one as the United States Custom House, and residence of the collector of the port and his staff of assistants, all comprised in the person of one—Drinkwater—an inspector reporting to the El Paso collector. Attached to this building was a brick "corral" [cattle pen,] having a large gate in front, and also an entrance from the saloon. This corral was used as a stable, a place in which to secure stock during Indian raids, and a fort from which to repulse the raiders.

The saloon room had a door and window in one of the longer sides facing the road. It was furnished with a dilapidated cook stove, a pine counter, eight or ten poisonous looking bottles, a few various sized, dirty glasses, a tin quart measure for water, several boxes for seats, and a barkeeper with unkempt hair, stubby beard, and a piratical breath. He was shod with dusty, cowhide boots, into the legs of which were stuffed the bottoms of a pair of faded overalls. He wore a dirty blue flannel shirt, open at the throat, exposing an equally dirty skin underneath. His head was covered with an old rust colored felt hat, the brim of which was tilted up behind and pulled down in front, a very fashionable and taking style of wearing the hat in such towns, being a sign occipital that the wearer is not stuck up, and has all the chivalry necessary for shooting any enemy he gets the "drop on." A couple of revolvers hung at his waist. The saloon was isolated from the room above by exposed floor joists overlaid with a shrunken, unmatched pine floor.

The upper room, from which the building took the name of Custom House, was approached by a set of rickety outside stairs, that ended at a landing and door directly over the saloon door. A window in the wall at each gable end admitted light.

The room was in keeping with our republican simplicity. In its center stood a pine table containing one drawer. Upon the table was a dusty ink bottle, two or three rusty pens, a pack of dirty playing cards, a few soiled blank forms, a "Mescal" [Mexican whisky] bottle and a goblet, which, having no foot, was reversed, showing that the user was a person well informed as to the social usage in high-toned clubs on festive occasions. A couple of rough boards, supported by hay rope, hung from the ceiling joists. These shelves held the library, blanks and records. A number of boxes, used as chairs, stood around the room. A disreputable looking oak chair, with a bottom made from one-half of a barrel head, was the official throne. The official couch, consisting of a very mangy moss mattress and a blanket seedy enough to plant, were rolled together and stood in one corner.

Hanging on the wall was a large map of Calabazas. Upon it was depicted a flourishing city. Great hotels towered up from the business thoroughfares—in black letters. Church steeples pierced the air in—blue letters. Handsome private residences graced the streets—in yellow letters. Palatial public edifices, and monuments, surrounded by parks, occupied squares—in red letters. Splendid avenues—in green letters, and double rows of black lines indicated street railways—in shaded letters.

On the map, Calabazas was many square miles in area, with presumably a large population; whereas the sole street was the stage road from Tucson to Hermosillo, Mexico, and five living souls comprised the entire white population,—Drinkwater, the saloon keeper, the store keeper, Crandall, the land agent, and myself.

In the suburbs (?) a quarter of a mile away, lived a few Chinese who had been making brick. Their time was now devoted to gambling and cutting railroad ties or cord wood in the adjoining scantily wooded gulches.

Near the town were scattered a few blasted Cottonwood trees, leafless and whitened by storm. These answered the purpose of telegraph poles in sudden emergencies, which were not infrequent later. Shallow wells supplied the little water needed for animals.

Calabazas bade fair to remain as it was, for it could never possibly live up to that gorgeous map. As a health resort, it would hardly be selected, though no one had ever died there, its citizens were too lazy to draw their last breath. It was a good place in which to take a Turkish bath, for the sun beat down with an intensity unequalled elsewhere; but to perspire in Calabazas was a shocking waste of whisky. Invalids requiring a low diet might have

come, if they could have survived the trip—they certainly would
have found the diet low enough. It might have been utilized as a
burial place for the millionaire dead. In its climate and alkaline
soil the bodies would have been incorruptible, and an incorruptible millionaire, dead or alive, would be worth a pilgrimage to see.

My arrival, as a permanency, was viewed with much suspicion,
until a few days intercourse convinced the older residents that I
was not a detective, revenue officer, or a special agent. For a small
monthly stipend paid Drinkwater, I was permitted to call the
southeast corner of the Custom House room my bedchamber, and
there roll up in my blankets; the pack of cards, the table desk and
the goblet were at my command. I could quench my eccentric
thirst at the saloon "olla" [pronounced oya] a porous and cooling
unglazed jar used for holding drinking water, or was welcome to
draw all the water I chose from the well. Occasionally my own
soap and towel were at my service; I could import mescal from the
Line, duty free, if I divided equally with Drinkwater, and could
borrow my shaving tools when not in use by my townsmen. I
could make coffee or tea on the bar-room stove, if enough was
made for all hands, and in fact, I was taken to their hearts as one
of themselves. The tri-weekly stage, which was a "buck-board," [an
Arizona instrument of torture,] brought the mail and stray travelers.

The Calabazas gamblers and saloon men were characteristic
ones of the far West. They would express unbounded affection
for each other one moment, and the very next, in a quarrel over
some trivial matter, use one another for targets. Of course the
survivor would pay all of the funeral expenses with no niggardly
hand, and, if possible, employ a brass band to express, with
trombone and bass drum, the intensity of his grief over his dead
friend. At the funeral he would be chief mourner—out on bonds,
or in charge of a deputy sheriff—and would bemoan the fate that
Jack or Bill had brought upon himself by being "too fresh" to
reach for, or too slow in drawing his gun from the hip. On one
occasion a "Sport," at the risk of his life, saved that of his chum or
"Pard." In talking of the occurrence, the saved friend, uneducated
save in cards and shooting, said, in blood-curdling language, "I
haven't never saw anything as nervy as Bill's throwing up Bob's
pistol hand." Bill was an educated man, and his ears had audibly

cracked at this exhibition of his "Pard's" grammar. He, in a friendly way corrected him. This was taken as offensive. To mollify him Bill tried the universal panacea of asking the crowd up to drink, and all accepted but his chum. Bill then asked why he did not drink, make friends or fight. The offended man without a word, gently slapped Bill's face with his finger tips, and both reached for their weapons. As quick as thought two shots were fired, and the ungrammatical man lay dead, while his former friend laid by his side mortally wounded. To be grammatical, in Calabazas, was to covet death.

They had no mercy on the enemy on whom they fortunately had the "drop," and feared no one but the enemy who unfortunately had the "drop" on them. This "drop" being the unpleasant predicament one was in who, unarmed or unready to shoot during a quarrel, was consequently forced to view the bullets cuddled up in the chambers of his enemy's revolver, well knowing that if the finger on the trigger should be crooked, fatal results would ensure. It was customary for the gentleman having the "drop" to give as a preliminary to the final act, a very farcical rendition, to outsiders, of the intensity of his feelings toward his helpless enemy. For any one to have had the "drop" on them was the cause of many wakeful nights, and the drinking of many cocktails, until the "drop" was returned with interest.

They detested nothing so much as deception. Should a man call for a drink and have no money with which to pay, it would insure him a bullet or broken head; yet, if he said was "broke" and wanted a "bracer" none of the better class would refuse him. They would have felt disgraced in their own estimation did they do so. "Any man was liable to be broke, but let him say so, like a man."

By some strange anomaly these people could not, unmoved, see human suffering, unless they were angry—always a fierce uncontrolled anger—nor could they hear of suffering without pecuniarily trying to relieve it. They were a strange compound of whims and fancies, and, under their varying impulses, were capable of the most generous and brave, or the meanest and most cowardly acts. A church—that they would sooner drink water than enter—would be amply subscribed for, irrespective of creed; and public improvements or holiday celebrations were generously contributed to.

In New Mexico and Arizona, strange to say, the most deadly ruffians were seldom over twenty-five years of age; very many not over eighteen or twenty. One that was scarcely twelve years old had quite a reputation, and was responsible for the conduct of two extra heavy revolvers, and a bowie-knife large enough for a hay scythe. Each of these desperadoes had his pistol handle notched for the men actually, or presumably killed by its owner. Their instincts were cowardly, and their delight was to abuse women or impose on civil, quiet persons. Upon the fears of such they played, until successful bluffing and continual practice with their recklessly handled weapons, gave them the necessary courage to clinch their record by assassinating some defenceless person, when assured of escape.

The generic name for these youths of evil fame, throughout the Territories was "Kid." As Calabazas increased in population, they became nearly as common as the almost equally annoying Calabazas fly. A new comer, to whom the honors were shown, would, at a cost for refreshments of from twenty-five cents to one dollar an acquaintance, be introduced to "New Mexican Kids," "Wyoming Kids," "Arizona Kids," "Colorado Kids," "Texas Kids," and such a variety of other kids, that he would be so bewildered between the effects of vile whisky and the Kid introductions, as to come to the conclusion that in Calabazas he had struck a human goat ranche.

The genus "kid" wore his hair long, and in curls upon his shoulder in cow-boy or scout fashion; had an incipient moustache, and sported a costume made of buckskin ornamented with fringe, tassels, and strings of the same material—the dirtier the better. His head was covered with a cow-boy's hat of phenomenal width of brim, having many metal stars, half moons, etc., around the crown. Upon his feet he wore either moccasins or very high heeled, stub toed boots, and an enormous pair of spurs, with little steel balls that jingled at each step. Buckled around his waist would be a cartridge belt holding two carefully sighted revolvers, and a bone handled bowie-knife in his boot leg, completed his dress. He was invariably the proud owner of a "cayuse" horse and Mexican saddle, a bridle with reins of plaited hair, and a "riata" [lariat] tied behind the saddle. The "cayuse" was never far from his master, for when that gentleman wanted a horse he wanted him badly; either to escape from a worse man than himself, or to escape the consequences of having killed one.

The arrival of the stage coach was a deliriously joyful event, for all of the new comers had to be carefully questioned and their reasons for coming summed up. The motive for his visit being shown, if one would attend to his own business, dissipate a little so as not to appear mean, and accept their rough jokes or horse play in a proper and *safe* spirit, he would not only get along, but would make some friends who would stand by him should the fact of his being quiet or not carrying a weapon, be taken advantage of by some "rustler" or "bluffer," to make a bad man's record by picking a quarrel with him.

At first, Calabazas was so quiet that Drinkwater's sprees were a relief, and his presence welcome. After the papers had been read, cards assisted in killing time. Each evening we indulged in games of poker (in which the stakes ran up to several thousands of dollars, represented by matches), until compelled, for comfort's sake, to extinguish the gnat-attracting lamp. Then, till the cool of morning, the sound of muttered oaths and spasmodic, ineffectual slaps would be wafted on the suffocating night air, as we battled with the bloodthirsty, voracious gnats that made night sleepless.

Very often, while having a game of cards in the Custom House, we would hear the gentle song of the Winchester bullet as it came in at one window and went out the other, some gentleman of humorous turn having fired at the lamp chimney for the purpose of "joshing" Drinkwater and myself. Quite often the report of the rifle was followed by the sound of shattering glass and a stygian darkness in the room. This, when an expert was at the other end of the rifle. Using the lamp for a target became so common that we found it dangerous to have a light, unless we moved the table into one of the corners where the bullet would have to pierce a brick wall before it could do any damage. Sometimes, when a particularly active game of cards was progressing in the saloon below, a dispute would arise as to the ownership of the "pot." Should the excitement become intense, bullets would presently come meandering up through the Custom House floor, very much to the disturbance of our peace of mind.

The bloods of the town would, toward morning, when business was slack, make social calls at each others saloons. Parties of these would drift into our saloon, and, occasionally, to show their good fellowship or high esteem, they would hail and desire me to come down and join them. Should the hail not be immediately answered, a few bullets would be jocularly sent crashing through the upper floor to expedite matters. Matters would invariably be expedited. With a series of appalling yells hurtling from my throat, I would hasten to the saloon, half dressed, pale and trembling, to be pulled to the bar by their friendly hands, while they cracked jokes concerning the mailing of an invitation from a revolver, and of how much quicker than the telegraph it brought an answer, with much more badinage to the same effect. That they were informed by Drinky as to the corner in which my bed was made, and fired into opposite corners, accounts for my having sustained no injuries other than to my nerves. These hospitalities could not be avoided. To sleep on the ground or from under cover, insured catching the prevalent ague, and a tent would have afforded no more privacy, nor as much protection from vagrant bullets. The Calabazans dearly loved the sound of pistol shots, and when not firing volleys into each other, were filling the air with random bullets.

Along the river bottom were hurdy-houses, an institution that is indigenous to the mining, railroad, or frontier town, and that merits a word of description. A large tent, supported by a framework of scantlings, is the ball room; around the sides are benches for onlookers and patrons, two or three hanging lamps dimly illuminating the interior. At the rear end is a counter and bar with shelves, and a mirror in a gilt frame. Upon this bar the owner makes his most enticing display of bottles, glass ware, and artificial flowers. A sawed off shot gun or a revolver occupies a special shelf under the counter, within easy reach of the bar-tender, but no one else. In a corner of the tent a much travelled, superannuated piano is placed diagonally; and behind the piano is a small platform upon which are chairs for the violin and banjo players, whom the pianist accompanies. In front of the piano is placed a row of chairs for the girls.

The musicians wear a fatigued air as befits the *creme de la creme* of hurdy society. It is an honor to have them accept a drink at your expense; and a friendly nod from one raises you to the same notch in your fellow's estimate as a free pass to a theater would in older communities. At eight o'clock P.M the house fills with roughly-clad, rude-mannered, foul-mouthed men. The musicians take their places and the fiddler calls out, "take your partners for a dance." With less bustle than in a city ballroom the dancers are in place, the floor manager, generally the proprietor assisted by a six shooter, winds his way among them to see that all is ready; to eliminate dead beats, and customers whose dance and bar bills are already large enough; or some fellow too attentive, and who may wed one of the girls, thus putting the hurdy-man to great expense in replacing her. A signal is given, the music strikes up, a rattling reel, a quadrille, or a well played waltz, and the rough shoes of the dancers beat the floor resoundingly.

At the end of the allotted fifteen minutes the music ends with a suddenness that stumbles. Each man takes his partner to the bar for refreshment. The men are handed any liquor they order. The girl's orders, varying from champagne to beer, are filled from one magical bottle containing innocuous, whisky looking, clarified and sugared coffee; for the reason that the women must be kept sober. A drunken woman cannot dance satisfactorily, and, as an irate hurdy-man was heard to remark, "A hurdy-girl with a gag, raises more ＿＿ than a rattle-weeded Texas steer."

There was a refreshing candor and freedom from constraint in the intercourse between the Calabazans. To refuse a drink was a shocking insult to the entertainer, for the water being bad, it was something to be avoided at all hazards. It was not in good form to pronounce the surname, if you knew it, of one whom you were addressing. Ignorance of this social custom sometimes brought new comers to grief. Many a quiet keen eyed stranger came to the town; men whose ears cocked sharply at the hearing of a proper name. Therefore, from the highest stratum to the lowest level of Calabazas society, none seemed gifted with a surname. It was Lizzie, Mollie, Sallie, or George, Pete, and Bob. As there might be two or more bearing these names, identity was made sure by a prefix, suggestive of some personal peculiarity, as Handsome George, Curly Pete, Spud Micky, or Charley's Jack,—referring to some saloon utility man. Ladies having the same names were distinguished one from the other by being known as "Splay-foot Sal," "Jag Lizzie," "The Widow," or "Birdie"—if given to singing.

Prefixes descriptive of personal deformity were common. "Sheeny," indicated a prominent nasal organ, "Conch" being substituted should the nasal organ be in the nature of a freak. "Limpy Bob" was a cripple, of course, and "Lucky" inferred very fortunate or unfortunate person, when attached to a name.

Calabazans used but few words to express a great deal. Experience had taught them the value of taciturnity; that the least said was the soonest mended, and the greater safety. Usually their remarks were limited to, "I don't care if I do," "make your game," or "whisky sour." The slang, profanity, and mixture of Mexican words and terms, made the vernacular language almost a foreign tongue.

Their favorite drink was Mescal, a fiery liquor made from a species of agave or cactus. It can only be kept in glass, and is sweetened with salt before swallowing. Three successive drinks of Mescal would drive a fellow into voluntarily kissing his mother-in-law, which is a valuable pointer for that necessary and much abused female.

Such was Calabazas during its short-lived boom. The whistle of the bullet was heard in the land; the clattering music of the faro and poker chips, as they were shuffled through the nervous fingers of the players, sounding from every side, as if beans were falling on a tin roof. "Keno;" "Make your game, gentleman;" "The black wins;" and "Drop that pot, you ____!" Bang! floated to the ear from the several tents after dark. Desperate men, never perfectly sober, carrying heavy revolvers and keen-edged bowie-knives in boot or breast, filled the tents and streets. Low-browed dogs, keepers of low drinking resorts, with huge pistols fastened to their waists by steel chains, slouched around their tent doors awaiting a chance to rob some laborer. At every turn men would be met whose crimes could not be atoned for by a life time of prison or a half dozen halters, they having been attracted to Calabazas by reason of its location near the Mexican boundary line, to where they could readily escape from American jurisdiction in case they were hunted for present or past offences. The average darkness of Calabazas humanity was illuminated by the flash light presence of some who were more eccentric, criminal, or specially gifted than the mass; of these I will attempt to give an account in the following chapters.

Those visiting the site of the former grandeur of Calabazas, as they ponder over its "kitchen middens," empty tins and early history, need not expect to find much but the name; for, upon the completion of the railroad, Calabazas became a dangerous way station; besides, a hurried trip to the Line was a wearisome and anxious one for those that prudential reasons compelled to make it. From time to time the best customers of the saloons and the flowers of society flitted to the Line. After the anti-Chinese riot, the people and tents moved to the new town of Nogales, whence it was but a step from the American sheriff to the Mexican safety over the Line. At the exodus, for obvious reasons, the Custom House and corral, the wells, and the hotel foundations were left behind. These are all that remain of the evanescent glories of Calabazas, unless, indeed, the map still hangs on the Custom House wall.

LIFE IN OLD TUCSON

John G. Bourke

WHEN PENNSYLVANIA-BORN JOHN G. BOURKE died in 1896 at the age of 49, he had compiled in his relatively short life an amazing record of achievement. Still in his teens, he enlisted in the Union Army. On the recommendation of his commanding officer, he went to West Point, graduating near the top of his class. His first tour of duty took him to the Southwest in 1871, where he became General George Crook's trusted aide. He fought through the Indian wars with distinction and at the same time carried on a second career as anthropologist and historian. He won many honors and wide acclaim in his second career but died an unhappy man because his outspokenness and quick temper, among other things, kept him from the promotion he deserved. He was more often repelled than amused by the weakness and duplicity of his fellow human beings. However, as his account of life in early-day Tucson shows, he was capable of viewing them with tolerant good humor. His portrait of Jack Long, though perhaps based on fact, presents the stereotyped westerner—just what readers elsewhere expected and enjoyed.

"See yar, muchacho, move roun' lively now, 'n' git me a Jinny Lin' steak." It was a strong, hearty voice which sounded in my ears from the table just behind me in the "Shoo Fly," and made me mechanically turn about, almost as much perplexed as was the waiter-boy, Miguel, by the strange request.

"Would you have any objection, sir, to letting me know what you mean by a Jenny Lind steak?"

From *On the Border with Crook*, by John G. Bourke, Chicago: Rio Grande Press, 1962, pp. 67–79.

"A Jinny Lin' steak, mee son, 's a steak cut from off a hoss's upper lip. I makes it a rule allers to git what I orders; 'n' ez far's I kin see, I'll get a Jinny Lin' steak anyhow in this yere outfit, so I'm kinder takin' time by the fetlock, 'n' orderin' jes' what I want. My name's Jack Long; what mout your'n be?"

It was apparent, at half a glance, that Jack Long was not "in sassiety," unless it might be a "sassiety" decidedly addicted to tobacco, given to the use of flannel instead of "b'iled" shirts, never without six-shooter on hip, and indulging in profanity by the wholesale.

A better acquaintance with old Jack showed that, like the chestnut, his roughest part was on the outside. Courage, tenderness, truth, and other manly attributes peered out from under roughness of garb and speech. He was one of Gray's "gems of purest ray serene," born in "the dark, unfathomed caves" of frontier isolation.

Jack Long had not always been "Jack" Long. Once, way back in the early fifties, he and his "podners" had struck it rich on some "placer" diggings which they had preempted on the Yuba, and in less than no time my friend was heralded to the mountain communities as "Jedge" Long. This title had never been sought, and, in justice to the recipient, it should be made known that he discarded it at once, and would none of it. The title "Jedge" on the frontier does not always imply respect, and Jack would tolerate nothing ambiguous.

He was bound to be a gentleman or nothing. Before the week was half over he was arrayed, not exactly like Solomon, but much more conspicuously, in the whitest of "b'iled" shirts, in the bosom of which glistened the most brilliant diamond cluster pin that money could procure from Sacramento. On the warty red fingers of his right hand sparkled its mate, and pendent from his waist a liberal handful of the old-fashioned seals and keys of the time attracted attention to the ponderous gold chain encircling his neck, and securing the biggest specimen of a watch known to fact or fiction since the days of Captain Cuttle.

Carelessly strolling up to the bar of the "Quartz Rock," the "Hanging Wall," or the "Golden West," he would say, in the cheeriest way:

"Gents, what'll yer all hev? It's mine this time, barkeep." And, spurning the change obsequiously tendered by the officiating genius of the gilded slaughter-house of morality, Jack would push back the twenty-dollar gold piece with which he usually began his evenings with "the boys," and ask, in a tone of injured pride: "Is there any use in insultin' a man when he wants to treat his friends?" And barkeeper and all in the den would voice the sentiment that a "gent" who was as liberal with his double eagles as Colonel Long was a gent indeed, and a man anybody could afford to tie to.

It was the local paper which gave Jack his military title, and alluded to the growing demand that the colonel should accept the nomination for Congress. And to Congress he would have gone, too, had not fickle Fortune turned her back upon her whilom favorite.

Jack had the bad luck to fall in love and to be married—not for the first time, as he had had previous experience in the same direction, his first wife being the youngest daughter of the great Indian chief "Cut-Mouth John," of the Rogue River tribe, who ran away from Jack and took to the mountains when her people went on the war-path. The then wife was a white woman from Missouri, and, from all I can learn, a very good mate for Jack, excepting that prosperity turned her head and made her very extravagant. So long as Jack's mine was panning out freely Jack didn't mind much what she spent, but when it petered, and economy became necessary, dissensions soon arose between them, and it was agreed that they were not compatible.

"If you don't like me," said Mrs. Long one day, "give me a divorce and one-half of what you have, and I'll leave you."

"'Nuff sed," was Jack's reply, "'n' here goes."

The sum total in the Long exchequer was not quite $200. Of this, Jack laid to one side a double eagle, for a purpose soon to be explained. The remainder was divided into two even piles, one of which was handed over to his spouse. The doors of the wardrobe stood open, disclosing all of Jack's regal raiment. He seized a pair of trousers, tore them leg from leg, and then served in much the same way every coat, waistcoat, or undergarment he owned. One pile of remnants was assigned to the stupefied woman, who ten minutes previously had been demanding a separation.

Before another ten had passed her own choicest treasures had shared the same fate, and her ex-liege lord was devoting his attention to breaking the cooking stove, with its superstructure of pots and pans and kettles, into two little hillocks of battered fragments; and no sooner through with that than at work sawing the tables and chairs in half and knocking the solitary mirror into smithereens.

"Thar yer are," said Jack. "Ye'v' got half th' money, 'n' yer kin now tek yer pick o' what's left."

The stage had come along on its way down to Sacramento, and Jack hailed the driver. "Mrs. Long's goin' down th' road a bit ter see some o' her kin, 'n' ter get a breath o' fresh air. Tek her ez fur ez this 'll pay fur, 'n' then *she*'ll tell whar else she wants ter go."

And that was Jack Long's divorce and the reason why he left the mining regions of California and wandered far and near, beginning the battle of life anew as packer and prospector, and drifting down into the drainage of the Gila and into the "Shoo Fly" restaurant, where we have just met him.

There shall be many other opportunities of meeting and conversing with old Jack before the campaigning against the Apaches is half through, so we need not urge him to remain now that he has finished his meal and is ready to sally forth. We return heartily the very cheery greeting tendered by the gentleman who enters the dining-room in his place. It is ex-Marshal Duffield, a very peculiar sort of a man, who stands credited in public opinion with having killed thirteen persons. How much of this is truth and how much is pure gossip, as meaningless as the chatter of the "pechotas" which gather along the walls of the corral every evening the moment the grain of the horses is dealt out to them, I cannot say; but if the reader desire to learn of a unique character in our frontier history he will kindly permit me to tell something of the only man in the Territory of Arizona, and I may say of New Mexico and western Texas as well, who dared wear a plug hat. There was nothing so obnoxious in the sight of people living along the border as the black silk tie. The ordinary man assuming such an addition to his attire would have done so at the risk of his life, but Duffield was no ordinary individual. He wore clothes to suit himself, and woe to the man who might fancy otherwise.

Who Duffield was before coming out to Arizona I never could learn to my own satisfaction. Indeed, I do not remember ever having any but the most languid interest in that part of his career, because he kept us so fully occupied in keeping track of his escapades in Arizona that there was very little time left for investigations into his earlier movements. Yet I do recall the whispered story that he had been one of President Lincoln's discoveries, and that the reason for his appointment lay in the courage Duffield had displayed in the New York riots during the war. It seems—and I tell the tale with many misgivings, as my memory does not retain all the circumstances—that Duffield was passing along one of the streets in which the rioters were having things their own way, and there he saw a poor devil of a colored man fleeing from some drunken pursuers, who were bent on hanging him to the nearest lamp-post. Duffield allowed the black man to pass him, and then, as the mob approached on a hot scent, he levelled his pistol—his constant companion—and blew out the brains of the one in advance, and, as the story goes, hit two others, as fast as he could draw bead on them, for I must take care to let my readers know that my friend was one of the crack shots of America, and was wont while he lived in Tucson to drive a ten-penny nail into an adobe wall every day before he would go into the house to eat his evening meal. At the present moment he was living at the "Shoo Fly," and was one of the most highly respected members of the mess that gathered there. He stood not less than six feet three in his stockings, was extremely broad-shouldered, powerful, muscular, and finely knit; dark complexion, black hair, eyes keen as briars and black as jet, fists as big as any two fists to be seen in the course of a day; disputatious, somewhat quarrelsome, but not without very amiable qualities. His bravery, at least, was never called in question. He was no longer United States marshal, but was holding the position of Mail Inspector, and the manner in which he discharged his delicate and dangerous duties was always commendable and very often amusing.

"You see, it's jest like this," he once remarked to the postmaster of one of the smallest stations in his jurisdiction, and in speaking the inspector's voice did not show the slightest sign of anger or excitement— "you see, the postmaster-general is growling at me because there is so much thieving going on along this line, so that I'm gittin' kind o' tired 'n' must git th' whole bizz off mee mind' 'n' ez I've looked into the whole thing and feel satisfied that you're the thief, I think you'd better be pilin' out o' here without any more nonsense."

The postmaster was gone inside of twelve hours, and there was no more stealing on that line while Duffield held his position. Either the rest of the twelve dollars per annum postmasters were an extremely honest set, or else they were scared by the mere presence of Duffield. He used to be very fond of showing his powerful muscle, and would often seize one of the heavy oak chairs in the "Congress Hall" bar-room in one hand, and lift it out at arm's length; or take some of the people who stood near him and lift them up, catching hold of the feet only.

How well I remember the excitement which arose in Tucson the day that "Waco Bill" arrived in town with a wagon train on its way to Los Angeles. Mr. "Waco Bill" was a "tough" in the truest sense of the term, and being from half to three-quarters full of the worst liquor to be found in Tucson—and I hope I am violating no confidence when I say that some of the vilest coffin varnish on the mundane sphere was to be found there by those who tried diligently—was anxious to meet and subdue this Duffield, of whom such exaggerated praise was sounding in his ears.

"Whar's Duffer?" he cried, or hiccoughed, as he approached the little group of which Duffield was the central figure. "I want Duffer (*hic*); he's my meat. Whoop!"

The words had hardly left his mouth before something shot out from Duffield's right shoulder. It was that awful fist, which could, upon emergency, have felled an ox, and down went our Texan sprawling upon the ground. No sooner had he touched Mother Earth than, true to his Texan instincts, his hand sought his revolver, and partly drew it out of holster. Duffield retained his preternatural calmness, and did not raise his voice above a whisper the whole time that his drunken opponent was hurling all kinds of anathemas at him; but now he saw that something must be done. In Arizona it was not customary to pull a pistol upon a man; that was regarded as an act both unchristian-like and wasteful of time—Arizonanas nearly always shot out of the pocket without drawing their weapons at all, and into Mr. "Waco Bill's" groin went the sure bullet of the man who, local wits used to say, wore crape upon his hat in memory of his departed virtues.

The bullet struck, and Duffield bent over with a most Chesterfieldian bow and wave of the hand: "My name's Duffield, sir," he said, "and them 'ere's mee visitin' card."

If there was one man in the world who despised another it was

Chief-Justice John Titus in his scorn for the ex-marshal, which found open expression on every occasion. Titus was a gentleman of the old school, educated in the City of Brotherly Love, and anxious to put down the least semblance of lawlessness and disorder; yet here was an officer of the Government whose quarrels were notorious and of every-day occurrence.

Persuasion, kindly remonstrance, earnest warning were alike ineffectual, and in time the relations between the two men became of the most formal, not to say rancorous, character. Judge Titus at last made up his mind that the very first excuse for so doing he would have Duffield hauled up for carrying deadly weapons, and an occasion arose much sooner than he imagined.

There was a "baile" given that same week, and Duffield was present with many others. People usually went on a peace footing to these assemblies—that is to say, all the heavy armament was left at home, and nothing taken along but a few Derringers, which would come handy in case of accident.

There were some five or six of us—all friends of Duffield—sitting in a little back room away from the long saloon in which the dance was going on, and we had Duffield in such good humor that he consented to produce some if not all of the weapons with which he was loaded. He drew them from the arm-holes of his waistcoat, from his boot-legs, from his hip-pockets, from the back of his neck, and there they all were—eleven lethal weapons, mostly small Derringers, with one knife. Comment was useless; for my own part, I did not feel called upon to criticise my friend's eccentricities or amiable weaknesses, whatever they might be, so I kept my mouth shut, and the others followed my example. I suppose that on a war-footing nothing less than a couple of Gatling guns would have served to round out the armament to be brought into play.

Whether it was a true alarm or a false one I couldn't tell, but the next day Judge Titus imagined that a movement of Duffield's hand was intended to bring to bear upon himself a portion of the Duffield ordnance, and he had the old man arrested and brought before him on the charge of carrying concealed deadly weapons.

The court-room was packed with a very orderly crowd, listening attentively to the long exordium from the lips of the judge upon the enormity and the uselessness of carrying concealed deadly weapons. The judge forgot that men would carry arms so long as danger real or imaginary encompassed them, and that the opinions prevailing upon that subject in older communities could not be expected to obtain in the wilder regions.

In Arizona, the reader should know, all the officers of the law were Americans. In New Mexico, on the contrary, they were almost without exception Mexicans, and the legal practice was entirely different from our own, as were the usages and customs of various kinds. For example, one could go before one of those Rio Grande alcaldes in Socorro, San Antonio, or Sabinal, and wear just what clothes he pleased, or not wear any if he didn't please; it would be all right. He might wear a hat, or go in his shirt sleeves, or go barefoot, or roll himself a cigarrito, and it would be all right. But let him dare enter with spurs, and the ushers would throw him out, and it was a matter of great good luck if he did not find himself in the calaboose to boot, for contempt of court.

"Call the first witness; call Charles O. Brown."

Mr. Charles O. Brown, under oath, stated his name, residence, and occupation, and was then directed to show to the judge and jury how the prisoner—Duffield—had drawn his revolver the day previous.

"Well, jedge, the way he drawed her was jest this." And suiting the action to the word, Mr. Charles O. Brown, the main witness for the prosecution, drew a six-shooter, fully cocked, from the holster on his hip. There was a ripple of laughter in the courtroom, as every one saw at once the absurdity of trying to hold one man responsible for the misdemeanor of which a whole community was guilty, and in a few minutes the matter was *nolle prossed.*

I will end up the career of the marshal in this chapter, as we shall have no further cause to introduce him in these pages. His courage was soon put to the severest sort of a test when a party of desperadoes from Sonora, who had been plundering in their own country until driven across the line, began their operations in Arizona. At the dead of night they entered Duffield's house, and made a most desperate assault upon him while asleep in his bed. By some sort of luck the blow aimed with a hatchet failed to hit him on head or neck—probably his assailants were too drunk to see what they were doing—and chopped out a frightful gash in the shoulder, which would have killed the general run of men. Duffield, as has been shown, was a giant in strength, and awakened by the pain, and at once realizing what had happened, he sprang from his couch and grappled with the nearest of the gang of burglars, choked him, and proceeded to use him as a weapon with which to sweep out of the premises the rest of the party, who, seeing that the household had been alarmed, made good their escape.

Duffield was too much exhausted from loss of blood to retain his hold upon the rascal whom he had first seized, so that Justice did not succeed in laying her hands upon any of the band. When Duffield recovered sufficiently to be able to reappear on the streets, he did not seem to be the same man. He no longer took pleasure in rows, but acted like one who had had enough of battles, and was willing to live at peace with his fellow-men. Unfortunately, if one acquire the reputation of being "a bad man" on the frontier, it will stick to him for a generation after he has sown his wild oats, and is trying to bring about a rotation of crops.

Duffield was killed at Tombstone ten years since, not far from the Contention Mine, by a young man named Holmes, who had taken up a claim in which Duffield asserted an interest. The moment he saw Duffield approaching he levelled a shot-gun upon him, and warned him not to move a foot, and upon Duffield's still advancing a few paces he filled him full of buckshot, and the coroner's jury, without leaving their seats, returned a verdict of justifiable homicide, because the old, old Duffield, who was "on the shoot," was still remembered, and the new man, who had turned over a new leaf and was trying to lead a new life, was still a stranger in the land.

Peace to his ashes!

There were military as well as non-military men in Tucson, and although the following incident did not occur under my personal observation, and was one of those stories that "leak out," I tell it as filling in a gap in the description of life as it was in Arizona twenty and twenty-five years ago. All the persons concerned were boarders at the "Shoo Fly," and all are now dead, or out of service years and years ago.

The first was the old field officer whom, for want of a better name, every one called "Old Uncle Billy N——." He had met with a grievous misfortune, and lost one of his eyes, but bore his trouble with stoicism and without complaint. During a brief visit to Boston, he had arranged with an oculist and optician to have made for him three glass eyes. "But I don't clearly understand what you want with so many," said the Boston man.

"Well, I'll tell you," replied the son of Mars. "You see, I want one for use when I'm sober, one when I'm drunk, and one when I'm p—— d—— drunk."

The glass eyes were soon ready to meet the varying conditions of the colonel's life, and gave the old man the liveliest satisfaction. Not long after his return to the bracing climate of Tucson he made the round of the gaming-tables at the Feast of Saint Augustine, which was then in full blast, and happened to "copper" the ace, when he should have bet "straight," and bet on the queen when that fickle lady was refusing the smile of her countenance to all her admirers. It was a gloomy day for the colonel when he awaked to find himself almost without a dollar, and no paymaster to be expected from San Francisco for a couple of months. A brilliant thought stuck him; he would economize by sending back to Boston two of his stock of glass eyes, which he did not really need, as the "sober" and "tolerably drunk" ones had never been used, and ought to fetch something of a price at second-hand.

The Boston dealer, however, curtly refused to negotiate a sale, saying that he did not do business in that way, and, as if to add insult to injury, enclosed the two eyes in a loose sheet of paper, which was inscribed with a pathetic story about "The Drunkard Saved." It took at least a dozen rounds of drinks before the colonel could drown his wrath, and satisfy the inquiries of condoling friends who had learned of the brutal treatment to which he had been subjected.

A great friend of the colonel's was Al. Garrett, who in stature was his elder's antithesis, being as short and wiry as the colonel was large and heavy. Garrett was an extremely goodhearted youngster, and one of the best horsemen in the whole army. His admirers used to claim that he could ride anything with four legs to it, from a tarantula to a megatherium. Semig, the third of the trio, was a Viennese, a very cultivated man, a graduate in medicine, an excellent musician, a graceful dancer, well versed in modern languages, and well educated in every respect. He was the post surgeon at Camp Crittenden, sixty miles to the south of Tucson, but was temporarily at the latter place.

He and Garrett and Uncle Billy were making the best of their way home from supper at the "Shoo Fly" late one evening, and had started to cut across lots after passing the "Plaza."

There were no fences, no covers—nothing at all to prevent pedestrians from falling into some one of the innumerable abandoned wells which were to be met with in every block, and it need surprise no one to be told that in the heat of argument about some trivial matter the worthy medical officer, who was walking in the middle, fell down plump some fifteen or twenty feet, landing in a more or less bruised condition upon a pile of adobes and pieces of rock at the bottom.

Garrett and his elderly companion lurched against each other and continued the discussion, oblivious of the withdrawal of their companion, who from his station at the bottom of the pit, like another Joseph, was bawling for his heartless brothers to return and take him out. After his voice failed he bethought him of his revolver, which he drew from hip, and with which he blazed away, attracting the attention of a party of Mexicans returning from a dance, who too hastily concluded that Semig was a "Gringo" spoiling for a fight, whereupon they gave him their best services in rolling down upon him great pieces of adobe, which imparted renewed vigor to Semig's vocalization and finally awakened the Mexicans to a suspicion of the true state of the case.

The poor doctor never heard the last of his mishap, and very likely was glad to receive the order which transferred him to the Modoc War, wherein he received the wounds of which he afterward died. He showed wonderful coolness in the Lava Beds, and even after the Indians had wounded him in the shoulder and he had been ordered off the field, he refused to leave the wounded under fire until a second shot broke his leg and knocked him senseless.

Associated with Semig in my recollection is the name of young Sherwood, a First Lieutenant in the Twenty-first Infantry, who met his death in the same campaign. He was a man of the best impulses, bright, brave, and generous, and a general favorite.

This rather undersized gentleman coming down the street is a man with a history—perhaps it might be perfectly correct to say with two or three histories. He is Don Estevan Ochoa, one of the most enterprising merchants, as he is admitted to be one of the coolest and bravest men, in all the southwestern country. He has a handsome face, a keen black eye, a quick, business-like air, with very polished and courteous manners.

During the war the Southern leaders thought they would establish a chain of posts across the continent from Texas to California, and one of their first movements was to send a brigade of Texans to occupy Tucson. The commanding general—Turner by name—sent for Don Estevan and told him that he had been informed that he was an outspoken sympathizer with the cause of the Union, but he hoped that Ochoa would see that the Union was a thing of the past, and reconcile himself to the new state of affairs, and take the oath to the Confederacy, and thus relieve the new commander from the disagreeable responsibility of confiscating his property and setting him adrift outside his lines.

Don Estevan never hesitated a moment. He was not that kind of a man. His reply was perfectly courteous, as I am told all the talk on the part of the Confederate officer had been. Ochoa owed all he had in the world to the Government of the United States, and it would be impossible for him to take an oath of fidelity to any hostile power or party. When would General Turner wish him to leave?

He was allowed to select one of his many horses, and to take a pair of saddle-bags filled with such clothing and food as he could get together on short notice, and then, with a rifle and twenty rounds of ammunition, was led outside the lines and started for the Rio Grande. How he ever made his way across those two hundred and fifty miles of desert and mountains which intervened between the town of Tucson and the Union outposts nearer to the Rio Grande, I do not know—nobody knows. The country was infested by the Apaches, and no one of those upon whom he turned his back expected to hear of his getting through alive. But he did succeed, and here he is, a proof of devotion to the cause of the nation for which it would be hard to find a parallel. When the Union troops reoccupied Tucson Don Estevan resumed business and was soon wealthy again, in spite of the tribute levied by the raiding Apaches, who once ran off every head of draught oxen the firm of Tully, Ochoa & De Long possessed, and never stopped until they had crossed the Rio Salado, or Salt River, where they killed and "jerked" the meat on the slope of that high mesa which to this day bears the name of "Jerked Beef Butte."

Another important factor in the formative period of Arizona's growth is this figure walking briskly by, clad in the cassock of an ecclesiastic. It is Bishop Salpointe, a man of learning, great administrative capacity, and devoted to the interests of his people. He preaches little, but practises much. In many ways unknown to his flock he is busy with plans for their spiritual and worldly advancement, and the work he accomplishes in establishing schools, both in Tucson and in the Papago village of San Xavier, is something which should not soon be forgotten by the people benefited. He is very poor. All that one can see in his house is a crucifix and a volume of precious manuscript notes upon the Apaches and Papagoes. He seems to be always cheerful. His poverty he freely shares with his flock, and I have often thought that if he ever had any wealth he would share that too.

This one whom we meet upon the street as we leave to visit one of the gambling saloons is Pete Kitchen. We shall be in luck if he invite us to visit him at his "ranch," which has all the airs of a feudal castle in the days of chivalry. Peter Kitchen has probably had more contests with Indians than any other settler in America. He comes from the same stock which sent out from the lovely vales and swales in the Tennessee Mountains the contingent of riflemen who were to cut such a conspicuous figure at the battle of New Orleans, and Peter finds just as steady employment for his trusty rifle as ever was essential in the Delta.

Approaching Pete Kitchen's ranch, one finds himself in a fertile valley, with a small hillock near one extremity. Upon the summit of this has been built the house from which no effort of the Apaches has ever succeeded in driving our friend. There is a sentinel posted on the roof, there is another out in the "cienaga" with the stock, and the men ploughing in the bottom are obliged to carry rifles, cocked and loaded, swung to the plough handle. Every man and boy is armed with one or two revolvers on hip. There are revolvers and rifles and shotguns along the walls and in every corner. Everything speaks of a land of warfare and bloodshed. The tile of "Dark and Bloody Ground" never fairly belonged to Kentucky. Kentucky never was anything except a Sunday-school convention in comparison with Arizona, every mile of whose surface could tell its tale of horror were the stones and gravel, the sage-brush and mescal, the mesquite and the yucca, only endowed with speech for one brief hour.

Within the hospitable walls of the Kitchen home the traveller was made to feel perfectly at ease. If food were not already on the fire, some of the women set about the preparation of the savory and spicy stews for which the Mexicans are deservedly famous, and others kneaded the dough and patted into shape the paper-like tortillas with which to eat the juicy frijoles or dip up the tempting chile colorado. There were women carding, spinning, sewing—doing the thousand and one duties of domestic life in a great ranch, which had its own blacksmith, saddler, and wagonmaker, and all other officials needed to keep the machinery running smoothly.

Between Pete Kitchen and the Apaches a ceaseless war was waged, with the advantages not all on the side of Kitchen. His employees were killed and wounded, his stock driven away, his pigs filled with arrows, making the suffering quadrupeds look like perambulating pin-cushions—everything that could be thought of to drive him away; but there he stayed, unconquered and unconquerable.

Men like Estevan Ochoa and Pete Kitchen merit a volume by themselves. Arizona and New Mexico were full of such people, not all as determined and resolute as Pete; not all, nor nearly all, so patriotic and self-denying as Don Estevan, but all with histories full of romance and excitement. Few of them yet remain, and their deeds of heroism will soon be forgotten, or, worse luck yet, some of the people who never dreamed of going down there until they could do so in a Pullman car will be setting themselves up as heroes, and having their puny biographies written for the benefit of the coming generations.

Strangest recollection of all that I have of those persons is the quietness of their manner and the low tone in which they usually spoke to their neighbors. They were quiet in dress, in speech, and in conduct—a marked difference from the more thoroughly dramatized border characters of later days.

TOMBSTONE IN 1879:
THE LIGHTER SIDE

D. S. Chamberlain

After five or six years in the mining camps of Montana and
Idaho, David Chamberlain moved west to Portland, Oregon,
lost interest in his job in a drug store, and tried out various
frontier communities in the West, including Ehrenberg, Tombstone, and Tucson, Arizona. He ended his career as a millionaire drug manufacturer in Des Moines, Iowa. Excerpts from
his autobiography were deposited by his son, L. H. Chamberlain, in the library of the Arizona Historical Society.

1879

I CLOSED UP ALL of my affairs in Aurora, Nevada, paid up everything I owed, and left for California, going to San Francisco, then
to Los Angeles, and from there out into the new, undeveloped
silver mining district of Tombstone, Arizona, arriving there with
less than $5.00 but with undaunted courage and good health.

The camp was new, growing rapidly. Some of the richest silver
mines ever found in the west were being developed there and
there were opportunities on all sides.

While others went to prospecting for silver the water for the
camp was hauled nearly three miles and sold for $2.00 a barrel. I
got a saddle horse and went out prospecting for water. I found a
spot not much over a mile from the center of the camp where the
grass was very green on a flat over one acre square. I concluded
that where the grass was green like that there must be moisture
coming up from below. I went and had a talk with a merchant who
had a small stock of goods there and told him what I proposed to

From the *Journal of Arizona History*, Winter, 1972, pp. 229–234.

do. I told him I wanted to put two men to work digging a well, that I believed I could get water which could be sold for less than they were paying for it at that time, but I might need $30.00 or $40.00 to pay wages with. He told me, all right, I could have $50.00 if I needed it. In two days we had developed a good well, clear, cold water, and from that start I finally had four wells, was selling water for $1.50 a barrel, and supplied the whole camp with water that summer. It was not long until I was on easy street compared with what I had when I came there. Afterward I bought an interest in the General Supply store.

The Contention Mine had sold for $1,000,000 to Disston & Sons, manufacturers, of Philadelphia. Their foreman, Mr. Ogden, in charge of a large force of miners, came to me one day and proposed that we fit up our own cook house, fire the cook and get our own meals. I was to supply the provisions out of the store at cost. We both had become tired of Chinese restaurant living. We paid the cook $40.00 a month. From that time on we lived on the fat of the land. We frequently had quail pot pies and sometimes we would go out and bring in a deer. By that time a butcher shop had been opened where we could buy beef or mutton. Just before the Fourth of July he proposed to me that we have a blow-out on the Fourth and a good chicken dinner and invite a number of our friends to dine with us, which we did, but had to send him twelve miles down to Charleston to get the chickens. He brought home three live chickens. We celebrated the Fourth of July with a big chicken dinner.

That fall he told me that his company was going to pipe the water to Tombstone from the Huachuca Mts. and that the pipe from Pittsburgh was then on the way, that I might quietly sell out before the news would get out. Within a week I found a buyer and sold out.

In the summer of 1879 there was no permanent building in Tombstone, no church, school or town organization—not even a justice of the peace or constable. Sam Danner's big tent saloon was general headquarters. Two or three tons of flour were hauled over from Hayden's mill at Phoenix and stored in one side of the saloon.

Sam Danner's tent saloon in Tombstone was quite an affair during the real early days of this widely known silver camp. This saloon was before the days of the Bird Cage Theatre, the Oriental Saloon or the Crystal Palace Bar, and was well known throughout Cochise County as a rendevous for some of the tough characters in the Southwest.

A string of planks laid on top of empty whiskey barrels formed the original front bar of this saloon. Lighting for the tent saloon was furnished by old time kerosene oil lamps hung from the ridge pole of the tent. All around the east side of the tent, which had nothing but a dirt floor, was a long bench with no back to it. This bench served as a seating place for miners, cow punchers, cattle rustlers and outlaws of every kind and description. I should say offhand that this tent was perhaps fifty feet long and nearly as wide. The long bench which served as a resting place for the thirsty imbibers of the early days of Tombstone was always well filled, and in addition thereto, the long bar was well patronized. No matter what drink might be called for, the price was the same—two bits. Most of the patrons drank straight whiskey and lots of it.

A little incident happened one night in Sam Danner's saloon that was quite amusing. A roughneck outlaw came into the front door of the tent and was looking for trouble and soon found it. After he had been beaten up and mauled around for a while and relieved of his brace of six shooters, he went over and sat down on the long bench. One patron of the saloon to whom this particular gentleman had been unusually abusive, decided to get even with him. He decided to go outside the tent and get hold of a good sized two-by-four, then he drove a spike into the two-by-four so that the nail would be protruding three or four inches. He then laid the two-by-four down outside the tent and walked within and counted from one end of the bench man by man until he counted the man that had been so abusive to him.

On account of the light shining through the tent and casting this man's shadow, it was very easy for the gentleman with the two-by-four to definitely locate the man that he wanted to get even with. He picked up his two-by-four and with one wallop imbedded the spike into the soft parts of this man's rear end and then made his getaway.

Quite naturally the man who had felt the sharp stab of the rusty spike got up with a howl of pain and started trying to locate the man who had stabbed him in his more or less tender parts. He went outside the saloon carrying his brace of six shooters, which had by that time been returned to him by the bartender or bouncer, looking all over town for the man who had inflicted this punishment upon him, cussing as he went, but the man was not to be found.

The consequence was that this particular fellow, although he patronized Sam Danner's saloon as faithfully as ever, never took occasion to sit down upon any bench in Sam Danner's saloon, as long as he remained in the camp.

This was just one of the amusing incidents that happened in the town of Tombstone during the days of seventy-nine.

Danner came from South Carolina. He had two barkeepers, one of them, I know, coming from Kentucky. Each of them had been brought up in ardent Methodist families. The one from Kentucky lived in the same locality where Peter Cartwright, the great Methodist evangelist lived. He was called the fighting parson.

They conceived the idea of holding the first religious services ever held in Tombstone, posted a notice that a class and prayer meeting would be held the next Saturday night from nine until ten o'clock. During this hour the bar would be closed. Every man in camp was invited to attend but had to have a ticket to gain admission. The ticket entitled them to a free drink of whisky after the meeting was over. The ticket consisted of old playing cards bearing Sam Danner's initials. A man sitting on a soap box outside the saloon distributed them.

The meeting was well attended and was opened promptly at nine o'clock by Danner repeating the following prayer: "Oh Lord, we pray for full forgiveness of all the sins we have committed, but what we most repent of is for those we have omitted." Some of the congregation were seated on bags of flour and others stood up. Wash Harris, a singer, banjo picker and entertainer, did the singing to the tune of his banjo. I do not remember all of the song but the following is a part of it:

> Glory, Glory, Hallelujahram!
> Man! Man! Glory Hallelujahram
> The poor man looked down on the rich man
>   and he said

I wish you were in Helloram.
Man! Man! Glory Hallelujahram.

Then Danner called on each one to confess their sins and the devilment they had committed back home when they were boys, including the watermelons and fruit they had stolen and tricks they had played on neighbors on Hallowe'en night. No one admitted that they had stolen anything for its value and all of them admitted that they had been brought up by good Christian mothers.

I told Mr. Danner that I was afraid they were carrying this meeting a little too far and that it was casting a slur on religion. No, he said it was all just for a little fun and to remind them of their boyhood days. It could not be objected to by the ladies—because there were none present; and it was not a bad example for the children—because there were none present. Finally the meeting was dismissed with a benediction.

After the congregation was dismissed they all lined up at the bar, presented their tickets, had their drink of whiskey and most of them departed. No one was intoxicated or used obscene or profane language. They were all far away from civilizing influences, every man for himself, and as a whole not a bad lot. Surely they were charitable, always saw that no one went hungry, and if they were sick or in distress there were always friends to take care of them.

THE GOSPEL AT GALEYVILLE

Jeanne Williams

BORN ON THE KANSAS-OKLAHOMA BORDER, Jeanne Williams has spent most of her life in the Southwest and her most successful characters are pioneer women who survive against heavy odds through great courage and endurance. Her novels are well researched and are basically serious, but she has an active sense of humor, as she demonstrates in the following excerpt.

The focus is on Katie MacLeod who comes to the mountains of southeastern Arizona to start a horse ranch. She spends some time at Galeyville, a town well known to Tombstone buffs as a haunt of rustlers and desperadoes. When Katie arrives, it is enjoying a short-lived mining boom. The local citizens befriend her and enjoy the music she makes with her Highland harp. When two fire-and-brimstone preachers preempt a saloon for a preaching duel, Katie agrees to furnish the music. We pick up the action as the crowd gathers at the saloon.

Tables had been pushed to the sides of the big room, and the floor was crowded with what looked like every chair in town, including Bride's. A black-moustached, balding man hastily finished shrouding a large painting above what Katie surmised was the bar—it, too, was draped with sheets—but she caught a glimpse that made her blush.

That painting! It was of a lady with not a stitch to her pink hide, sprawling in some bushes with a bunch of grapes in her hand! If she'd tried that in this country, she'd have been too busy pulling thorns out of her backside to loll around eating grapes!

Some women sat together in the back of the room, nicely

From *Home Mountain* New York: St. Martin's Press, 1990, pp. 34–38; 84–85.

dressed and quite ordinary-looking except for lips and cheeks a bit redder than was natural. These, thought Katie, stealing fascinated glances, must be whores and harlots. Only they didn't look the way they should, weren't glittering with diamonds and rubies, or posing in filmy lace to display maddeningly beautiful bodies. They weren't beautiful, in fact, just average.

Disillusioned, Katie turned to see the black-moustached man place a box on a small table in front of the decorously hidden bar. "There you are, Brother Thomas," he said, wiping his brow and smoothing another sheet over the improvised stand. "That whiskey carton'll make a good place to put your Bible."

"Thanks, Brother Babcock." The Reverend Thomas had a booming voice that reverberated like the blasting charges in the mine. Made to look even taller and more cadaverous by a black linen duster worn over black trousers and a white shirt with black string tie, he had a bushy black beard and hair peppered with gray. His piercing dark eyes noted each face in the assembling crowd with a strange mixture of excitement and disgust. "Brands for the burning," he whispered as if to himself and swung to Radnor in a stance as challenging as if he'd raised his fists. "Welcome, Brother Radnor. I'm glad the Lord has moved you to seek truth and mercy and get yourself a new hand."

Katie thought Radnor stiffened the slightest fraction, but his smile was genial. "Don't stick your iron in the fire for me yet, Reverend. I'm escorting the ladies. I reckon you've stuck your feet under Mrs. Malone's table a few times so you know her, but Miss Kate MacLeod just got to Galeyville night before last."

"Hah, the young lady with the harp, King David's instrument!" Black eyes drove into hers with physical impact. She was close enough to see thready little broken veins in his nose and the large, coarse pores of his skin. A sour, disappointed smell rose from the black duster. Katie wished she could step back, but there wasn't enough room. "Are you saved, Sister Kate?"

Pa had intoned long graces over their meals, and once, years ago, a preacher on his way west had stayed all night and read his Bible and prayed with the family, but that was Katie's total religious education. Puzzled, she said, "I'm not lost. We never were, really, just caught without water in the desert."

Bride's laughter pealed, Radnor's lip twitched, Mr. Babcock

snickered, and the minister reddened. "Would you joke about your soul's salvation or are you that ignorant?"

Katie flushed, hurt and bewildered. "I didn't know you were talking about my soul, Reverend Thomas. But I guess, yes, I am pretty ignorant. Mama taught us to read and cipher and write a little, but there wasn't a school close enough for us to go."

Shamefaced under Radnor's cold stare, Reverend Thomas said, "Never mind, child, I see you're an innocent. But that innocence could be your destruction so you listen careful to the sermon."

Stepping behind the improvised pulpit, the preacher thumped his Bible down and raised his arms. "Rise up on your hind laigs, brothers and sisters, bow your heads, and join me in prayer." A hush fell as the minister's voice resounded. "Our Father, Thou art the Great Dealer and knowest all our hands and what we need to fill 'em. We know, Oh Lord, Thou wouldn't cold-card us though our mortal minds cain't figger why some are dealt aces full while others get a pair of deuces or wind up with busted straights and flushes. We believe, Lord, that Thou only expects us to play our hands the best we can without poor-mouthin' or blaming Thee for not givin' us better cards. We know we can't bluff that final hand, that Thou wilt call every bet and we better have what we claimed we did. Lord, Thou didst hang around with barkeeps and sinners so Thou shouldst be right at home here. Set Thy charges in these stony hearts, Father, that hanker overmuch for the riches of this world, and blast out the gold and silver of the spirit! Amen."

Lifting his head amid the scuffling of people taking seats or, failing that, some comfortable perch or leaning-place, Reverend Thomas scanned the crowd and took a deck of cards out of his vest. He splayed them out, flinging them to the floor and grinding them under his boot. "I preach in the language of cards so you'll understand better, my dear brothers and sisters, but cards are evil. They turn your minds from the things of God, they cause cheating and swearing and killing, and they lure you into swilling the devil's juice. Yes, verily, wine is a mocker; strong drink is raging! There's a rattler coiled at the bottom of every glass! Whosoever looketh upon it is not only not wise, he's dumber 'n the tinhorn that draws four cards when there's aces showing."

His heel and the rough plank floor mutilated the cards, and in utter repudiation, he trampled them underfoot. Katie expected

Mr. Babcock to jump up and protest the condemnation of his business, but the saloon owner placidly shifted his tobacco to his other cheek and settled more comfortably in his chair as Reverend Thomas opened his Bible.

"Dearly beloved, all the gospels tell us the soldiers cast lots for Jesus' garments, but John tells us why. His robe was woven without a seam from top to bottom—we'd reckon His mother made it for Him, wouldn't we, just like your mothers made you the nicest clothes they could. So after the soldiers split up His other garments, there was this dandy robe left, and rather then ruin it by dividing, they gambled for it."

He paused sorrowfully. "Yes, right there, they flocked like a bunch of buzzards and shot craps for Jesus' robe. All of you that's been through a mesquite thicket know what thorns feel like. How'd you like to have a wreath of them jammed down over your forehead? How'd you like to drag your cross up a rocky, bare hill like those we got out toward the flats and then be hung up betwixt two cow-thieves—"

There was a shuffling of boots, but the Methodist thundered on. "Yes, Jesus was put to death with a rap-scallion on either hand, and one mocked Him, but the other, who must've had some good in his heart, told his pard to lay off and asked Jesus to remember him when He came into His Kingdom. Now even in His pain, brothers and sisters, even in His sweat and blood, with flies swarmin' and so thirsty He must have just croaked the words, Jesus pitied that thief and said, 'Today Thou shalt be with Me in Paradise.' And we can believe that rustler didn't hurt so bad then and died with the promise of salvation. But those soldiers, those blind prideful Romans all stuck up from conquerin' the world, the four hunkerin' down at the foot of the cross—you can bet they damned themselves that day. They're burning in hell right now for that one little game, tormented forever in that lake of fire that's a sight worse than any desert you've ever panted across. Won't be no waterhole for them, not even alkali water. They been in hell nigh two thousand years, and that's the wink of an eye in eternity. Eternity never ends, beloved. Not a one of us can know when it's going to start for us! This is the best chance you'll ever have to toss away your cards and whiskey!"

He stretched out his arms as his fiery gaze ranged from face to face. "You gamblers and winebibbers and cowboys who know more'n you should about back trails to Mexico—you folks who look decent as white-washed tombstones while within your breasts your hearts are deceitful above all things and desperately wicked— you women livin' where the lights are red and the carpets soft—I say to you, come forward and confess your sins and the Lord will be merciful to you just like He was to that thief."

Some of the men glanced sideways at each other, swallowed, or moved uneasily, but no one accepted the invitation. Katie had never thought before about Jesus' really suffering. She hurt to think about it and burned with indignation at the callous soldiers and those who'd sent Him to such a slow, nasty death, but if He'd die like that for people, would He condemn them to torment forever and ever?

She couldn't believe that; neither could she think of any big sins except being ready to kill Missou if he wouldn't let the animals drink. She wasn't sorry for that, so she sat tight while Reverend Thomas exhorted, pacing up and down.

At last, a lanky red-headed man with a drooping moustache and cowboy garb stood up at the back of the room. "Brother Thomas, that was a mighty good sermon for a Methodist one, but it looks like no one wants to get sprinkled. Could be they crave baptism like the Lord got from John the Baptist, the kind that's plumb complete so they'll know they've been saved. Anyhow, there's a young lady supposed to play a harp in between you and me. Ain't fair for you to use up the whole mornin'."

Thomas glared, but several of the crowd called, "That's right!" and someone yelled, "I came to hear that gal play her harp! Don't mind givin' you parsons a chance to rope me, but you oughta be fair!"

"Fair!" rumbled Thomas. "Shame, Brother Daggett! Lo, I've plowed deep, harrowed up the rocky soil, and now you'll plant your seed and reap the harvest."

Daggett went so red his freckles disappeared, and his hand dropped to where a holster would have hung had he worn one. "I'll forgive that slander, brother, since you're upset over not stampedin' a herd into the Methodist corral. Tell you what let's do. I won't ask anyone to get saved today—though if they want to foller me down to the creek afterward I'll sure baptize them, hoof to horn, total, entire, whole hog, and thorough, and you can do the same for any as can't wait to get sprinkled." He cocked his head and set his hands on his narrow hips. "Here's my proposition, Brother Thomas. Next Saturday, you dally your rope first, brand all the prime stock you can in an hour, and I'll see what I can do with the drags and the dogies."

For a moment, light blue eyes contended with smoldering black ones, but the congregation was nodding approval and Mr. Babcock got out his pocketwatch. "Sounds like a fair shuffle to me, Reverends, but if it don't suit you, Brother Thomas, we'd be obliged if you'd go outside to argufy on account of it's past time for the lady to sing."

Thomas closed his Bible and stepped back from the disguised whiskey crate. "I'll call you, Brother Daggett! I'm withdrawin' to commune with the Lord, but I'll be back in time to make sure you don't go gatherin' up my sheaves!"

He stumped out. Brother Daggett unfolded himself onto a stool, and Katie noticed that one of his scuffed, split-leather boots had a knife sheathed inside it. He grinned at Katie, and she blushed for it suddenly seemed that all eyes were fixed on her.

[A week later the crowd gathers for Round Two]

As the sisters followed Bride out the door, there was a drumming of hoofs, uproarious shouts, and in a flurry of dust, six horses flashed by and were reined in by their riders at the hitching rail in front of Babcock's. Laughing and joking, the horsemen swung from their saddles, loosened the cinches and hitched their mounts.

Sweeping off their hats, they stood back to let the womenfolk enter the building first. Five of the men were young, and one with sandy hair, blue eyes, freckles, and a big grin, was little more than a boy. The eldest, whose shaggy white hair, beard, and moustache revealed only a little leathery skin, stared at Bride with shrewd dark eyes in which unwilling admiration mixed with the amusement that resounded in his voice.

"Howdy, Mrs. Malone."

Urging Katie and Melissa in front of her, Bride said frostily, "Good day, Mr. Clanton."

The old man chortled. "Well, boys," he said without lowering his voice, "did you ever see ladies in such a rush to get inside a saloon?"

"In case you don't know it, there's preaching going on," Bride flung over her shoulder. "You can't get a drink till afternoon, sir, so you'd best take your thirst down to Evilsizer's."

"Why, ma'am, the boys and me rode in to hear the parsons," said Clanton piously. "Here, Ike, Billy, hold the doors so Mrs. Malone and the gals won't get smacked by 'em when they swing back. Saloon doors are plumb treacherous 'less you're used to 'em. Why, in Tombstone, ma'am, there's so many swingin' doors that ladies walk in the street and leave the boardwalk to men and dogs who don't mind gettin' knocked down."

"Folks," he said in a conversational tone, "Our Methodist brother has used up his time and mine, too, but that's all right. Won't take long to put it to you straight why you'd better head for the Baptist corral before Death's pale rider throws his rope on you. Baptists wait till a person's old enough to know what they're doin' when they get baptized—and when we do it, you know you've had your sins washed away, hoof to horn. What good's a little sprinkle? No use a'tall in the desert of sin! When you're really baptized, when the Great Stockman marks you for his own, folks, you don't fall from grace the way Methodists do, you're branded for good. You don't have to fret about back-slidin' and goin' back for a dinky little wettin' down. I've dug out a hole in the creek deep enough to dunk the biggest of you. You'll never have a better chance—and you may not get another chance. Jump out of the devil's pasture, brother man, sister woman, and follow me to the water!"

He strode toward the door. No one moved. Beaming, Reverend Thomas rose and held wide his arms. "I've got a pitcher of water right here, beloved. No need to drown yourself to get a new hand."

Nobody stirred. As the minister's face reddened, Sarah Metzger called, "Bless you, Brother Thomas, your preachin's so good I wish I could come to the mourners' bench, but I've been a Methodist twenty years, feet dug down and resting on the solid rock of Gospel!"

"We be Methodists, Reverend," said a Cornish miner whose companions nodded. "Amen, that we be!"

"And I've been a Baptist since I attained the age of reason," declared Myra Firbank.

"She must have 'tained it and loped right into unreasonableness," whispered a cowboy. "Ever try askin' her for credit?"

The youngest of the five men who'd ridden in with the white-haired Clanton had been lounging against the wall with the others. Now he straightened. "Somebody's got to get baptized by someone." His blue eyes sparkled, and his snub nose wrinkled in a grin as he drew his pearl-handled revolver. "You fellas there on the front row, if you're that keen on hearin' the preachers, you'd ought to be ready to get sprinkled or dipped."

Myra Firbank screeched more loudly than the saloon girls. Men sort of melted out of their seats, Diamond placed Rosie in Katie's arms. "Stay put," he commanded softly and started toward the young man, who swiveled his gun toward the gambler. Johnny Ringo had his hand on his holster when the door shadowed.

"Billy." Radnor's voice was mild. "This is same as a church whilst there's preachin' going on, and I know you'd never pull a gun in a church. You bet a bundle on this contest?"

"We all did." Billy Clanton stared at Radnor; after a moment, he shrugged and holstered the gun. "Shucks, Lord Bill, we heard you put a hundred dollars on the Baptist parson."

Radnor's ears went pink. "You heard right and I've got a proposition to put to all of you. The reverends have put in well nigh a month combing the draws and thickets from here to the Peloncillos and well nigh to Mexico, and they've preached to us three Sundays. It's not their fault most of us know we couldn't stay on the straight trail now if we took it. I reckon we ought to thank them for worrying about us, and right now I'm putting my hundred on the pulpit here and invitin' you to do the same—whatever it is you bet. My notion is to split it between Brother Thomas and Brother Daggett so they can maybe start churches where the ground's not so stony, or use it to help widows and orphans."

Even covered by a sheet, the whiskey crate resounded with the jangle of a spilled-out bag of silver dollars. In an instant, Ringo tossed down a handful of gold pieces. "More where this came from," grinned Billy Clanton, and added a heap of big Mexican pesos. John Diamond's greenbacks were quickly buried by more coins while Mr. Babcock, bald head glistening, sorted the array into two equal piles. Katie stared, mesmerized. She hadn't known even banks had that much money. It looked a fortune.

"Two thousand, nine hundred, and seventy dollars," called Babcock. "I'll round it off to three thousand—that's fifteen hundred apiece." He stepped around the bar and, producing two sacks, began to fill them.

The room, so full of explosive tension minutes ago, buzzed with laughter, ministers vying with their audience to thank each other. "Katie," whispered Bride. "Let me hold Rosie and you fetch your harp. This would be a good time to sing 'Amazing Grace.'"

INDIANS YESTERDAY

Pasqual muttered, between the paroxysms of his affliction, "Ugh! Muchee pepper! Belly strong dust! Burn 'um Injun nose!"

THE ARIZONA PIONEERS saw nothing humorous in the local Indians, especially the Apaches. It is difficult to joke about a "naked savage" who is intent on taking your life and property. The Apaches had harried the Mexicans for almost two centuries before the Anglos arrived, and they attacked the new invaders with equal enthusiasm. There were raids and massacres on both sides and when troops were withdrawn from Arizona at the outbreak of the Civil War, life was grim indeed for the settlers who chose to remain.

After Appomatox the real struggle began. Reservations were set up under military supervision, but the wild ones refused to put up with confinement, supervision and cheating by a few rascally whites. They were highly skilled desert fighters and kept ahead of government forces until 1886 when Geronimo and Naiche finally surrendered and were sent off to permanent exile.

When a humorist like J. Ross Browne turned his attention to his Apache neighbors, he naturally viewed them as less than human and found amusement in their ignorance. As the Indian wars receded and more was revealed about Indian culture, later authors were able to depict the tribesmen with more kindly amusement.

INDIANS AT YUMA

J. Ross Browne

J. Ross Browne made his living as a government functionary in early-day California and traveled the world for pleasure, gathering material for books and articles. In 1864 he visited Fort Yuma on the Colorado River with his friend Charles D. Poston, "the Father of Arizona" and the Territory's first Indian agent. Poston was planning to become acquainted with the leaders of Indian tribes in his district. Browne intended to gather material for a series of articles which were assembled in 1867 as *Adventures in the Apache Country*. The high point of their stay at the Fort was a Christmas *baile*, where Browne had his first look at the inhabitants of the area. A few Sonoran ladies did their best to make the event enjoyable but Browne saw them only as "dusky belles," suggesting that they belonged to an inferior human stock. He was even more condescending to the Indian leaders whom he met the next morning when he and Poston delivered their presents to the assembled tribesmen. He concentrated on the dress and ornaments of the chiefs, finding ridiculous what the visitors no doubt considered elegant and tasteful. It has taken almost a century for the white man to give the Indians credit for doing the best they could with what they had.

Christmas Day came, and with it some natural longings for home and the familiar faces of the family circle. Yet we were not so badly off as one might suppose in this region of drought and desert. Colonel Bennett and his amiable wife got up an excellent dinner at the fort; and in the evening we had a *báile*, or Spanish dance, at which there were several very dusky belles of the Sonoranian race. Unfortunately two Jesuit Padres, attached to the

From *Adventures in the Apache Country*. New York: Harper & Brothers, 1867; Tucson: University of Arizona Press, 1973, pp. 57–65.

Arizona command, had previously secured the attention of the principal Señoritas in the neighborhood; and what with baptizing and marrying and confessing, it was difficult to get up a quorum at the dance. However, there were plenty of officers, and what the ladies lacked in number they made up in spirit. The fiddlers scraped with an inspiring vim; whisky flowed, and egg-shells, containing dust and gilt-paper, were broken in the true Spanish style upon the heads of handsome gallants.

Not aspiring to distinction in that way, I was quietly seated on a bench, enjoying the dance, and unsuspicious of this peculiar custom, when a lovely belle of the darkest hue whirled by in the giddy waltz, dexterously cracking an egg on the crown of my head as she passed, and leaving me a spectacle of confusion and astonishment before the eyes of the crowd. The mischievous beauty struck me exactly on the spot where Time has already laid his relentless hand; and I was not surprised at the merry shouts of laughter that ensued; for if my head looked like any thing upon earth, it must have borne a close resemblance to a boulder surmounted by croppings of gold and silver.

Next day Superintendent Poston and myself held a grand pow-wow with the Yuma chiefs and their people. From all parts of the neighborhood they came; warriors, squaws, and children; from the mesquit bushes and mudholes of the Colorado; from the sloos and the arroyas of the Gila; the cotton-woods and the deserts and the mountains of Castle Dome. Every village had its delegation of dusky tatterdemalions. Lizards and snakes and mice were hastily cast aside in the wild anticipation of muck-a-muck from the Great Father. Hungry and lean, painted and bedizened with ornaments, they came in to receive the bounty of the mighty Federal chief.

Great were the rejoicings when we opened the boxes and bales of merchandise so liberally furnished by the Government contractors, Cronin, Huxtall, & Sears, of New York. Red, white, green, and gray blankets; military suits, glittering with tinsel; old swords, four feet long; sun-glasses for lighting cigars; and penny whistles for the small fry. It was indeed a wonderful display of the artistic triumphs of civilization, well calculated to impress the savage tribes of the Pacific with awe and admiration. There were axes of the best Collins brand, that flew to pieces like glass against the iron timbers of this anomalous region; and hats made by steam, and flaming red vests stitched by magic, and tobacco-boxes and tin kettles that might be opened, but never upon earth shut again. Surrounded by all the military paraphernalia of Fort Yuma, and with ceremony the most profound and impressive, we delivered our speeches and dry goods to the various chiefs; we gave them damaged hominy and hoes, and spades and shovels, and sashes and military buttons, charms, amulets, tobacco-boxes, and beads; shook them by the hand collectively and in detail, and pow-wowed generally in the approved style.

Pasqual, the doughty head-chief of all the Yumas, long known to fame as the longest of his tribe, predominated over the ceremonies. A grave, cadaverous, leathery old gentleman, with hollow, wrinkled cheeks, and a prodigious nose, through the cartilage of which, between the nostrils, he wears a white bone ornamented with swinging pendants, is Pasqual the doughty. On account of the length of his arms and legs—which, when stretched out altogether, bear a strong similitude to the wind-mill against which Don Quixote ran a tilt—the mighty Pasqual is regarded with much respect and veneration by his tribe. His costume, on the present occasion, consisted of a shabby military coat, doubtless the same worn in ancient times by his friend, Major Heintzelman, the embroidery of which has long since been fretted out by wear and tear, and the elbows rubbed off by long collision with the multitudes of office-seekers among his tribe. Of pantaloons he had but a remnant; and of boots or shoes he had none at all, save those originally furnished him by nature. But chiefly was Pasqual conspicuous for the ponderous bone and appendages that hung from his nose. A slight catarrh afflicted him at the time of our pow-wow, and it was not without great inconvenience that he managed the ornamental part of his countenance—turning repeatedly away to blow it, or adjust the awkward pendants that swung from it, and always re-appearing with tears of anguish in his eyes. I took pity upon his sufferings and gave him some snuff, assuring him it was a sovereign remedy for colds in the head. The result was such a series of explosions, contortions of the facial muscles, and rattling of the ornamental bones, as to alarm me for the sanity of the doughty chief, who seemed quite wild with the accumulation of his agonies. The assembled wisdom of the nation grunted repeatedly in token of amazement; and Pasqual muttered, between the paroxysms of his affliction, "Ugh! muchee pepper! belly strong dust! Burn 'um Injun nose!"

Vincente, the next chief in command, dressed in a blue cotton shirt of the scantiest pattern. It reached only a short distance below his waist, and, for the matter of respect to the prejudices of civilization, might have ended at the collar. I really wish the contractors would furnish longer shirts for the Indians. The Yumas are tall, and I know of no tribe on this coast averaging only fourteen inches from the crown of the head to the soles of the feet. Vincente had probably received a hint that the distribution would be honored by the presence of ladies. What he lacked in costume he made up in paint. Both his eyes were encircled with yellow ochre; blue streaks adorned his cheeks; his nose was of a dazzling vermillion, and his legs were gorgeously striped with mud. His only additional article of costume, visible to the eye, was a dusky cotton diaper, ingeniously tied behind, leaving a long tail to flutter majestically in the breeze.

Tebarro, the next great chief, wrapped himself in an American blanket, and dyed his face a gloomy black. I think he was in mourning. He wore tar on his head, and tar on his cheeks, and tar on his nose and chin, which becoming mingled with the grit and dust of the Colorado desert, gave him a sort of asphaltum look, like the house-tops and pavements of Los Angeles. When he stood in the sun he melted—such was the force of his grief. Black tears ran down from his head and cheeks and chin, and mingled with the wool of his blanket. Literally he wept tar.

Antonio, the fourth great chief, wore a strap round his waist, with a rusty old sword tied to it by means of rawhide. He didn't wear any thing else, save the usual girdle of manta upon his loins, that could be considered an article of costume; but his eyes were gorgeously encircled by a cloud of blue paint fringed with vermilion. Like his illustrious superior, Pasqual, he wore pendent ornaments in his nose, of the most inconvenient pattern. I should judge Antonio carried a quarter of a pound of native jewelry, consisting of bone and lead, upon the cartilage of his proboscis.

Juan, the fifth and last of noted warriors and head-men, was redundant in gamoose breeches and cotton rags. On his head he wore a helmet of Colorado mud, dried into the roots of his hair by the action of the sun. This I believe is accounted by the Yumas a sovereign remedy for vermin. The liveliest skipper is forever deprived of locomotion by the conglomerate of dried mud. When the helmet is broken off in segments, like a piece of baked crockery, it must present a curious spectacle of embalmed bodies.

These distinguished chiefs and their people received the presents allotted to them with great dignity and good-humor. There was no grabbing or stealing, nor any sign of discontent. Every man received his share with satisfaction, and with gratitude to the Great Father in Washington. When they shook hands with us for the last time, and we were about to part, the scene was really affecting. I almost shed tears at it myself, unused as I am to crying about what can't be helped. In squads, and couples, and one by one, they affectionately took their leave, with their hoes and axes, spades and shovels, gimcracks and charms stuck all over them—in their sashes, breeches, clouties, blankets, and pinafores. One went with a necklace of mattocks around his neck and three Collins axes in his girdle; another with his head thrust into a glittering pile of tin-ware; while a third, one of the unbreeched multitude, wore a frying-pan in front by way of an apron, and a corn-hoe behind, in the usual fashion of a rudder. Old men and young were tuning their jews'-harps; luxurious squaws were peeping at the redundant beauties reflected by their little zinc looking-glasses; children were blowing their tin whistles, and small fat papooses were hanging their heads out of compressed bundles behind their mothers, wondering, with open mouths and great round eyes, what could be the cause of all the hubbub. It was an impressive scene of barbarous happiness not easily forgotten. And so ended the Grand Pow-wow.

Our unhappy driver, George, who had never smiled during the whole course of the ceremonies, now turned away with an expression of the most profound and confirmed melancholy. Not even the warrior with the rudder, nor the chief with the mud roof to his head, could dissipate the intensity of his gloom. Nor were the blandishments of the dusky Yuma belles of any greater avail. With his hand pressed upon the pit of his stomach he groaned in agony of spirit as he descended the hill; and I fancied the plaintive words reached my ears, "Oh! Mary Jane, how could you? Think of him that loves you, and he among Injuns and savigges!"

DANGEROUS MAN

Oliver La Farge

OLIVER LA FARGE CAME of a distinguished eastern family and was educated at Groton school and at Harvard. He graduated in anthropology and did field work in Guatemala and the American Southwest, eventually settling in Santa Fe. He spent his life learning about Indians, writing about Indians, and fighting for Indian rights. As much as any white man could, he understood Indians, especially the Navajos in Arizona and New Mexico. He wrote two well-known novels and three collections of short stories about them. *LAUGHING BOY*, his best-known book, won a Pulitzer Prize in 1930. Critics charge him with sentimentalism and an overly romantic point of view in this love story, but the short stories are closer to truth and reality. "Dangerous Man" is anything but funny as it examines the failure of two cultures to find common ground, but there is a grim humor in the misconceptions the white man and the young Navajos have about each other.

This was the heart of the Indian country, the land of the Navajo, still unperturbed, unconscious of the slow-advancing, irresistible empire of the Americans. Badger Killer sat on a rock in the moonlight, singing. In his intention, the high-pitched, quavering love-song, which travelled nearly as far around as would a coyote's yelping, was projected only to the ears of one broad-faced young woman sitting among her family in their hut some fifty feet away.

Walter Mather, rolled up in his poncho, wished to heaven the buck would shut up; he was tired, he wanted to sleep. The figure against the sky did not look romantic to him, nor hardly lovable,

From *All the Young Men*. Boston: Houghton Mifflin, 1935, pp. 128–132. First published in *Scribner's Magazine*.

though it might seem different to that dish-faced, cow-hocked squaw over in the hut. The young man was one of those heavy-faced Indians, long-lipped, heavy-lidded, broad-nosed, stupid and insolent-looking. One saw in him the doltish rustic and the savage. And that singing was really terrible.

Badger Killer had apparently sung himself out. He went away in the direction of his own camp. Mather rolled over with a sigh, then he grunted and sat up. There was another seated Indian in a blanket, about twenty yards away, not singing. He saw the formless, wrapped, still figure bisected by the sharp line, with a glint of moonlight on it, of a muzzle-loading rifle; on watch, plainly. He pulled his saddle to him and made himself comfortable: no sleep tonight.

He hadn't known for the last two days whether he was a prisoner or a guest. There wasn't any gold hereabouts anyway. He was a fool to have come here. Himself and Pennsylvania and his father's house and his girl had nothing to do with all this. It was unreal. Tomorrow he was going to get away from this menacing unreality; he couldn't get to Santa Fe and the stage line fast enough. The country was all right, if you liked desert, but these Indians—well, they just weren't people.

Be nice to get back home and eat real food and see a lot of grass again. Here, mustn't sleep.

Another Indian came to relieve the one who was watching him. After ages it grew light. He rose and cooked his breakfast as though everything were usual; then he went to saddle his horse. Spear Thrower, the chief of the settlement, walked up to Mather. Behind the old Indian stood two braves. Spear Thrower said in mutilated Spanish: "*Penga conmigo, chiquito hablamos.*" He pointed toward the largest hut.

Mather looked at him, then he looked at the young men. One of them had an ancient gun, a flintlock with a bell mouth and elaborate brass decorations on the stock. It was an ornamental piece, much too damn ornamental. Looking at it and at its owner, with the wisps of hair hanging over his eyes, the dirty shirt of red-dyed, rough buckskin, one imagined him shooting that gun. It would spout fire and smoke and a handful of miscellaneous missiles, nails, shot, pebbles, anything. He rolled a cigarette slowly.

"*Buenos pues, vamonos.*"

There were twelve men, old and young, inside the hut, sitting in a ring. Spear Thrower politely indicated a seat on a pile of sheepskins. Looking around, the American saw that every man there had a weapon of some kind across his knees. With a pleasant smile, he drew his Colt's revolver and laid it in his lap. He rolled another cigarette, and passed tobacco and papers.

Neither he nor any of the Indians were really at home in Spanish; he spoke practically no Navajo, and none of them had mastered English. Conversation proceeded with difficulty. They wanted to know what he was doing in their country, why he was poking all the time in odd corners.

He explained that he had been looking for a yellow metal which the Americans valued highly. He had not found any, so he was going to Santa Fe for a rest and more supplies. If he should find some, it would be a good thing for them; they would be paid blankets, copper, knives, gunpowder, many gifts, for the right to mine it. He was not a soldier, he was a friend; he wished them no harm.

They heard him quietly, then they began to talk among themselves. He wished he knew what they were saying. This was all so grotesque. He was Walter Mather, on his way back to Pennsylvania, where he belonged. Now this bad dream of dark, heavy faces in a half-lit brush hut was menacing him. He stroked the handle of his revolver. Hello, there was the love-song fellow making a speech. Bovine face, wonder what he's saying?

Badger Killer spoke directly to Spear Thrower. "What are you waiting about? We know all about that metal, we have seen it when we visited the Apaches. They come in great numbers, they bring soldiers. When we visited the Apaches that time, where the Americans were digging up that metal, they shot at us with one of those great big guns on wheels. We do not want them looking for it here, we do not want those gifts. We take what we need from the Mexicans, from the Zuñis and the Hopis; we do not want him here. Say the word, Grandfather, and I shall walk to the door. From the door I shall put an arrow into him. This is too much talk, I think."

Spear Thrower answered: "You speak quickly, my son, I think. Look, he has one of those new gun's-children that shoots six times just like that. He has it in his hand. Which six of us want to be shot at? Let us let him go, I think."

Several others agreed.

Badger Killer spat on the floor. "Let him go then. Tell him to get out. Tell him my friend over there and I shall ride with him as far as the pass, so as to see that he really goes. Let us attend to it. I shall ride back to camp on his horse."

"Good, that is well spoken. Does your friend want to go?"

Slender Hand, a tall, lanky brave with a hawk nose, said: "Yes. He has a plan, I think. I shall be glad to go with you, elder brother."

Everyone assented. Spear Thrower turned to the American and told him in lame Spanish:

"You go now. You leave this country, you not return to it. These two young men ride with you as far as the pass, to see that you really go. Saddle your horse. Give me some tobacco."

Mather suppressed a sigh of relief as he passed over a full sack. "Keep it, my friend."

Evidently the ugly young buck's oration had been in his favour—probably had had experience with the soldiers, or else being in love had an effect even on the saddle-faced sons of the desert. He made fast his few goods and mounted with a swing of the leg. It was fine to be started, it would be fine to get through the pass and out of the Navajo country. His two escorts were conversing across him; they sounded cheerful. What a hell of an ugly language! Well, not as bad as Ute.

Badger Killer rode on his right, Slender Hand on his left. They were discussing the merits of Mather's iron-grey horse. Slender Hand changed the topic.

"What are you going to do? What can we do with only our bows?"

"Wait and see; I shall do it. I have a plan. I am a dangerous man. When we get to that flat place, let us trot; that is all."

Badger Killer felt delightfully excited, a stirring in the pit of his stomach as the moment approached. He stretched his legs, pointed his toes in the stirrups, and leaned far back, so that the sun bathed his face. With half-closed eyes and his face upturned, he sang the song about the magpie, and the one that makes fun of the wildcat. Now they were at the flat place and began to trot.

"*Nashto, shichai,*" he said to the American, holding his right hand toward him across his reins and moving his index finger in a small circle upon the ball of his thumb. *"Cigalo, amigo."* He held his reins and his quirt in his left hand.

Mather reached for his tobacco. They were such children, such frank and constant beggars! The Navajo reined his horse in sharply, and at the same time his outstretched right hand descended, to close upon the revolver in its holster. The horse stopped short; Mather's carried him a length ahead before he realized that he was disarmed.

The unreality had suddenly risen up like a grey cloud to overwhelm him; this was the impossible, the ridiculous end. He saw his front door and the Pennsylvania street and his father in a grey beaver hat, as he brought the quirt down frantically across his horse's quarters, across his neck.

With entranced, surprised delight, Badger Killer realized that the revolver was working for him, that it had fired, and again, and a third time, that he had hit, that the American was falling from the saddle. His pony, startled, was leaping sideways. He let out a whoop, and then emptied the remaining three chambers into the air while he gave the long-drawn, Navajo wolf-howl. Slender Hand caught the grey horse.

"I am a dangerous man. I took his gun's-child; while he was awake and watching I seized his gun's-child. It shot from my hand six times, pouring forth lightning. From my hand I sent lightning six times. In a handsome way, with my horse dancing, I killed him. I have a gun's-child; I can make it talk; I am a dangerous man."

"All right, Dangerous Man, come and divide these goods. Come and take the scalp."

"The horse is mine, and that American hat. We shall divide the rest evenly."

They went through his few belongings, commenting excitedly. Slender Hand reached into one pocket.

"Look at these cigarette-papers!"

"Ei-yei! They are handsome! Look, they have pictures on them. Do you suppose they are holy?"

"I do not know, but they will make big cigarettes."

"Here is one, yellow on one side, green on the other. I want that. I shall smoke that where people can see. You may have the rest."

"Good."

"Look, look at this ornament. I shall hang it from my necklace."

"This is his god, I think. He prays to it."

"It speaks; listen! It says, 'tick-tock, tick-tick.'"

"Yes, and see, that little stick goes around."

"How does he pray to it?"

"I saw him when he went to bed. He took out a piece of iron and turned it in this hole, and the thing made a singing noise. And when he got up, he looked at it the first thing. He takes it out and looks at it; then he looks at the sun."

"It is for him, I think. It might be bad medicine for us."

"Perhaps you are right."

"I am afraid of it." Dangerous Man threw it away; it struck a rock and spouted wheels and springs.

"Ei! Look at how much was in it. Did you see those gleaming snakes? It is a bad thing."

They rode back to camp, leading the captured horse.

Dangerous Man sang: "I have a gun's-child. I have an American hat. I am a dangerous man. From his side I took his gun's-child; with a well-made plan I took his gun's-child, bravely. A-yé-yé-yé-ya-hai! It shot, from my hand it shot forth lightning; from my hand three times lightning went forth and struck him; while my horse danced, lightning went forth and struck him. I have killed a Mexican, I have killed a Zuñi, I have killed an American. I have a gun's-child that shoots six times, I have an American hat, I have a blue horse. I am a dangerous man. A-yé-yé-yé-ya-hai!"

"That is all right, Grandfather, but you will not sing that song in camp tonight. You have blood on you; we are not clean."

He came back to earth. "You are right. Let us find Tall Singer to make the songs over us." He flicked at his pony's mane with his quirt. "Then, when I sing at that place, I shall be heard. That girl will speak to her parents now, I think."

PAPAGO WEDDING

Mary Hunter Austin

THOUGH BORN IN ILLINOIS, Mary Hunter Austin could claim to be a naturalized citizen of the Southwest. She loved the deserts and the mountains, and she loved the people who lived in harmony with the lonely and rugged terrain. She gained national importance as a writer about these people and places. Her later years were spent in Santa Fe, where she became the Grand Dame of the pueblo, a formidable figure in the life of New Mexico. Her life was not a happy or a peaceful one, but her values were stable. She tried to romanticize or even mysticize the southwestern Indians, but her sense of humor kept her from going too far. *One Smoke Stories* is a collection of earthy, humorous tales told, supposedly, by Indians around a campfire, the length of the tales measured by the time it took to smoke a corn-husk cigarette.

There was a Papago woman out of Pantak who had a marriage paper from a white man after she had borne him five children, and the man himself was in love with another woman. This Shuler was the first to raise cotton for selling in the Gila Valley—but the Pimas and Papagos had raised it long before that—and the girl went with him willingly. As to the writing of marriage, it was not then understood that the white man is not master of his heart, but is mastered by it, so that if it is not fixed in writing it becomes unstable like water and is puddled in the lowest place. The Sisters at San Xavier del Bac had taught her to clean and cook. Shuler called her Susie, which was nearest to her Papago name, and was fond of the children. He sent them to school as they came along, and had carpets in the house.

In all things Susie was a good wife to him, though she had no

From *One-Smoke Stories*. Boston: Houghton Mifflin, 1934, pp. 243–249.

writing of marriage and she never wore a hat. This was a mistake which she learned from the Sisters. They, being holy women, had no notion of the *brujería* which is worked in the heart of the white man by a hat. Into the presence of their God also, without that which passes for a hat they do not go. Even after her children were old enough to notice it, Susie went about the country with a handkerchief tied over her hair, which was long and smooth on either side of her face, like the shut wings of a raven.

By the time Susie's children were as tall as their mother, there were many white ranchers in the Gila country, with their white wives, who are like Papago women in this, that, if they see a man upstanding and prosperous, they think only that he might make some woman happy, and if they have a cousin or a friend, that she should be the woman. Also the white ones think it so shameful for a man to take a woman to his house without a writing that they have no scruple to take him away from her. At Rinconada there was a woman with large breasts, surpassing well-looking, and with many hats. She had no husband, and was new to the country, and when Shuler drove her about to look at it, she wore each time a different hat.

This the Papagos observed, and, not having visited Susie when she was happy with her man, they went now in numbers, and by this Susie understood that it was in their hearts that she might have need of them. For it was well known that the white woman had told Shuler that it was a shame for him to have his children going about with a Papago woman who had only a handkerchief to cover her head. She said it was keeping Shuler back from being the principal man among the cotton-growers of Gila Valley, to have in his house a woman who would come there without a writing. And when the other white women heard that she had said that, they said the same thing. Shuler said, 'My God, this is the truth, I know it,' and the woman said that she would go to Susie and tell her that she ought to go back to her own people and not be a shame to her children and Shuler. There was a man of Panták on the road, who saw them go, and turned in his tracks and went back, in case Susie should need him, for the Papagos, when it is their kin against whom there is *brujería* made, have in-knowing hearts. Susie sat in the best room with the woman and was polite. 'If you want Shuler,' she said, 'you can have him, but I stay with my children.' The white woman grew red in the face and went out to Shuler in the field where he was pretending to look after something, and they went away together.

After that Shuler would not go to the ranch except of necessity. He went around talking to his white friends. 'My God,' he kept saying, 'what can I do, with my children in the hands of that Papago?' Then he sent a lawyer to Susie to say that if she would go away and not shame his children with a mother who had no marriage writing and no hat, he would give her money, so much every month. But the children all came in the room and stood by her, and Susie said, 'What I want with money when I got my children and this good ranch?' Then Shuler said, 'My God!' again, and, 'What can I do?'

The lawyer said he could tell the Judge that Susie was not a proper person to have care of his children, and the Judge would take them away from Susie and give them to Shuler. But when the day came for Susie to come into court, it was seen that, though she had a handkerchief on her hair, her dress was good, and the fringe of her shawl was long and fine. All the five children came also, with new clothes, well-looking. 'My God!' said Shuler, 'I must get those kids away from that Papago and into the hands of a white woman.' But the white people who had come to see the children taken away saw that, although the five looked like Shuler, they had their mouths shut like Papagos; so they waited to see how things turned out.

Shuler's lawyer makes a long speech about how Shuler loves his children, and how sorry he is in his heart to see them growing up like Papagos, and water is coming out of Shuler's eyes. Then the Judge asks Susie if she has anything to say why her children shall not be taken away.

'You want to take thees children away and giff them to Shuler?" Susie asks him. 'What for you giff them to Shuler?' says Susie, and the white people are listening. She says, 'Shuler's not the father of them. Thees children all got different fathers,' says Susie. 'Shuler——'

Then she makes a sign with her hand. I tell you if a woman makes that sign to a Papago he could laugh himself dead, but he would not laugh off that. Some of the white people who have been in the country a long time know that sign and they begin to laugh.

Shuler's lawyer jumps up . . . 'Your Honor, I object——'

The Judge waves his hand. 'I warn you the court cannot go behind the testimony of the mother in such a case...'

By this time everybody is laughing, so that they do not hear what the lawyer says. Shuler is trying to get out of the side door, and the Judge is shaking hands with Susie.

'You tell Shuler,' she says, 'if he wants people to think hees the father of thees children he better giff me a writing. Then maybe I think so myself.'

'I *will*,' said the Judge, and maybe two-three days after that he takes Shuler out to the ranch and makes the marriage writing.

Then all the children come around Susie and say, 'Now, Mother, you will have to wear a hat.'

Susie, she says, 'Go, children, and ask your father.'

But it is not known to the Papagos what happened after that.

INDIANS TODAY

He found himself tied to a stake, with considerable quantities of dried brush piled around his legs.

A STARTLING DEVELOPMENT in American history is the complete reversal, over the last century, of our assumptions about the First Americans. The howling savage of yesterday is now a "pre-industrial" whose lifeway is better than the white man's. He is the abused gentleman; the white man is the savage—cruel, greedy and aggressive.

This did not occur overnight, of course. In fiction the first clear statement came in 1923 in Harold Bell Wright's *The Mine with the Iron Door*, set in the mountains near Tucson. Natachee, an educated Apache who considers himself an outcast from both races, blames the white man's greed for ruining his people and his homeland. After that the floodgates opened and in such novels as W. I. Comfort's *Apache* (1931), Elliot Arnold's *Blood Brother* (1947), and Jane Barry's *A Time in the Sun* (1962) the white man on the way down and the Indian on the way up pass each other like buckets in a well. Geronimo, once damned by General George Crook as "the worst Indian who ever lived," became a symbol of heroic resistance to oppression and injustice. He became, in fact, in the view of one novelist (Forrest Carter, *Watch for Me on the Mountain*, 1978) the Apache George Washington or even the Apache Moses, leading his people to a Promised Land in Mexico.

The humorists have been slow to find anything amusing in these forbidding facts, but several have tried. Byrd Baylor sees her Papagos as victims of a white bureaucracy so inept as to be comical. John Templeton's Indians can beat the whites at their own games, including golf. The Arizona pioneers never imagined anything like this.

JUDGE STILLWELL'S INDIAN SCARE

Charles U. Pickrell

BORN IN NEBRASKA, CHARLES U. (PICK) PICKRELL grew up on a ranch near Tempe and worked as a cowboy and teacher before enrolling at the University of Arizona. After graduation he served for two years in the Field Artillery and returned from France to a job with the Agricultural Extension Service. In 1937 he became its head. He was widely acquainted in Arizona and everywhere he went he heard true stories which he loved to retell. In fact, his career as a storyteller ran neck and neck with his career as a livestock specialist. When he died in 1962, he left a legacy of humorous anecdotes which will enrich the state's culture for a long time.

This is a story told to me by the late Mary Stillwell Buell. Mrs. Buell was a native daughter of Tombstone and for many years preceding her death was head of the Extension work in Home Economics at the University of Nevada. My first acquaintance with her was as my teacher in the eighth grade.

Her father, William H. Stillwell was Associate Justice of the Territorial Supreme Court of Arizona during the period 1881-1885 and later he enjoyed a fine legal practice in Arizona.

The story took place during the time his assignment included the counties of Cochise and Graham.

On this occasion the Judge had closed the session at Tombstone and was proceeding from there to Solomonville to convene another session of court—at that time Solomonville was the county seat of Graham County. This being before Greenlee County was created.

He was driving two horses to a buckboard and had already passed through Bowie and was on the last stretch of his journey.

From a talk given to the Arizona Historical Convention, March 26, 1960. Ms., Arizona Historical Society.

For some reason, he looked back and was horror stricken at what he saw—two Indians on horseback were rapidly approaching his vehicle.

The judge not being one proficient in the use of firearms, soon decided to employ the speed of his pair of horses as a possible means of escape, hoping to reach a ranch or another traveler before he was captured by the redskins. Although the horses, with the aid of the whip, put forth a noble burst of speed, it was not long before the Indians caught up with the judge. But, instead of filling him with arrows or bullets, they returned to him one of his law books that had dropped out of the buckboard.

MRS. DOMINGO FACES LIFE IN TUCSON

Byrd Baylor

BYRD BAYLOR, BORN IN TEXAS, at home in New Mexico and Old
Mexico, and now a resident of Arizona, made a reputation as an
author of books for children before writing *Yes Is Better Than No,*
her first adult novel. Her characters are displaced Papago Indians,
living off the reservation and trying to keep their lives and
families together in a poor district of Tucson. They had to cope
with the puzzling ways of the white people who pass out welfare
checks and tell them what to do. Mrs. Domingo and her friends
find it is better to say yes to whatever these people propose, and
then find ways to circumvent them. Mrs. Domingo has won a
swimming pool in a contest. She has no use for it, so she covers it
over and lives in it. Sue Mills, the social worker, visits her there.

Since this Manny Escalante figured out the way to get an
address for Maria to give to the welfare lady, word has spread that
he has the knack of understanding how Anglos think. Mrs.
Domingo admires this talent, and she likes to question him. She
herself enjoys discovering hidden meanings, omens, signs. She's
wise, but wise in Indian ways, not Anglo ways.

Indians know that a white person will choose whatever makes
the most trouble for everyone; he'll never think of the natural
easy way that would come first to an Indian's mind. So it's not just
anyone who can ever guess how those minds are working, what
strange paths they follow.

Today Mrs. Domingo is sitting in a rocking chair down in the
deep end of the swimming pool. Rose and Lopez are stretched

From *Yes Is Better Than No*. New York: Charles Scribner's Sons, 1977. The
passage quoted is Chapter 8, pp. 70-83.

out on the slanting cement floor asleep, their heavy shoes touching. Manny and Maria are in the two straight chairs facing Mrs. Domingo, watching as she rolls a Bull Durham cigarette. She'd never smoke out in the sunlight, but now that she's old she can take that kind of pleasure in private among her friends.

It's dark down here, secret and magical with just the flickering light of the candles grouped around the pictures of St. Jude and St. Francis Xavier and the Virgin of Guadalupe.

They've moved a few of Maria's cardboard boxes down into the swimming pool, and the pictures of the saints are propped up on them. If anybody from welfare comes around, Maria knows what she is supposed to say: "See, that's my stuff. I live right here."

She's practiced saying it to Manny. A whisper. She can't bring her voice up out of her throat when she thinks of speaking to a social worker, but Manny tells her, "You got to speak out the way *they* do. They'll never believe you unless you talk loud."

Now Manny is leaning forward explaining again how the idea of the address came into his mind. It's something you can discuss many times.

"That's just one of the regular rules over there at welfare," he says. "No rent money to be given out to anybody who hasn't got a house."

"Seems to me they'd give you the money quicker than ever if they knew you didn't have a roof over your head." She draws on her cigarette, holding it carefully between her thumb and forefinger.

"Not them," Manny says. "They got a whole different way of seeing things."

Mrs. Domingo considers it from another angle. "What if she'd said she had a house all right but there just wasn't a number on it anywhere? I've seen houses like that."

"That wouldn't help," he says. "If their rule says they want a number, then you got to get one for them. Never mind the house. Just so you got the number. They really stick to things like that."

"They do," Maria nods.

They sit awhile in silence, hearing the slow steady whine of Lopez' breathing and the voices of the children above ground, outside. But all three of them suddenly tense and Manny stands up. The children's voices have changed. You catch the tight careful sound that moves into Indian voices when an Anglo is present.

"It could be somebody to see you," Mrs. Domingo whispers to Maria. "Remember, you just act like this is your place right here. Don't even look over at the alley."

Maria nods.

They can't quite hear what the children are saying, but there's no doubt they aren't talking to an Indian. You can tell that.

In this part of town even the youngest children know about answering questions and opening doors. You learn to peek out first. Just the slightest flutter of the curtains, the faintest whisper behind the door. If it's a white face, you wait for it to go away. Five. Ten. Fifteen minutes. White people don't like to wait long. But if they do wait and you finally open the door an inch, you pretend not to speak English. Or if you do speak English, you say (even if it's your brother they're asking for), "No I wouldn't know that name. I never heard of that one around here. No. I don't know."

Mrs. Domingo gets up stiffly, hands her cigarette to Manny. "I'm the one to find out," she says.

The floor of the pool slants so it's like climbing a steep little hill. The blue steps don't reach all the way to the floor, and there is an old bucket below the steps to climb onto first. It takes awhile.

As you come up you have to stoop to keep from hitting your head against the telephone poles and corrugated tin Pepsi Cola sign and cardboard that make the roof. You fold yourself over like any desert creature coming out of his burrow. Small as a gopher, you reach up toward sunlight. It is good to go from darkness to light; it recalls those first Papagos who struggled upward from the underworld.

But Mrs. Domingo has to wait a moment more to reach the light because the entrance to the pool now has a little shack built over it to keep the rain out. From the street it looks like any outhouse rising unsteadily from any pile of junk.

Mrs. Domingo peers out through the holes in this door before she pushes it open.

At first she can't even guess that the girl standing there in the sun talking to the children might be a social worker. They're so skinny and small, these white girls, how can you tell whether they're children or women? They dress like children anyway. Look at this one...bare suntanned legs, sandals, short red dress way above her knees, long blonde hair swinging loose. An Indian has sense enough to know when she changes from girl to women. Not these Anglos. They don't know the pleasures of the many seasons of life, don't know the satisfaction of ripening.

The girl has a puzzled look on her face. She is smiling at the children and now she turns quickly to smile at Mrs. Domingo too. But Mrs. Domingo is old enough that she doesn't have to smile for nothing the way white women do whether they mean it or not. So she waits. Just stands there.

This girl has an armful of papers. "I'm Sue Mills...from the welfare department."

The children move back and look at her, expectant, as though she might play a game with them. Even so, they're wary.

She's still smiling toward the children, first one and then another. Seven of them.

"They don't all live here, do they?"

"*Them?*" Mrs. Domingo glances around the yard as though she had never before noticed these shabby barefoot ones. Her grandchildren. She peers into their round dark faces.

Three of them are Rose's kids. Four are Lupe's. Lupe's little ones are still so young they can't understand that their mother has been taken away and they have looked for her all day—behind trees, in abandoned cars, in the ruins of the unfinished adobe house. Poor Lupe, locked up now in that hospital where Anglos put crazy people. If only they had waited until the medicine man had a chance to cure her...but Lupe had gone running through the streets at night. Of course they found her. And now nobody knows when she'll be home again.

"Mrs. Domingo?"

"Yes."

"I really have to ask. How many children are living here with you?"

Mrs. Domingo shrugs. "These kids from down the street? But they're just hanging around. That's all." She waves her arms, shouts at them in Papago, again roughly in English. "Go on home, you kids. Beat it."

And they go, bare feet kicking up dust as they streak across the vacant lot. Mrs. Domingo knows they'll run around the corner and wait until the white girl has gone. They all have sense enough for that. Even the three-year-old, Josefina. She is right behind the others, not looking back.

But this Sue Mills says in her excited little-girl voice, "The thing is, Mrs. Domingo, we've already had a complaint from the health department."

Mrs. Domingo sits down slowly on a log in the woodpile. "I got a few complaints myself," she says. She won't let them frighten her the way the younger women are always frightened.

Still smiling (Holy Mother, doesn't she ever stop that!) Sue Mills flings back her hair and sits down beside Mrs. Domingo, crossing her long suntanned legs in the sand. She hands two papers to Mrs. Domingo—one yellow, one white. But Mrs. Domingo doesn't even glance down at them. She waits for the girl to tell her.

"Inadequate plumbing...lack of running water...improper...."

"But we got an outhouse," Mrs. Domingo says.

"Yes, I see you have two of them." She smiles enthusiastically.

But Mrs. Domingo corrects her. "Only one. Why would we want two?"

Sue Mills glances toward the privy behind the two-room tin shack, then toward the thin little building huddled at the entrance of the swimming pool.

"Oh, that," Mrs. Domingo says. "That's to the swimming pool."

The girl jumps up and starts toward it, hesitates when she notices that the earth around it is covered with layers of tin and boards and palm fronds. Tacked to the door is a Virgin of Guadalupe poster which says THIS IS A CATHOLIC HOUSE. Someone has crossed out the word, HOUSE, and pencilled above it, SWIM POOL.

Mrs. Domingo watches the young social worker standing there in the sun squinting at the rough splintery boards of that doorway. But she does not make any explanation and the girl doesn't turn around for a long time. When she does, all she says is, "Wow!"

Mrs. Domingo usually brings out a chair when any important person comes to the house but this afternoon she doesn't because the two straight chairs and the rocking chair are all down in the swimming pool. Anyway, this girl is so young...and she doesn't stay anywhere for very long.

They sit down on pieces of mesquite in the woodpile and Sue Mills chews on her large pink sunglasses as she talks.

"I really hate to bring bad news," she says. "But the health department says the house has been known to be substandard for a long time and when you wash there's water running in the alley and...." She studies the papers. "And in a substandard two-room house, you cannot take in other people's children."

Mrs. Domingo relaxes, feels the muscles of her neck loosen. "It's okay then. I don't want to take in other people's children. To tell the truth, I never thought of it. I got enough trouble feeding my own grandkids."

The girls begins to shake her head even before she says anything. "But that's what they're talking about. Grandchildren."

"Them?"

"Now that your daughter...." She studies the yellow paper for the name. "Now that Lupe has been committed to the state hospital her children are eligible to be placed in foster homes and taken care of."

Mrs. Domingo doesn't speak yet. Just looks at the girl, looks at the sky, looks at the brown earth.

"Then, of course, the welfare department would pay for their care."

After a while Mrs. Domingo says, "Well, if welfare wants to pay somebody, let welfare pay me for their food. Two or three dollars now and then. That would do."

Sue Mills leans forward, her blue eyes round and bright. "Oh, a *relative* can't be certified as a foster parent."

Mrs. Domingo's face is blank, expressionless. She is glad to feel the sun on her, hot as it is; that's something she can understand.

"It's a rule, you know," the girl says finally.

"Who made that rule?" But she asks it quietly under her breath. Who thought of that one? Surely not an Indian. There's not an Indian in Arizona dumb enough to make a rule like that.

Mrs. Domingo thinks of the round one-room house where she was born out there on the reservation, a place made of bent ocotillo sticks covered with bunches of grass. A family in a room together...what's bad about that? It is a very good thing for a family to come together into its own small circle of light. It is a very good thing to hear each other's nighttime breathing. And who stays in a house so much anyway—except white people. An Indian is outside most of the time.

"Tell them we don't need that money," Mrs. Domingo says.

The girl looks distressed. Her smile is gone. "Really, I know how you feel. But the health department seems to think that..."

The papers lie between them on the ground. They both glance toward them. The girl seems lost in thought now but Mrs. Domingo knows something must be done, so she pulls herself up and leads the way over to the tin shack.

"Look here," she says, poking at a cardboard patch in the wall with the mesquite stick she is leaning on. "We're thinking of fixing this place up. It's already planned."

The girl looks doubtful, puts her own small smooth hand up to stroke a kitten which pushes under a torn piece of screen sagging limply from an open window.

"Paint and everything," Mrs. Domingo says.

"Then I can mention that in my report. That's good."

They walk over to the old adobe walls of the unfinished house. Mrs. Domingo never passes by without touching those walls, caressing their roughness, fingering the bits of straw still in the adobe.

"This is our real house, this one," Mrs. Domingo says. "But it never got itself finished."

They glance up, shading their eyes from the sun that shines down where the roof should be. "It would have been a good house. Three rooms," Mrs. Domingo says.

Sue Mills writes in her notebook. "Maybe I could call it a three-room house under construction."

Mrs. Domingo shrugs.

"When was this house started? I should mention that too."

"Twenty-three years ago."

"Well, perhaps I should just say *under construction*."

It doesn't matter to Elma Domingo. To her it's simply The House. They walk back toward the two-room shack and stand facing it. It's so quiet here now without the children, Mrs. Domingo feels lonely. A social worker is not much for company, she thinks, still looking straight ahead.

"Now that's how many people in these two rooms, Mrs. Domingo?"

"Who says they're all in there at the same time?"

"Well, *if* they are, how many?"

"To tell the truth, I never counted them up. I never thought of it."

"Would you count them up now, Mrs. Domingo?"

"Anyway, some sleep down in the swimming pool. And now that it's so hot, of course some sleep outside by the mesquite tree. Should I go counting in all those places?"

Sue Mills nods. "If you would. And then let me know." She begins to write, chews her orange pen, writes again very very slowly. "Another thing, Mrs. Domingo. For that many children I'm sure we ought to be able to say you have two bedrooms at the very least."

"But this little house here—that's two rooms. You can sure count those rooms in if you want to. Two."

"But are they *bedrooms*? Don't you cook in there too?"

"Sure, we cook in there. But there are beds all around."

"See, Mrs. Domingo, there's not supposed to be cooking in a sleeping room."

"No?" Well, her ancestors out there in the desert didn't know that either. "I got to remember that," she says.

"It would be just wonderful if in your remodeling you could build another bedroom. Then you'd have one for the boys and one for the girls."

"That's better, huh?"

"Well...yes."

Mrs. Domingo shakes her head. There's so much to remember, so many rules. You don't know whether to act like they make sense or not. It's like talking to a crazy person...like talking to Lupe.

The girl is walking back and forth, squinting in the sun. "That pool, Mrs. Domingo...whatever is under all that? It really is a pool? An empty pool?"

"Sure." Mrs. Domingo isn't going to explain everything in the world to this girl. "A swimming pool."

"Could I possibly have a look down there? It might help if I could mention it in my report, but I don't know quite how to...."

So they walk over to the door and Mrs. Domingo pulls it open.

"You have to go down backwards." She waits for the girl to go in and disappear down the blue steps.

There is a thin mattress at the shallow end. "Careful," Mrs. Domingo calls down to her. "You can't stand up very well right there. It's a real good place for sleeping though."

In the deep end, Maria and Manny sit in the two straight chairs which have had the front legs shortened so they now rest fairly steadily against the slope of the pool. In the dim light it takes a minute or two before the girl can see. A chicken steps daintily over the two sleeping figures—Rose and Lopez, their heads slanting downward, arms wide apart for balance—and moves toward the social worker.

Maria and Manny do not look up. They sit there formally, sit there looking into space, straight, silent, unmoving. Sue Mills turns quickly away, moves back toward the steps.

"Of course there's still a lot to be done," Mrs. Domingo says. "Someday we might get a real long electric cord so we could hang a light down from outside. Some people say we could even hook up a TV."

The girl is back up the blue steps even before Mrs. Domingo has started down.

"Well," Sue Mills says. "My...!"

Mrs. Domingo follows her slowly, slowly. Outside in the sunlight they look again at those papers, the white one and the yellow one. The girl is very quiet now, very thoughtful. Finally she says, "How about this? Two-room house with separate recreation room...."

Now Mrs. Domingo is willing to smile at the girl a little. Not much, but a little—the way you'd smile at a foolish child who still has much to learn. Of course, that's the way it is with so many of these Anglos who tell people what the rules are; they may know the rules all right, but they don't know anything else. You almost feel sorry for them the way they make such a fuss over things that don't matter at all.

"Recreation room...or maybe family room. And I'll be sure to mention that you're making some repairs."

"Many repairs," Mrs. Domingo says.

Sue Mills nods. "Extensive repairs. That's what I'm saying."

Mrs. Domingo stands in the shade and watches as the girl drives away. As soon as she is out of sight, the children begin peering around the greasewood bushes in the vacant lot. By the time she is a block away, they are all back asking, "Is it okay?"

Rose and Lopez come up from the swimming pool, still sleepy, blinking in the sun, worried. Maria and Manny stand beside them and Ignacio comes around the corner of the shack. Maria's two oldest girls, Anna and Amelia, run across the alley. They've been hiding behind the abandoned car, listening.

Everybody gathers now, slowly, casually, as though they just happened to be passing the palo verde tree, pausing for a moment in its thin shade.

"I'll tell you what," Mrs. Domingo says. "It would be a very good thing if we could find that boy that paints so pretty and he would come over here and put a lot of paint on this place." She lifts her hand toward the two-room shack. "A lot of paint to cover the boards and tin and everything."

"What color?" one of the children asks.

"Maybe blue. Maybe yellow. Pink would be okay. Green."

"I'll go get that boy then," Anna says. "I know where he is—hiding over at the Gomez place, but he can't come out until dark."

There are always boys in hiding, living at somebody else's house, avoiding probation officers, schools, police, foster homes ... anything that traps you. Mrs. Domingo doesn't remember what this one, this Gabriel, is hiding from, but she wouldn't want him to take a chance on getting caught. "Tell him to come down the alley," she calls after Anna. "Tell him to be careful."

Then Mrs. Domingo turns to the rest of them. "We got to get a little money for some paint."

"I go to work for a lady tomorrow," Maria says. "I could give some."

But Manny and Lopez and Ignacio, the three men, shake their heads.

"Forget it," Manny says. "We'll go find paint. We'll get it today."

"You got money?"

"We'll find some that somebody isn't using. We'll look around."

Ignacio puts on his straw hat and goes in one direction, Lopez in another, but Mrs. Domingo signals Manny to wait. She wants to talk to him. First, however, she puts the children to work carrying rocks to make a border around the house, a little mound three or four inches high. Even stones lining the path to the outhouse, the path to the woodpile.

Then she comes back to the shade and Manny and Maria follow her.

"I'll tell you this other rule they got. Maybe you can figure something out."

"He can," Maria says.

"This house is not supposed to be just any two rooms. It's supposed to be two *bedrooms*." She says it slowly as though she herself isn't sure what the words mean.

Maria doesn't understand it either. "But people do sleep in both of those rooms."

"Sure, I told her that. But the rule says you got to sleep in rooms just made for sleeping. No stove or sink. No kitchen stuff. I guess that's it."

The children are listening too as they carry rocks. Amelia calls to them, "What if you said the stove wasn't really for cooking, just to keep warm with?"

Manny shakes his head. "No use. If they got that rule, you can't make them change it."

They walk over to the house, open the door, stare in at the old stove with the pot of beans on it, the table with the tin coffee cups and the plate of tortillas and the bowl of ground red chiles and the sugar. The boxes turned to sit on. The pots and pans hanging on the wall. The buckets for carrying water. The large round washtub for bathing. The shrine with its lighted candles, its paper flowers. The cigar box nailed to the wall for important papers. The three sagging beds, the mattresses on the dirt floor. The old refrigerator with the door propped open, a place for storing flour and beans and lard and coffee.

"Two bedrooms, eh?" Manny ponders it.

Mrs. Domingo repeats it. "Two. They aren't supposed to sleep in the same room...the girls and the boys." She shrugs.

"Even the babies?" Maria asks.

"Anybody," Mrs. Domingo says. "Any age."

They smile.

"Listen," Manny says. "You just got to think of that rule. No matter how crazy. Just think of that rule and we'll find some way to beat it."

They walk slowly around the house, back out the front door, over to the mesquite tree.

"Sure," Manny says. "You just take the stove and the icebox outside."

"Then we got no kitchen."

"No, but there's no rule says you got to have a kitchen. Then at least you got you a two-bedroom house."

So it is settled. "I never minded cooking outside anyway," Mrs. Domingo says.

Manny and Rose and Maria begin pulling the stove across the dirt floor and out the door, getting the stovepipe down, dragging out the boxes of pots and pans, the refrigerator. All this goes under the ramada now, under the trees. Anywhere.

"What about the table? Can you have a table in a bedroom?"

"No, I don't think so," Manny decides. "Just beds. Nothing but where they're going to sleep. Boys and girls...."

"And the saints," Mrs. Domingo says. "I know it's okay to have saints in there."

The artist, Gabriel, arrives while they are still bringing out boxes of dishes. He doesn't want to wait until night after all. Somebody drives him over in a red Ford and they wheel around the corner in a haze of exhaust smoke and the rumbling noise of a dragging muffler. The car roars through the alley, stops by the woodpile. When the dust settles, two boys crawl under the car to tie the muffler up again with a piece of wire from the neighbor's fence while another raises the hood and unscrews the radiator cap. Gabriel gets out and the children all put down their rocks and come to stand beside him.

He looks at the tin and plywood and cardboard of that shack and shakes his head and laughs. "They're going to say you're crazy to try to paint up that pile of junk. Man, you need a lot more than paint."

Mrs. Domingo gives him a straight old-lady stare, acts as though she had not heard him. She wants more respect from the young ones, doesn't like to see Papago boys acting like Anglos—not speaking properly to their elders. She makes him wait for awhile before she speaks to him.

"You an artist?"

"I can paint any picture," Gabriel says. "Give me anything to copy, a postcard or a holy picture or a girl or mountains and cactus."

"Which ones do you do best?"

"Holy pictures, I guess." He spits in the dust. "That or girls."

Mrs. Domingo points with her mesquite stick to a large piece of tin wired to the wall near the door—a faint white and red reminder that it was once part of an advertisement for chewing tobacco.

"That would be a good place for a picture," Mrs. Domingo tells him. She backs off and squints. "Most of the boards will just be painted, maybe blue...whatever colors they find around today. But it would be a very pretty thing to have some real pictures too."

Gabriel stands back considering the project, hands deep in the pockets of his skintight levis. He slowly ties his unbuttoned flowered shirt at the waist, lights a cigarette and nods. "I did the Garden of Gethsemane for my mother for Christmas and once I did St. Teresa for my probation officer."

One of the boys gets up from under the car and comes over and kicks at the cardboard walls of the house. "He does horses good too," he tells them. "Maybe he could put some way back behind the Jesus or something."

Mrs. Domingo goes inside, comes out again with a 1958 calendar of religious pictures. "I wonder what *they'd* like."

Everybody looks at the pictures. Mrs. Domingo keeps coming back to St. Martin cutting his cloak in two with a sword, wrapping half of the red scrap around the shoulders of a beggar—almost naked, poor man.

"That's dumb," the children keep saying. "Now he's ruined his coat and the naked guy is still cold with just that rag around him."

Even so, there is a fine prancing white horse which St. Martin is riding and this is a good saint for the poor. Everybody knows that.

St. Martin then.

Gabriel sharpens his pencil with a green switchblade knife, props the calendar up against the wall, and begins to draw on the tin.

"I still don't think it's going to do any good," he says.

"You do it anyway," Mrs. Domingo says quietly. "We got to try."

"Okay."

"And remember, you've always got this for a place to come to any time you got to hide from somebody."

"Thank you very much." He is polite now, treating her as an old woman should be treated.

"How about house numbers?" she asks him. "Can you paint them very pretty over the door?"

"Sure I can. But it's not going to do any good."

Now Mrs. Domingo walks away from all of them, walks down the street to her old friend, Jude. Saint of the impossible. Staring straight ahead, as always. A little dusty, a little faded.

The thing is, she tells him, we don't know yet just exactly what those rules are. We don't know what we have to do to keep Lupe's kids. But maybe the little paths will help, and of course we'll rake the dirt nice and smooth. And then the paint. White people always like a painted house.

What's your suggestion, Jude?

She walks home across the vacant lots, down the dusty alleys. Her old feet prefer the feeling of earth under them, not sidewalks. Not cement.

CHARLIE EAGLETOOTH TAKES ON THE GOVERNMENT

John Templeton

ADVERTISING MAN JOHN TEMPLETON, educated in California and based in Nevada, takes the humorous approach to Indian problems in his first novel. The scene is the Zapi Reservation, populated by affluent, tourist-supported, university-educated delightful tribesmen. They drive Cadillacs and take their pleasure at the Bent Arrow Country Club on the reservation, but they are concerned about their less-prosperous Indian neighbors. Five years before, the government had planned the Coyote Canyon Dam, which would benefit these indigent tribesmen, but nothing had been done. When the tribal council learns that a new superhighway has reached the edge of the reservation and is surveying on Indian land without tribal approval, Charlie Porter (Eagletooth), Dr. Gene Blackhawk, and visiting journalist Doris Evans plot to take advantage of an 1877 treaty which gives the tribe status as an independent nation if the whites should ever encroach on their territory. To kick off the campaign, the entire male population of the reservation—all eighty of them—dress up in Indian costume, mount a string of rented horses, and raid a surveying party. Harley Burton, State Department bigwig, is sent to suppress the "Indian rebellion." He gets suppressed himself. It takes a visit from the president of the United States to achieve a satisfactory solution.

Harley Burton was in a bad mood. He had considered the breakfast one of the worst he was ever forced to endure. It only went to prove a pet theory, he reflected, on how the culture and civilization of a society can best be determined by its ability to cook

From *Charlie Eagletooth's War.* New York: William Morrow, 1969, pp. 109–120.

a three-minute egg. The particular stratum into which this present insidious block of humanity must be relegated became fairly obvious after he was forced to send back nine eggs as totally unfit for human consumption. Ultimately he gave up in disgust, having only toast and coffee. If this were not enough humiliation, he was still irritated over the absurd indignities he was forced to undergo in that grimy little room with no bathroom and its rickety, antique bed. People who lived in such uncivilized squalor were little better than animals, he finally concluded.

Standing up from the table, he meticulously put on his homburg, picked up his brief case, and strode belligerently from the room. In the hotel lobby he discovered his two deputies. Everett Williams and Eddie Meadows, nervously waiting for him. On a brief visual inspection of their persons, his eyes widened in horror on seeing how each man, in addition to carrying a rifle, had a revolver plus an oversized hunting knife hanging from a belt at his waist. Burton walked quickly across the room, to stand in front of them menacingly.

"Would you two mentally incompetent morons get rid of those guns immediately? This is a peace mission, and there is no place in it for firearms."

"I don't think you understand, Mr. Burton," Everett intoned plaintively. "If we don't go in there armed, it's doubtful we will ever come back out."

"He ain't just whistling 'Dixie,'" Eddie Meadows added anxiously. "We ain't got much chance as it is, but without guns we're just askin' to get our hair parted with a tommy hawk."

Harley suppressed the anger he felt welling up in his throat, since it was not good to lose your temper in front of subordinates. He spoke levelly. "Take those guns off immediately and leave them here in the hotel. That is an order."

Both men looked at each other questioningly before laying the rifles against a table and unbuckling their gun belts. Neither spoke. Their expressions of condemned helplessness said all that was necessary. Harley watched their movements as they slowly obeyed his commands, sensing from the looks given him by the other people in the lobby that nobody agreed with him. This made him feel good, because any course of action this rabble considered wrong must in its final analysis be correct. When the disarming process was completed, he turned abruptly on his heel and headed for the main entrance.

It was on his arrival on the front porch that the second shock of this troubled morning awaited him. Standing in dusty elegance by the steps was a long, black Cadillac. This, on top of everything else, made Harley want to scream in anguish. Its age was doubtful; however, as to the car's primary function, there was no doubt. It was a hearse. Not only was this quite sufficient to be in bad taste, but faded white lettering on its side proclaimed to all the world that this vehicle was the property of the Embassy Embalming Parlor. Adding insult to injury, beneath those big six-inch-high letters appeared a phrase in neatly painted script, "We bury you in style. You harvest the happiness of knowing you had the best."

A crowd of people gathered to watch Harley's departure stared in fascination as he stood frozen in front of the car. His first reaction was to turn around and go back inside, but this course of action was discarded when he noted movie cameras and television trucks all jockeying for position to film him. Jamming in around the car's doors were other reporters, all eager for a word or statement about his proposed encounter. He realized any show of indecision on his part might be misinterpreted, so with bold strides he walked down the stairs, past reporters with their shouted questions, and slid into the hearse's front seat. In trying to remain aloof while ignoring a blatantly impolite press, he almost made the mistake of trying to enter the car's rear door. This would have been disastrous. He fortunately had seen in time that there was no back seat, only a large, carpet-covered pallet. Everett Williams and Eddie Meadows jointed him in the front seat, as Everett started the car and drove quickly away.

Once out of sight from Salt Wells, Harley raised his voice in an angry command. "Stop the car!"

When Everett braked it quickly, almost running off the road in his haste to comply, Harley snapped again. "I won't ask where you found this hideous example of a vehicle, but since I must ride in it, you"—he nodded his head defiantly at Eddie Meadows—"get in back."

"Not me," Eddie objected, with fear. "I ain't gettin' back there. That's for dead people, and maybe I ain't far from it, but you're not stuffin' me back there."

"Don't argue with me—move!"

Meadows looked forlornly at his friend Everett, and after seeing the resignation in his eyes, shrugged his shoulders dejectedly before climbing over the seat. There was insufficient room to sit up, and this forced him to stretch out on the padded partition. It seemed, as he stared furtively around with a fear-crazed look in his eyes, that he fully expected to meet many of the Embassy Embalming Parlor's former customers. Everett Williams felt a great deal of sympathy for his pal, but at the moment he was more convinced than ever that Eddie was right in his first reaction to this trip. They should have taken the twenty years in prison.

Charlie felt rivulets of sweat running down his back and chest as he stood beside a huge protective boulder to survey a narrow dirt road twisting below him. Kelly Grinning Fox relaxed comfortably in the rock's shadow, smoking a cigarette. At his feet rested a square, black box with a plunger and wires running out from its base down the hill. Charlie felt more than a little bit uneasy, since even though they were a good hundred yards away; and over fifty feet above the road, he was uncertain as to exactly what those boxes of dynamite would do when touched off. Kelly's assurances that everything would be all right did little to soothe an increasing anxiety. Shifting his gaze, he looked behind a small hill and saw the twenty horses and men of his raiding party waiting patiently. Checking his watch for what seemed like the fiftieth time in the past hour, he cursed silently at the slow passage of time. By his calculations they still had at least ten minutes to go.

Kelly shifted his position on the rocky ground, groaned, pulled out a small, sharp-edged rock from where he was sitting, and spoke confidently. "Would you take it easy, Charlie? Everything's going to be all right."

"You're a fine one to be talking so lightly," Charlie said caustically. "Hell, you're not even sure what all that damned dynamite will do when it blows. Besides, are you certain it will go off when you push that plunger? We only want to stop that car, not blow it up."

"I tried to explain to you a dozen times before, a match-type fuse is unreliable. These electrical demo caps are the only way to fly. Now don't worry. You signal when the car is fifty feet from that draw, and I'll touch it off like the Fourth of July."

"Okay," Charlie said unhappily, "but I can't help but think that two whole boxes of that stuff is too much. We just want an explosion sufficient to stop the car, not dig a subterranean crater."

"Would you leave it up to me? The full force of that stuff should go straight up in the air, making nothing but a damned big noise and a lot of dust. Settle down. You're running this war like you play golf—in a sweat about everything."

Charlie glowered at his diminutive companion and contemplated making a nasty remark but decided to forget the whole thing. When it came to golf, Kelly was the one guy who drove him absolutely crazy. He was physically superior to the small man in almost every respect, but only about six times in the last five years had he ever been able to beat him. In fact, if Peg ever learned how much money he had blown to Kelly out on the course, then all hell would really break loose. Hastily he jerked to attention, scanning the horizon intently. There was no doubt about it, he thought excitedly, it has to be Harley Burton, as in the distance a small cloud of white, powdery dust began spiraling skyward from the desert floor.

Harley Burton leaned forward to knock his cigar ash into a small dashboard ash tray while staring impassively at a bleak desert landscape jouncing past his window. He could feel streams of perspiration running beneath his shirt, and he bemoaned the fact there was no air conditioner in the car. It was his understanding that they were standard equipment on all vehicles manufactured after 1950.

Once again he returned his thoughts to the countryside moving past him and cursed the land along with everything connected with bringing him here. This property was too damned good for these troublemakers, he reflected. By God, if he had anything to say about it, he would see that this entire tribe was transported to the windswept Arctic tundra and ice floes. If nothing else, they would quickly learn respect for their betters. He let his eyes glance covertly at Everett Williams, who was fighting the automobile's steering wheel as if it had suddenly come to life as a twisting monster. Harley was silently cheerful that both Williams and his obnoxious friend in the back had chosen to remain quiet during the trip. He was not interested in listening to any further cowardly remarks on their part.

The road had just completed a long, gradual turn and was heading again for open country when it happened. Everything in front of the long, black hood erupted in a mighty roar of rock, sand, and sagebrush. The hearse came to an abrupt stop as its front end was lifted high into the air like a toy and slammed back to earth in a loud, bone-rattling crash. Harley sat in startled dismay, trying to see through a brown cloud of dust engulfing them, while Everett Williams stared blankly through the yellowed windshield as if trying to comprehend what had happened to the road.

Above the ear-shattering boom and sound of falling boulders came the terrified voice of Eddie Meadows shouting from in back. "I knew it would happen—I knew it—those damned red savages have the atom bomb!"

His words fell on deaf ears, as both Everett and Harley were staring mutely out a side window. Their eyes were hypnotically glued to a scene of pure terror: a blood-curdling charge by a horde of mounted, murderous Indians. Many experts claim that a man's reaction to danger is almost always the same. It is an irrevocable pattern within himself which can never be altered. But Everett Williams proved this theory to be totally erroneous. Reversing his previous reaction to those plunging wild-eyed devils, he quickly opened the car's door and sprinted up the road, creating his own cloud of dust. Eddie Meadows, extricating himself from the rear of the hearse like a greased eel leaving a pipe, followed his friend with equal vigor. When last seen both men were heading back toward Salt Wells at a speed that would have done credit to a stakes horse setting a new track record.

Harley, on the other hand, was too stunned either to run or yell or, for that matter, even breathe. He merely sat there in weak obedience until his captors yanked him unceremoniously from the car. Years of training came momentarily to his aid as he tried to retain some form of dignity while being dragged toward a waiting horse. Regardless, his efforts quickly deserted him when he was gagged, blindfolded, and tied belly-down on the animal. Fortunately, when the full realization of his danger ultimately filtered into his mind, he passed out.

Charlie walked over to check his prisoner's welfare and was quite pleased to see he was unconscious. Turning with an angry shout, he directed the full extent of his wrath at Kelly Grinning Fox.

"Of all the stupid, lame-brained jerks in the world, Kelly, you are the biggest. I thought that stuff was only supposed to make some noise. Why, hell, man, in addition to being heard three states away, you've blown a damned hole fifty feet across in this abandoned road."

"What the devil are you mad about?" Kelly shouted over the noise of men trying to control their obstinate horses. "Nobody got hurt, did they?" After a great deal of cursing and pleading in conjunction with plain old-fashioned begging, the Zapi warriors got their horses all going in the right direction, and trotted off after Kelly. Charlie watched balefully for a moment before mounting his own animal to follow. The remainder of the trip was uneventful, as most of the participating parties were concerned only with their own immediate survival while perched precariously on the backs of those unpredictable beasts.

When Harley raised his head, swimming upward from a blessed blackness of escape, he viewed his surroundings with a total lack of comprehension. He found himself tied to a stake, with considerable quantities of dried brush piled around his legs. Walking disinterestedly past him were scores of painted savages, both male and female, while a huge fire blazed about ten feet away. Probably a prime factor contributing to his confusion was the startling authenticity of the Indian village in which he found himself. Giant, white circular teepees, approximately fifteen in number, stretched across his vision, with an assortment of skin-drying racks, pottery, council fires, and hitching poles scattered about the premises.

A light breeze fanned the fire, and he felt a warm gust of air waft across his chest. Glancing down, he was shocked to discover that he was stripped to the waist. It must have been approximately at this point when Harley understood this all to be no dream or hallucination, because he raised his shiny bald head to the heavens, let forth a piercing scream, and began to fight wildly at the ropes holding him. During a lull in his hysteria, he looked up to see a tall, regal-appearing Indian standing in front of him. The savage raised his hand in a gesture of silence before speaking haughtily.

"Me Eagletooth, Great War Chief Zapi Nation. You gettum war lance saying we only talk with great white father in eastern castle. Why you come here? Why you spy on my people?" Sweeping his hand in a dramatic movement of kingly quality, Charlie spoke flatly, as if this were all a great bother to him. "We council now, to see if you live or die." Turning abruptly, he walked away with his arms folded across his chest, back ramrod straight, and a face that was doing its best to keep from being convulsed in laughter.

Harley watched his captor's stately retreat with a feeling that his doom was sealed. Shortly after Charlie's departure, two ferocious squaws came toward him and placed three large branding irons in the flames. They grunted in unintelligible phrases, apparently preparing themselves to enjoy the imminent festivities. His blood ran cold as they moved closer, speculatively prodding his ribs with jabbing fingers. What Harley had no way of knowing was that these two berserk, mumbling females were in reality Fran Singing Bird, president of the local P.T.A., and Janet Hamilton, a Brownie Scout leader.

While he stood frozen in terror, no longer conscious of the ropes restricting him, he watched the two women return to the fire, each giggling with insane glee over some private joke. As they stirred those long, brutal irons among the glowing coals, he could not help but equate them with those witches stirring a caldron in Shakespeare's *Macbeth*. He noticed how the branding irons were now pulsating in a white heat, and his Adam's apple seemed to be stuck in a parched, dry throat.

Fran Singing Bird, shuffling to some unheard melody, which in reality was a Watusi to a current rock 'n' roll hit, moved over to one side and picked up a large, hairy steer hide. Janet Hamilton caught her cue and stooped down to remove one of those glowing torture instruments from the fire. With a bloodthirsty leer, she moved toward the extended hide which Fran was waving like a practiced toreador. She feinted and parried the metal rod, and Harley felt an increased tension as its hot tip, in dramatic effect, approached closer and closer to the furry cow skin. With a final orgiastic scream, Janet plunged the weapon into the hide, from which there came a steaming cloud of black smoke. Burton had little difficulty in imagining that this was his own flesh, as a putrid smell of burning hide filled his nostrils. This, then, was the final act required to shove Harley over the brink, into a world of peaceful, velvet oblivion.

From a main tent Charlie and several other members of the tribal council watched the proceedings with clinical eyes. Some were obviously enjoying this spectacle, while others were fearful that they might overdo scaring the poor guy. When the two girls realized their act was over, they smiled conspiratorially before collapsing into each other's arms in gales of hysterical laughter.

"What do we do now, Charlie?" inquired Marty Black Cloud as they walked to a cooler in the rear of a central command teepee to get a cold beer.

"Gene's going to give him a sedative to make certain he'll be out for at least a few hours, and we'll take him back to Salt Wells. I think when Mr. Harley Burton regains consciousness, he will have changed his mind about our being serious."

Dan Evans scratched his head thoughtfully before muttering in a voice definitely tinged with worry, "You're probably right, but let's hope the pompous ass doesn't panic and call in the whole damned army to wipe us out."

Charlie chuckled at his friend's concern and returned his thoughts to the very convincing act just put on by Fran Singing Bird and Janet Hamilton. He had known both women personally for many years, and there was no doubt about their being two of the mildest souls around. Either they were damned good actresses, he reflected, or quite possibly it was all only an insight into their true hidden natures. The thought caused a cold chill to vibrate up his spine. Pulling off an aluminum tab on the beer can's top, he tilted it to his mouth and let its cool liquid caress his throat. Lowering the can, he looked seriously at Marty Black Cloud and spoke in terms of finality, tinged with dismay.

"Any time some idiot tries to con you into believing that women are the weaker, gentler sex, you tell him to go suck an egg."

COUNTRY ROADS

He was stirrin' the beans with a six-shooter when I rode into camp.

ARIZONA IS, AND WILL ALWAYS BE, mostly country. The cities are deceptive. They seem enormous, and they are, but the desert and the mountains are too rough and resistent for the kind of living most people prefer. True, Phoenix smog is drifting south almost to Tucson, and dirt bikes are tearing up the desert and the dry washes within reach from Broadway and Main, but the vast desert west of Yuma, the endless flats and slopes between Phoenix and Kingman, and the rocky canyons of the Mazatzals will remain inaccessible to the multitude. The miners and cattle ranchers and loggers are still at work, however, in the lonely places, and their talk and tales still go on, adding to the rich store of country humor that makes Arizona a good place to talk and write about.

THE MOVIES COMES TO SALOME

Dick Wick Hall

DEFOREST (DICK WICK) HALL, Iowa born, came to Arizona about the turn of the century and began a career as newsman, mining and real-estate promoter, and popular humorist. In 1906 he founded the desert hamlet of Salome on the proposed route of a railroad from Phoenix to California. Emigrants in Tin Lizzies were already heading for the Promised Land. Hall offered a store, a restaurant, a post office, gasoline, and a one-page newspaper called the *Salome Sun,* filled with country humor, cracker-barrel philosophy, along with glimpses of Arizona's unreconstructed population. Before long a wide range of newspapers were reprinting it, and it became a regular feature of the *Saturday Evening Post.* At the height of a promising career, Hall died in a Los Angeles hospital in 1926. His Salome frog, seven years old and unable to swim, was and is his most famous piece.

A Big Crowd of about Sixty Folks, including those from Gold Gulch, Cactus Flats and Buzzard's Roost, and Mr. and Mrs. Three Fingered Jack Martin and children from the Hip O Circle Ranch, was at the Moving Picture Show at the Salome School House Wednesday Night, give by Mr. Mallory from Los Angeles, as advertised exclusively in the Salome Sun last week, which shows it pays to Advertise.

Mr. Mallory has a Portable Outfit run off from his automobile and made a purpose to give Moving Pictures at Places like Salome that haven't never had none yet. All he has to do is to drive his car up to the School House and Jack Up his Back End and put a Belt

From *Dick Wick Hall: Stories from the Salome Sun by Arizona's most famous humorist.* Collected by Frances Dorothy Nutt. Flagstaff: Northland Press, 1963, pp, 23-25.

onto his Hind Wheel and this makes the Electricity that runs the machine in the School House on a wire and then turns a crank and Grinds out the Pictures.

It didn't get Dark until near Train Time, but everybody was at the School House by Sundown, except Snappy Dan, the Agent, who has to meet the Train or lose his job. Mallory borrowed some blankets from the Blue Rock Inne, where he stopped, to cover up the Window and make it Dark so some of the Buzzard Roosters couldn't see in for Nothing, and a sheet to hang up in the back end of the school house to see the Pictures on. The section boss loaned him some railroad ties and some planks to make extra seats out of and the rest of the Folks took turns on the outside looking through the door, those that couldn't get in.

After everybody had got set that could get in, Mr. Mallory Jacked Up his Back End and put the belt on and started to make the Electricity and it comes into the School House on the wire and the Machine started to Buzz like a rattlesnake and everybody turned around or got up to look at it and all of a Sudden the back end of the School House all Lit Up and here comes our Train about a hundred yards down the track a running like the Devil and getting closer and closer and coming Right At Us and just as it looked like it was coming into the School House, the engineer Whistles—and That was All we saw, because Everybody was Gone by then, and those that got out first run around behind the school house to see the Wreck, thinking the Train had Jumped the Track, which it hadn't done at all as it was just pulling into the Depot.

Somebody had knocked the Picture Machine down in their Hurry to Get Out and it took Mr. Mallory quite awhile to get it set up again and coax some of the Folks back inside again, so this time he runs the Train sideways so as not to Scare some of the Women that was Nervous. The Train hadn't No More than got to going good again when it was Held Up and Robbed and two or three of the Passengers shot.

Some of the Gold Gulch boys that had their Guns on started to shooting at the Hold Ups and the Women and Kids and some of the rest of us that couldn't get out of the windows got in under the seats and the Leader of the Gang of Train Robbers, who looked a little like Buckskin Charley, he got Sore at the Gold Gulch boys mixing in on the Hold Up and he turned around and come running towards us and threw down on with a Gun that looked as big as a Stove Pipe and Blazed Away but Nobody got hurt this time either because there wasn't anybody left there but Mr. Mallory. There wasn't any Dance after the Show as advertised and No Show on Thursday Night either because Mr. Mallory left sometime during the night and took everything with him before anybody was up the Next Morning. Folks will have something to Talk About all Winter now.

THE FLYING COWBOY

Marguerite Noble

THE RUGGED RANGE COUNTRY north of Globe was home to Marguerite Noble during her growing up, and ranchmen and ranch women were the people she knew best. After a long career as a junior-high teacher in Phoenix she began to write about what she remembered, and when a short piece appeared in the *New York Times,* she wrote her novel *Filaree,* which has become an Arizona classic. It is a rather grim story about her mother's successful struggle for survival and happiness after her cowboy husband deserted his family, but Marguerite knew the other side of ranch life too, and described the life-saving humor of these often hard-pressed country people with equal skill.

The late Duck Robbins, cowboy and rodeo hand, tells of an event when he was rodeoing. After the show was finished, several of the contestants gathered in Dick's room to relax with a snort or more of panther juice.

Dick was traveling with his partner. They worked as one, sharing expenses, sharing their horse, pooling their entry fees, and splitting equally their winnings. Their first loyalty was to their buddy.

After a few more swallows of panther elixer the merriment increased. Dick's partner said, "I bet I could jump out this window and fly around this here hotel." The bets were on. "Here's ten dollars says you can't. "Here's ten dollars says you can."

The braggart took one final nip of that wonderful drink and stepped to the open window. He raised his arms, and with a mighty jump sailed into the wild blue yonder. A screeching wail rent the air and all was still.

From *The Payson Review,* January 24, 1989.

The cowboys rushed outside and dragged their unfortunate companion from the bushes under the window. It is amazing how the episode cleared the "flyer's" thinking. He turned to his buddy Dick and said, "You're sure a helluva partner! What'd you let me do that for?"

Dick replied, "Why, I thought you could. I lost ten dollars on you."

IT TAKES TIME

Budge Ruffner

LESTER WARD "BUDGE" RUFFNER of Prescott would be a candidate for the position of Humorist Laureate of Arizona, if there was such a post. Arizona born, with a family background going back to 1867, Budge spent his boyhood years on Arizona cattle ranches and Indian reservations where he began collecting and recording the lore and language of the country people he loved. He tapped this storehouse for a column signed "Budge" which for years decorated the pages of the *Prescott Courier,* and for his two books: *All Hell Needs Is Water* (1972) and *Shot in the Ass with Pesos* (1979), both little compendiums of Arizona humor.

There aren't many like him left. Quiet, but not without humor, and just enough meat on his frame to round out the legs of his Levi's.

I was sitting underneath a big juniper tree when he drove up. What had been a dry wash now ran bank to bank, severing the dirt road with a roaring ribbon of dirty water; until it receded, our separate journeys had ended. He squatted on his boot heels and we started the trivial talk the occasion demanded. The weather: how dry the country had been and how grateful we were for the rain. The creek went down some, but its volume of flow still forced more time-killing conversation. He mentioned a favorite book he had bought in 1939 and how much he had enjoyed it.

It had been a source of discussion on many bunkhouse nights or when he was out someplace on the ranch with the wagon. Most of the cowboys he worked with had read it. He talked about it.

"About a year before Pearl Harbor I lent the book to an ol' boy

From *All Hell Needs Is Water,* by Budge Ruffner. Tucson: University of Arizona Press, 1972, pp. 61-63.

who was workin' for an outfit at Camp Wood. He was batchin' there that winter and told me he would like to read it and return it to me. I went to his wedding at Skull Valley in 1948 but didn't think to ask him about it. A few years later I saw his oldest boy at the 4-H calf sale in Prescott; he told me he thought he had seen the book around the house and would try and remember to ask his dad about it, but I never heard no more about it. In 1960, we hired a fella from Peach Springs to help us work the fall roundup and he knew this guy I had lent the book to. He told me he thought his first wife had left him but he had married again and was running a little outfit for someone down around Kirkland. I don't get down around there very often, but I figured I might see him in town someday and ask him about it. I sure didn't want him to lose that book.

"The next year I spotted him at the Labor Day Rodeo in Williams. He was back of the buckin' chutes, but by the time I got over there he was nowhere in sight. I saw his ex-wife on The Row one night and she told me she was sure he had took the book with him when they had 'split the blanket.' It was December, wasn't it? Nineteen and sixty-seven when the big snow hit? A fella came through the ranch one day about a month later, with the county road grader. He told me the ol' boy who borrowed the book from me had moved back to Camp Wood and was working at the old Hill place. I think it was almost the end of June when I got a chance to get over there. I found him out on one of them granite ridges building fence. We talked awhile, then finally I got around to askin' him if he remembered borrowin' the book from me. He said he sure did and he thought old Mr. Favour had wrote it real well and he sure did respect old Bill Williams who Mr. Favour had writ about, and how interesting it was. 'Well, when are you going to return it?' I asked him.

"'Just as soon as I finish it,' he said."

The water was low now, we walked back to our cars and eased them down the sloping bank and into the rocky water. I followed his car on up the hill through the cedars, moving again towards my destination. Twenty-nine years had passed. What a beautiful way to wait for a creek to go down.

COME AN' GET IT

Ross Santee

ROSS SANTEE WAS A CONVERT to the Southwest. Growing up in his native Iowa, he was ambitious to become a cartoonist, attended the Chicago Art Institute, and tried his wings in New York. When that venture failed in 1915, he decided to visit his sister in Arizona and found his true vocation. Starting as a horse wrangler, he made himself at home on the range and became one of it's leading interpreters in line, color and in words. He was neither a romantic nor a realist; however, he viewed his subjects with sharp-eyed humor and enjoyed their quirks and oddities. He showed a particular fondness for the lordly cowboy cook and shows him in the round in "Come An' Get It."

Mr. Jones was his name. An' Mr. Jones was what the punchers always called him. Mr. Jones was a good cook. The punchers all admitted that. An' what's more Mr. Jones admitted it himself. When it come to cookin' spoon vittles an' fancy things like that I've never seen his equal as a round-up cook before. For he cooked doughnuts as well as any woman. An' we never killed a beef but what he made a tallow pudding. But Mr. Jones was n't what you'd call popular with the men. Slim Higgins said he did n't mind tippin' his hat to any one, but he did hate to just stand round and hold it in his hand.

The outfit was camped down by the big corral when Mr. Jones first came. A nester's hogs had been so bad at gettin' into the posts at night we had to swing the stuff all up on ropes to keep 'em from carryin' off the place. The first night Mr. Jones was there we had n't any more'n got to sleep when the hogs all come a-troopin'

From *Men and Horses*. New York: Century, 1928; Lincoln, Nebraska: University of Nebraska Press, 1987, pp. 251-267.

into camp. None of us paid 'em any mind exceptin' Mr. Jones. It was evident he did n't care for hogs. For when one of them started rootin' round his bed he started shootin'. Me an' Slim Higgins was sleepin' together, an' our bed was closer to the cook's than any of the rest, an' mebbe you think we did n't flatten out. The first shot woke me up. An' I thought the second shot had hit me in the eye. But it was just a hog that stepped on me. Slim thought he was shot half a dozen times, but it was nothin' but the hogs a-passin' over us. I've seen some cattle run at night, but that was nothin' to the way these hogs went through our camp. When the shootin' stopped, me an' Slim dragged our bed behind the biggest oak-tree we could find. The boys was all a-movin' round a bit. An' Shorty tried to talk us out of this oak-tree of ours. But we told him to find one for himself.

It was just before daylight when the hogs came back again. But me an' Slim was sittin' pretty good this time. For that oak was thick enough to stop a forty-five. An' nary a hog run over us. Slim said it was the first time in his life he was ever glad that he was thin. For when it come light enough for us to see, there was two dead hogs in camp.

I'll admit we all slept better after Mr. Jones had left. For too much of this night shootin' is wearin' on the nerves. We only camped a week down by the big corral. But by the time we left, no puncher in the outfit could have approached within' shootin' distance of a hog on the fastest horse he had.

Mr. Jones cooked for the outfit just two months, an' he never did no shootin' after we left the big corral. But the boys all watched him mighty close a-figgerin' he might break out again. It was one rainy night, when we moved into Tin Cup Springs, that Mr. Jones blowed up an' quit. For Mr. Jones refused to cook with juniper. An' there was no other wood within fifteen miles.

The boys took turns a-cookin' after Mr. Jones had left. But that did n't set too well with none of us. An' Shorty finally went to town an' brought us out another cook.

George was the new cook's name. An' he was n't the kind of man who'd ever get up an' go to shootin' in the night. For old George was the mildest-mannered round-up cook I've ever seen. Slim said it was probably because he had n't been cookin' long enough to get hard-boiled. "Wait till he's here a while," says Slim.

For old George told us he had never cooked for a cow outfit before. "I punched cow some when I was a kid in Texas," old George says. "But this is my first job cookin' for a spread. I told Shorty when he hired me I could n't cook spoon vittles or fancy things like that. But Shorty says as long as I slung out the beef an' bread an' was able to cook frijole beans an' was n't too particular, he reckoned I'd get by."

Now, I'll admit old George was n't what you'd call a particular man. For he was n't particular in sortin' the gravel from the frijoles. An' he was n't none too particular when he washed. Speakin' of a shot Shorty made one night when we killed a beef, Slim said the beef went down just like he'd been hit in the head with one of old George's biscuits. But at that I've seen a heap worse round-up cooks than old George. For if there's anything a cow-puncher likes better than havin' a fiddler in camp it's drinkin' coffee between meals. An' any time a round-up cook stands for that the punchers are usually for him. Even if they do crack a tooth occasionally on a gravel he's cooked in the beans. Old George was just that way, an' no matter how late a puncher got in he always found a pot of coffee, an' old George always stirred a little something up for him to eat. Dogie, the horse-wrangler, lost more horses while old George was with the outfit than he ever had before or since. For Dogie spent most all his time in camp a-augerin' old George an' playin' the coffeepot. An' when old George left, Dogie was all upset. For Dogie says the chances are he'll never find a round-up cook like George again.

But it was the manner of old George's leaving that interested me. For when he came George told me he had took the job to get away from his wife.

"You ain't married, are ya?" says old George. "Well, take my advice an' don't, for I ain't had no peace since then. Chances are I'd still be punchin' cows if it was n't for my ole woman. She made me give it up right after we got married. She made me quite playin' for dances, too. An' I was a pretty good fiddler, if I do say so myself. For I could play all night an' not play the same tune more'n twice. This woman o' mine is always walkin' on my tail. She won't even let me play the fiddle in the house no more. Since we came to Arizona I've been workin' in the mine. It's goin' on fifteen years this fall since I started rootin' in the bottom of a shaft. An' except for an occasional shift the only time I've lost since then was durin' a strike in 1917. An' durin' the strike my ole woman like to run me wild. I tried to tell her I was just workin' there an' they'd probably settle things without consultin' me. But you can't reason with a woman. She's always sayin' what she'd do if she was just a man. It was just a happen-so that I met up with Shorty when he was in town lookin' for a cook. I never told the ole woman I was comin' either until just before I left. For I knowed she would n't let me come. Say, you don't have no idea how good it feels to be out in the hills with a cow outfit again. An' to be able to play the fiddle every night without some woman chargin' you."

Old George had been with the outfit just a week when the first letter come from his wife.

"She wants me to come on back home," says George. "She's writin' awful pitiful. But I ain't goin' back until this round-up's over.

Another week went by, an' old George got another one.

"But I ain't goin' back," says George.

Four letters came for George all told, at intervals of a week apart. The outfit was camped in the Spur Camp the night the last one came Shorty an' I were the first two punchers in that night. We did n't see the Indian who brought the letter out. But when we got a look at George's face we knowed he'd had another letter from his wife. When we asked him what the trouble was George never said a word when he handed me the note. I never saw the other ones. But this note was short an' what you'd call right to the point. For all it says was:

"George come home at once or I'll sell the furniture."

We caught him up a horse, an' after old George left of course we laughed. But as we watched him ridin' down the trail towards town it was Shorty who spoke the thing we was all thinkin' of.

"Mebbe it ain't so funny after all," he says.

Just one month's freedom in twenty years.

A cook named Tommie Johnson finally finished out the work that fall. An' Tommie never quit until the day the outfit loaded out, down at the shipping-pens. Tommie could cook all right, but he was poison on Indians an' folks who came from town. As long as it was just the outfit he was cookin' for, a man could get along with him. But just let one outsider drop in for a meal an' Tommie was always on the prod.

There's a dish that's made in the cow-camp when the outfit kills a beef. It's made of the brains an' sweetbreads an' choice pieces of the steer. If there happens to be a woman around it's called a son-of-a-gun. But if there ain't no woman present the punchers calls it somethin' else that's always been a fightin' word.

Tommie was cookin' one night when a stranger who was driftin' through stopped off to get a meal. Tommie never said a word, but he started swellin' up. "Well, cook," says the stranger, a-tryin' to be sociable, "I see you goin' to have a son-of-a——for supper. "Yaas," drawls Tommie kind of slow. "If any more keeps droppin' in we're liable to have half a dozen."

When the outfit went down to the shipping-pens that fall Tommie had no more than seen the place than he started swellin' up. For when an outfit ships there's always lots of folks comes out from town to watch 'em load. An' every man an' his brother usually drops in for a meal. It was late when we got to the pens that night. For we'd had some trouble with the herd. An' Tommie was swelled up like a poisoned pup when we come in to eat. But he never said nothin' until next mornin' when we started loadin' out. Then Tommie said he'd quit if Shorty didn't put somebody helpin' him. The outfit was short-handed anyway, but Shorty finally wished the job on Slim. An' you can bet it did n't sit too well with him. Shorty said he figured the two of them would fight before the day was over, but it never occurred to him that they'd pull out together. But when the outfit come for dinner the two of them was gone. We did n't understand the thing at first, an' we figured of course they'd both be back. But a stranger who was there said he 'lowed they'd gone for good.

"I just drove down from town to see the cattle loaded when I heard them two arguin', an' I stopped to watch the fun. Finally I heard the cook say, 'Tell Shorty I've quit, an' he can send my check to town.' An' then I heard this skinny feller say, 'You can tell him yourself, for I'm goin' with you.'"

About the cleanest round-up cook I ever saw was one we had one fall named Smith. Smith ain't his name, but it will do. I've heard punchers kick about 'most everything. But this was the first time in my life I ever heard the punchers kick about a cook a-keepin' clean. But you can bet your life that any kickin' we did was done behind his back. For Bill Smith was a regular round-up cook. Just where Bill came from I never did find out. For in any of his talk he never did go back that far. An' personal questions are never a healthy thing in any outfit. But from his talk I gathered that Bill had done most everything from pullin' teeth to tendin' bar. For one night in camp when Bill was cuttin' Slim Higgins's hair I heard Bill say that he could do 'most anything an' do it well.

"I never seen nothin' yet I couldn't do," says Bill, "an' make a hand at it besides. I've got some forceps in my war-bag there, an' I can pull a tooth as well as any doc." Slim offered to take Bill's word for this. For Slim was mighty quick in tellin' Bill that all his teeth was good.

"It was interestin' the way I picked it up," says Bill. "I had a toothache once that came near killin' me. I was on a round-up at the time an' could n't leave at first. But finally I could n't stand it any longer, an' I rode in town to see a doc. I had a few drinks in town before I went to see this bird. But I pointed him out the tooth that hurt. When he pulled the tooth I took a few more drinks an' went on back to camp. But when I woke up in the mornin' it was hurtin' worse than ever. For come to find out, this doc had pulled the wrong tooth on me. I saddled up an' rode on into town again. An' when I told him what the trouble was he sort of smiles an' says he'll get the right one now. 'Mebbe you'll look 'em over close next time,' says I. He put up quite a fight at that. But I finally got him down flat on the floor and pulled out six of his."

It was while we was camped at Sycamore that the boys all took exception to Bill's cleanliness. There's lots of deep water-holes in there, an' the boys all played 'em pretty strong whenever we was in camp. But the rest of us all put on our clothes when we come in to eat, 'cept Bill. An' the only clothes Bill wore while we was there was his hat an' a pair of boots. We finally did get used to it. But I'll admit it did seem queer at first. For when we all come in to eat, there'd be the cook a-shufflin' the skillet lids, not wearin' nothin' 'cept his hat an' boots.

One night when Slim an' Ben Hicks an' me was on wrangle we asked Bill if he would let us eat before we took the horses out, for we knowed it would be two hours anyway before we got back again an' supper was almost ready then. But old Bill would n't let us eat. "Yez'll get no duff till you get back," he says.

The three of us was ridin' mules, an' they all was pretty salty. An' while we was augerin' the cook Ben Hicks reached down and hung a spur in the mule that Slim was ridin'. Ben jigged Slim's mule right in the flank, an' things began to happen then. For this mule of Slim's bogged down his head an' bucked right through the pots and pans. The coffee-pot was the first thing they upset, and the Dutch oven with the bread went next. But none of us waited to see no more. I never saw Slim make a better ride in all his life. But Slim said afterwards he was afraid the cook might kill him if the mule unloaded him in camp. An' you can bet the three of us did some tall explainin' to the cook when we got back to camp that night.

It was while we was camped at Sycamore that me an' Slim brought the bull in camp, an' Slim was to blame for this, for I'd of never thought of it.

The outfit was workin' up on the rim of Black River the day it come about. An' it was along the middle of the evenin' when Shorty told Slim an' me to go into camp an' get the night horses up. Slim an' me was n't long in pullin' out for camp. For we had n't none of us had anything to eat since mornin'.

We was just about a quarter from camp when we jumped this maverick bull. He was just about two years old, an' we didn't have no trouble ketchin' him. I started to build a fire, but Slim says: "No. There's no use waitin' here for the iron to heat. Let's take him into camp an' brand him there, for we can both be eatin' while the iron is gettin' hot."

"What in the blankety blank do you mean by bringin' that thing in camp?" was the first thing the cook says. We told him we was only tryin' to save a little time, but we was n't gettin' anywhere until Ben Hicks spoke up.

Ben had crippled a horse that mornin', an' Ben had come on back afoot. "You all go in an' eat," says Ben, "an' let me brand the bull."

That sort of pacified the cook, an' me an' Slim was just about half finished with our meal when I saw Hicks turn the critter loose. An' when Hicks tailed him up he pointed the bull t'wards camp. Of course you could n't blame the bull. For he was on the prod from bein' led , an' when Ben burned the Cross S in his hide it did n't help his feelings none.

My pony was the first thing the bull seen after Hicks had turned him loose. But that pony knowed considerable about bulls, an there was no chance of hookin' him. Just then the bull looked up an' spied the cook, an' right down through the camp he come a-knockin' the pots an' pans four ways at once. Slim got down behind some pack-saddles, an' I was hidin' behind a little cedar-brush. But it happened so quick the cook never had no chance to hide. For the bull went right through camp an' right on out the other side with the cook in front of him. I've heard both plain an' fancy cussin' from round-up cooks before, but it all sounded like a talk in Sunday-school 'longside of this cook of ours. There was a cat-claw thicket at the edge of camp, but they went through it as if it was n't there at all. When they come out the cook was still up in the lead. The cat-claw thorns had scratched him some. For he was n't wearin' no clothes that cluttered up his speed. When they finally disappeared from view the cook had lost his hat. But he was still a-runnin' like a quarter horse with the bull right at his heels.

This was the last I seen. For me an' Slim decided we'd both be better off if we was some place else.

It was late when we come back to camp that night, an' the cook had cooled off some by then. It seems the bull had finally put him up a tree, so Ben Hicks went an' drove the critter off. But before he did, Ben made the cook promise there would n't be no shootin' done when he got back to his gun.

We was makin' a drive at the Seneca one mornin' when a puncher named Steve Johnson happened into us. Steve had been reppin' for our outfit at the Terrapins, an' none of us had seen him in two months.

"As soon as I go to camp an' get a bite to eat I'll come on back and give you all a hand," says Steve.

"Not with that cook you won't," we says.

An' then we told him the only time a puncher dared to come within ten feet of the coffee-pot was when the cook yelled at us to come an' get it or he'd throw it out.

"Oh, that's all right," says Steve. For Steve is kinda hard himself.

While we was augerin' with Steve, Ben Hicks rode back to camp an' told the cook that a puncher was comin' down the trail, an' this puncher said he was stoppin' for a meal, an' what's more he wanted it right now.

"Well," says the cook, a-strappin' on his forty-five, "just let him come an' see what kind of luck he has."

Steve had n't been gone long, at least not long enough for a healthy man to eat, when he come a-ridin' back again.

"That cook is crazy as a hoot-owl," was the first thing that Steve says. "He was stirrin' the beans with a six-shooter when I rode into camp. I've seen tough round-up cooks before, but the only thing this cook had on was his hat an' a pair of boots. It sort of took my breath away. Then all at once he bawls at me. 'Git down, you blankety blank,' he says; 'we're goin' to eat here pretty soon.'"

Of course we laughed. But it did n't seem to bother Steve. For Steve says anybody 'cept a fool will change his mind occasionally.

THE ROAD TO IMURIS

Allan K. Perry

ROADS IN ARIZONA SOMETIMES CROSS the border and wander into
Mexico. Phoenix lawyer Al Perry's humorous novel follows one of
them south to the Sea of Cortez. Narrator Donald Van Deusen III
of a New York law firm comes to Tucson to assist at a trial
involving one of the firm's clients. Local attorney Wallace K.
Wallace, known as "Bill," wins the case handily and takes Van
Deusen, known as Pete, into Mexico for a celebration. With the
aid of some interesting Mexican characters, they drink and party
their way south to Mazatlan, where Pete takes passage for Los
Angeles on a shark-hunting ship captained by a beautiful half-
Chinese woman. Transformed by his experience, Pete is planning
at the end of the story to open an office in Tucson.

Perry's approach to Mexico seems at first like a real put-down,
but in reality he really loves the country and its people. Writing in
the late 1940s, it seemed to him that the Country "has made more
progress" since the Revolution "than it has made in the three
hundred years before." Old Mexico hands find his period piece
true and highly amusing.

As I sat on the running board of the Chevrolet, eating my
sandwich and drinking my beer, I endeavored, without much
success, to converse with the friendly officers in charge of the
station. When they spoke slowly and distinctly I was able to
understand a great deal of what they said, but when I tried to
convey some thought to them, employing the Spanish I had
learned at college, they did not seem to understand me. They
would, however, laugh good-naturedly and pretend they did.

From *Winners Get Lost,* New York: Exposition Press, 1950, pp. 45–55.
Reprinted by Arizona Silhouettes, Tucson, Arizona, 1964.

There was very little for them to do. The whole time we were with them, only one truck checked in at their station, and its cargo and papers were quickly examined and approved.

Suddenly, from within the station, came a quaint character who spoke English after his own fashion. He was short, fat, and good-humored, with a heavy black moustache on his lip and a gold star upon his chest. He was attired in levi pants and a faded red silk shirt. Around his waist he wore a wide belt, completely filled with cartridges, and from his hips hung two immense revolvers. He grinned constantly, showing great white teeth that resembled those of a young horse. Upon his head he wore the most disreputable-looking straw hat I have ever seen. It had apparently survived many a hot summer and many a cold rain. It should have been abandoned years before, but it must have suited the wearer. He bounced out of the station and up to the car like a rubber ball.

"Hi, gentlemans!" he cried, in a clear, high voice. "Good mornings. You go south? You take me 'long? I eenjoy ride weeth you. I Sonora State Policemans. G-Mans you call heem. *Bueno! Listo!* Let's go!"

"It will indeed be our extreme pleasure," answered Bill. "May I offer you a cold bottle of beer?"

"Your pleasures ees my pleasures," responded the weird individual. "I weel have two, plees, one for dreenk and one for how you call 'tracer'."

"My name is Bill and this is my friend Pete," Bill introduced us.

"I am most by God honored," said the officer. "My name, she ees Jesus, Jesus the G-Mans. *Bueno! Listo!* Let's go!"

With his drink in one hand and his "tracer" in the other, he climbed into the back seat, as Bill again stepped across the road to buy a case of good, cold beer to take with us as we proceeded south. Soon we were off, the Mexican officials waving their arms at us, and shouting their wishes for a pleasant journey.

Our way now lay along the bed of what I would call a small creek, but which Bill and Jesus insisted was the Imuris River. Irregular patches of green marked the small farms that were irrigated by its waters.

The journey was very pleasant. The "G-Man" sang many songs and we drank many beers. Then he and Bill rendered a duet entitled *"Me Gustan tus Ojos Negros"*—"I Love Thy Black Eyes," many of the words of which I could understand. The chorus may be thus translated:

> *"I love thy black eyes.*
> *Please give them to me;*
> *Because, if I have them, then*
> *You will love me as I now love thee."*

They sang it very well indeed, Bill's deep baritone blending excellently with the high tenor of Jesus.

They also sang a long, involved and rollicking number entitled *"Un palo blanc le hizo cinco disparos a su novia,"* which, Bill said, might be freely translated as "A pimp has shot his sweetheart five times." That song had at least thirty verses, all devoted to the mystery of why the panderer, who had six bullets in his gun, had only employed five of them against the person of his sweetheart. Each verse had the same ending:

> *"A pimp has shot his sweetheart five times;*
> *Oh, why didn't he shoot her six?"*

"Beel," said Jesus, as we drove slowly along, "we stop up here leetle way pretty soon so fren of mine honor you, too. He go south with us also, *bueno?*"

"*Bueno!*" said Bill.

Soon we turned off the main road, down closer to the creek, or river, whichever term is proper, and there, set among a grove of old and heavy cottonwood trees, which were now almost in full leaf, we stopped at a little ranch house with white walls and red-tiled roof, flower-draped and beautiful. As an added touch of color, great strings of red pepper pods were hanging on the exterior walls, presumably to dry, but probably to satisfy the inhabitants' love of beauty and vivid color. Jesus' friend came out of the door, a young Mexican customs officer, immaculate in his white duck uniform, slight of build, straight as an arrow, and with the smallest moustache any man ever wore in public.

"Hi, Ernesto!" shouted Jesus. "Meet my frens." Ernesto clicked his heels, saluted, and bowed from the waist. He spoke no English.

"He wait for that bus all morning, I bet you," said Jesus. "That bus she always come late. I hees good fren. We take heem long south. *Bueno!* Four good pipples. Four good frens. We seeng some more. You got more beers, Beel?"

We were out of beer. This displeased us, but we tried to show our new friend Ernesto that we enjoyed his company even as we continued our way.

"Hi, Beel, pretty soon you see leetle, theen road, goes off to the left," (he pointed directly to the right) "you take that leetle, theen road. Lives on it, one buttlegger. Good fren of mine. We get some *habanero.*"

We did. We found the bootlegger's establishment almost hidden in a grove of cottonwoods. It had a dirt floor, upon which we squatted. We all drank from the same tin cup, which was passed around and around. Jesus explained that, while the sale of liquor was legal in Sonora, the State Government was endeavoring to discourage the consumption of all kinds of intoxicants except beer. Licenses for all other liquors had been raised to such a height, with corresponding increase in retail prices, that the bootleggers were heavily patronized by the poorer people in the country.

The proprietor of the establishment was clad only in duck pants that had been white some years before. There were three or four black hairs upon his dirty, skinny chest, and the outline of his ribs showed plainly under his dark brown skin. Acne had invaded, infested and infected his face. There was some sort of rash upon his hands and thin arms.

"Pete," said Bill, "take a look at that feller's hands. I think he has a slight touch of syphilis."

"Hell, no, Beel," said Jesus. "That feller, she's just got leetle leprosy. That's all them sores ees."

I did not care for anything more to drink. We left the bootlegger's. Ernesto and I climbed into the back seat and slept. Bill and Jesus drove on into the south. Ernesto's stiff white uniform wilted and died.

How long I dozed I do not know. Jesus awakened me. "Thees next town Imuris," he informed me, "leetle bit of damn town but very fine. Have beeg country club fair, what you call heem. The Mayor, she's a good feller. Very good fren of mine. Mexican citizen all right but Greek as hell just the same. We make heem feed us. *Bueno!*"

"How can he possibly be a Greek and at the same time mayor of a Mexican town?" I inquired.

"Ho! Ho! You crazee feller, Pete, you don't have no Irish mayors and no Dutchman mayors in the United States, no?"

"Well, certainly, we have officials who were born abroad," I replied, "but I didn't know the same practice prevailed in Mexico."

"*Si, señor,* she does. Thees here feller we go see, hee's name she ees now Proto, but was born Protopopolus. Started een selling leetle bread loaves in Nogales. Saves hees money like hell. Pretty soon has beeg bakery and lots of dough een the bank, too. Revolution, she comes. He peeks the right side. Loans 'em money and geeves bread to the soldiers. Right side weens out. Makes Proto citizen, geeves heem beeg ranch. Makes heem good feller. Quits saving all hees money, helps the little pipples like hell. Gets heemself elected Mayor of Imuris. Someday he be governor, maybe president, *quien sabe?*"

I really looked forward to meeting the Mayor, but suddenly, out of some dark recess of my mind, assuming I still had one, came a recollection of some of the conversation I had heard the night before. "Jesus," I said, "I have never had a drink of *tequila.* I heard about it last night. Can we get some at Imuris? I believe it may settle my stomach."

"Ho! Ho! You funnee feller, Pete, you never dreenk *tequila,* no? Hell, we stop at the first *cantina,* Beel, we get thees funny feller some *tequila.* Where he been all hees life, he never dreenk *tequila?*" Then he went off into uncontrollable laughter.

Just at the edge of town, we stopped at the Cantina Molina Verde—the Green Mill Bar—a little adobe saloon of no particular distinction whatever. Ernesto could not, or would not, be awakened. Bill, Jesus and I entered through a swinging door, and I was introduced to *tequila.*

The barroom was plain and clean. Other than the bar and back-bar, it was devoid of furniture. The walls bore posters, such as those that had been given me by Pepe. In one corner of the room, two musicians, one with a wooden leg and a scarred face, played a homemade guitar and violin. Until we entered, the Molina Verde was without customers.

Bill purchased beer for the music-makers and then demanded

of the bartender, *"Tres tequila simples."* The bartender appeared tired and uninterested in life.

"O.K., chum," he replied in English.

"Look here, Señor Dead Pan," admonished Jesus, "you use them good Herradura *tequila,* not no old Jose Curevo brand, for my frens, or I lock you up teel you treep on your own wheeskers."

The bartender was apparently unimpressed by either the admonition or the threat. He placed three little whiskey glasses on the bar and poured into each of them a certain red liquid. Into three others, he poured a colorless liquid which I assumed was water.

Bill and Jesus hesitated a moment, but I raised one of the red drinks, smelled it, tried it with the tip of my tongue and then drank it down. I was vastly disappointed. It was neither fiery nor bitter, as I had thought it would be. In fact, it did not taste like much of anything.

I drank the other glass in one swallow. Instantly, fire broke out in my intestines, my throat and my mouth. I yelled and danced with pain. "Great God," I gasped, "I'm poisoned!"

The bartender, completely expressionless, handed me the remainder of the bottle of red liquid which relieved my suffering a little.

Bill and Jesus rolled on the floor with laughter. The musicians slapped each other on the back, laughing and chattering in Spanish.

"Ho! Ho!" yelled Jesus, between paroxysms of laughter. "I'm poison, Beel, Great God, I'm poison! That's the best. Pete, she's poison. She's dead." Over and over he rolled upon the barroom floor.

Eventually, Bill was able to explain the matter to me. The red liquor was soda pop, intended by the bartender as a "chaser," and the colorless article was the genuine *tequila.*

"Hell, Pete," said Bill, "you just started a new fad, that's all. You drink the chaser first and then chase it with the drink. May prove to be a hell of a good way to get drunk in a hurry, but I ain't about tight enough to try it. You were the funniest-looking son of a bitch I ever saw when that *tequila* hit your stomach. Your whole system was anticipating water and you fed it fire."

Although the soda pop the bartender had given me had extinguished the fire within me, my insides seemed to have undergone some tremendous chemical change. Everything was wrong. I could retaste the beer, onions, *habanero* and *tequila*, which I had had that day. My throat felt raw and rough. I had a dull headache and my knees buckled and trembled as we left the *cantina* to return to Bill's car.

As we entered the little town of Imuris, I felt, to borrow one of Bill's inelegant expressions, "like a skunk had crawled up inside of me and died." The town was small and not overly attractive. I noticed how narrow the streets were and how the houses and stores were built flush with the sidewalks. I also noticed how rough the streets were and how they jarred a poor devil who was suffering as I was.

Soon we came to an immense hedge of oleanders, in front of which flowed a small irrigation ditch. We crossed the ditch and entered the grounds surrounding the Mayor's house. Flowers of every description grew in abundance just within the hedge. An artificial pond, surrounded by broad, flat stones, contained water lilies and fish of many brilliant colors. Great cottonwood trees provided shade for the white ranch-style house where Mayor Proto lived.

Before the car had quite stopped, at the side of the dwelling, the Major came out to greet us. He was a tall, thin, stoop-shouldered old gentleman, dark and hook-nosed. He was well tailored and his white Oxfords were spotless. He and Jesus embraced, after the Mexican fashion, slapping each other's back affectionately. He and Bill saluted one another in the most friendly fashion, and I was presented. His English was excellent and his manner most courteous.

We were shown into the living room, the walls of which were dark green and unadorned. We sat in deep, dark green leather chairs. The floor was of stone, with great hand-woven Indian rugs scattered about. At one end of the room was a grand piano and near it, a harp. Bookcases filled one entire wall. The books ranged from the current Who-Done-Its to Aristotle. The room showed that it had been lived in.

A manservant accompanied by a young girl were dispatched to the car to get Ernesto and escort him to one of the cool bedrooms, so that he might finish his nap in comfort.

We relaxed, although I still suffered from the effects of the morning.

"Sam," said Bill, addressing the Mayor, "you look younger every time we meet."

"Bill," replied His Honor, "you get a little crazier all the time, as you get older."

"Gentlemens," said Jesus, "you ees both nuts!"

Everyone laughed but me. I had a feeling I might become sick again as I had at the international boundary.

"Mr. Pete," observed His Honor, "you are not feeling so well. Does not our Sonora sunshine agree with you?"

"Hell, yes," responded Bill, before I could frame a reply. "The son of a bitch has been drinking soda pop with *tequila* chasers. That's all that's the matter with him." They then told Mr. Proto of my experience.

"Permit me to prescribe," said the Mayor. He clapped his hands gently and the manservant again appeared. Mayor Proto spoke to him rapidly in Spanish. He returned in a few moments bearing a tray which contained small glasses of brandy for Jesus and Bill, buttermilk for our host, and a tall, thin glass of amber-colored liquid for me. I sipped it slowly, trying to identify the taste. It seemed to have some licorice in it, but beyond that I could not tell what it did contain. It felt cool to my raw throat, but produced a gentle warmth and relaxation. The pain seemed to subside almost with the first sip.

"That," I told Mr. Proto, "is the finest medicine I have ever tasted."

"It should be very good," he replied. "Its base is a very, very old, imported dry wine, called, in English, 'the tears of Christ.' To that we add just a dash of absinthe and a drop or two of bitters. It never seems to fail in a case like yours. The wine causes the digestive juices to flow more freely, and the absinthe acts as a mild narcotic."

I was indeed surprised to hear such language come from the lips of a Greek mayor of a small Mexican town. I commented upon it and Mr. Proto told me, with a smile: "You will be more surprised to learn, my friend, that until I was almost fifty, I had never been to school, although I spoke modern Greek, Mexican-Spanish, and some practical English. Then our Government inaugurated

its program of free education for all who would take advantage
of it, from six to sixty. Some of our people here at Imuris
were suspicious of the program, and some were just too lazy to
attend the school. I was not then in public office but I had
more of the world's goods than most of the others and they were
inclined to respect my judgment. I attended the Federal School
that was established here, and I studied reading, writing, Spanish
grammar and arithmetic. Many of the adult illiterates then followed
my example. I became so interested in an education that at
fifty-two I enrolled in the High School at Santa Ana. Later I
studied at the State University at Hermosillo. Now I consider that
I have sufficient formal education to converse with gentlemen like
you, who are my very welcome guests."

Slowly the thought came to me that Bill, in his wild outbursts,
might have been right. Perhaps the study of people is a necessary
part of a lawyer's education. Certainly I had learned a few things
on this trip that might prove of value to me later.

Mr. Proto then suggested that we have a "bit of luncheon"
before we attended the fair, which, as Jesus had said, was then in
progress at Imuris.

Our luncheon was brought in to us, there in the living room, by
the little barefoot maidservant who had assisted in the bedding
down of Ernesto. The meal was served from pottery plates, some
brown, some green, and some dark blue. It consisted of a half-
avocado, stuffed with shrimp; breast of quail wrapped and cooked
in slices of bacon; some sort of tough cornmeal cake called
"tortilla"; and sliced pineapple. There were brandies for Bill and
Jesus, and another glass of medicine for me. I was surprised at
the amount of food I could eat without discomfort. My stomach
trouble had left me.

After lunch, the Mayor rode with us to the plaza, or town
square, where the fair was being held. As we drove along the
rough road into town, he explained the purpose of the exhibition
to me.

"Our people here at Imuris are simple souls, with their own
peculiar sense of humor. We are not essentially an agricultural
people. Most of our little wealth comes from the raising of cattle
upon the ranges. Yet, as you may have noticed, there are little
farms along the river bed. Magdalena, however, is in the center of

a large agricultural territory. Every fall, the people there have a fair, at which is exhibited the produce of their valley. Substantial prizes are given for the largest melon, the best corn, the finest milch cow, the cotton having the longest fiber, and so on.

"So, our people decided to hold a fair each spring and exhibit the early produce as a joke. It is really a burlesque of the Magdalena exhibition. Here, the smallest of the early green melons receives the grand award; the cow who shows the most ribs protruding through her skin, and who gives the least milk, will win the blue ribbon. Our people consider it a great deal of fun and the fair has become something of a local *fiesta*. I request you, sir, as a particular favor, to play their little game with them. Pretend to be amazed at the wonderful exhibits and compliment them highly. It will both please and amuse them to have a stranger enter into the spirit of their little play."

I was ready, able and willing to enter into the spirit of the *fiesta* and I so informed Mr. Proto.

"Hell," said Bill, "why don't you get Pete up on a stand and let him give an exhibition of how to drink *tequila?*"

"No, no, Beel," grinned Jesus, "Papa Proto, he don't like for hees pipples dreenk *tequila*. More better Pete show 'em how dreenk soda pop."

We reached the plaza where the little show was in progress. Around the outside of the square booths had been erected where cakes, candies, *tortillas*, soda, beer, children's toys, and gay flags could be purchased. Within the square, the exhibits had been arranged upon tables. They had been previously judged and several of the poorer specimens, as Mr. Proto had told us, bore blue ribbons testifying that they had won first prize, or purple ones stating that they were the grand champion or sweepstake winner.

Many of the spectators were cowboys, wearing the inevitable levi pants and jackets, boots and spurs. Each wore a small, round, black felt hat, held in place by a thong running under the chin. The townspeople dressed much as anyone would in a similarly sized community in the United States. The farmers, however, were nearly all barefoot and wore the white trousers and shirts that appeared so common in this vicinity, their faces being shaded by large, wide-brimmed white straw hats with conical crowns.

Their womenfolk were attired in black dresses or skirts and clean white blouses. None of them wore shoes. Everyone seemed happy and imbued with the spirit of the fair.

I was presented to a tall old Indian, clad entirely in white, with beard to match, who, the Mayor stated, was the Commissioner of the Imuris Spring Fair. He accompanied us around and through the exhibits, Mr. Proto acting as interpreter for my special benefit as the different prize-winning products were pointed out to us. We were followed by perhaps twenty to twenty-five men, a few of the women, and a host of chattering children, who were dressed in the exact costumes of their parents.

A small, green melon, perhaps the size of an egg, had been awarded a blue ribbon.

"What does the North American gentleman think of that?" inquired the Commissioner, through the good offices of the Mayor and ex-officio interpreter.

I endeavored to maintain what Bill terms a "perfect poker face" as I replied, "That, my friend, is the largest grape I have ever seen. We grow some large grapes in New York, where I come from, but this is the largest single specimen I have ever observed. I congratulate the people of the Imuris Valley upon their production of such a giant grape."

Just how Mr. Proto translated this from English into Spanish, I do not know. The Commissioner appeared extremely puzzled but I noticed, nevertheless, a slight twinkle in his eye as the Mayor repeated my little speech to him. Several of our faithful followers snickered audibly.

We came next to an early spring cucumber, tiny and almost round. It, too, had been awarded a first prize.

"Ah!" I exclaimed. "What a tremendous pea! Now, in New York, we grow some very large and excellent peas, but none, I am sure, that could compete with this one. Again I congratulate you, Mr. Commissioner, as well as the exhibitor of this wonderful pea."

Before Mr. Proto had completed his translation, the crowd was laughing openly; the Commissioner endeavored to maintain his dignity, but I am afraid I had some trouble maintaining my "poker face." I was enjoying myself among these simple people, and they, too, seemed to be having a good time.

A wizened red tomato, draped in a purple ribbon, was next. I assured the Commissioner that, although we grew some very large cherries in New York, some running only six to the box, still I had never seen the equal to this one.

A yellow, Indian pumpkin, about the size of a tennis ball, I examined carefully and then informed the Commissioner that it was a very beautiful lime; not, perhaps, as large as the limes we grew in New York, but a very fair specimen of those grown so far south of Manhattan.

With the crowd now laughing and joking behind us, we next visited the livestock exhibits.

A sick lamb, apparently suffering from some form of mange, had won the grand award. It was indeed a poor little thing, tottering on its spindly legs and bleating piteously.

"My goodness," I sputtered, "a white mouse! One of my little friends raises them in New York, where, of course, the very finest of white mice come from, and he has the finest that are to be found there, but nothing like this one. Certainly this mouse has earned the decoration he has received."

The crowd roared. Even Bill and Jesus were laughing, but the Commissioner, except for the sparkle in his eye, was almost expressionless.

The grand champion cow, a dirty gray object, with, as Mr. Proto had said, her ribs protruding through the hide, her bag dried up, and great patches of hair rubbed off her sides, one horn pointed up, the other twisted down, almost stopped me. I could think of nothing in New York with which to compare her, so I said to the Commissioner: "At last I have seen a real Mexican hairless dog. I have often heard of them but this is the first I have ever seen."

Amid the laughing and wisecracking of the spectators, the Commissioner then delivered a little speech, which Mr. Proto translated for may benefit, thus:

"Gentleman from New York, sir, I greet you. The people of Imuris greet you. You have apparently enjoyed our exhibition and we have enjoyed having you with us. Now, by virtue of the authority vested in me, as High Commissioner of the Imuris Spring Fair, I appoint you Honorary Deputy Commissioner. This means you must return here for our fair each year at this time and must tell us again those big lies about the fruits you grow in

New York. For those you have told us today, I award you two first prizes and one grand sweepstakes."

Thereupon he pinned two blue ribbons and a purple and yellow affair upon my shirt front, threw his arms around my shoulders and kissed me upon both cheeks, his beard tickling like everything. The crowd, including Bill, the irrepressible Jesus and the dignified Mayor, cheered wildly and laughed heartily. In the excitement, some of the smaller children wet their pants.

Mr. Proto then placed his arm across my shoulders as he said: "My son, whatever sins you may have committed in the past, you have this day atoned. You have made a little town very happy. My people will talk for months about the peas and the cherries and the stranger who told such tall tales about the fruits that are grown in New York. By the time you return, for our next spring fair, some of them will have composed a little song about this first visit of yours, and it will be sung for you. You have, indeed, done well today. Accept my thanks and the thanks of my people."

I felt good all over. It was better than winning a lawsuit.

But we had to leave Imuris and its fair. I suggested we should return to Mr. Proto's house and pick up Ernesto, but the Mayor vetoed the proposal.

"No," he said, "it is better for him to complete his sleep. I will have his clothing washed and pressed and see that he is in good shape before I put him on the bus. The customs service is very strict about the habits and appearance of its officers. He might get into serious trouble if he went on with you gentlemen in his present condition."

So, with much handshaking and backslapping, we said goodbye to the Mayor, the Commissioner, the cowboys, farmers and townspeople. We climbed into the Chevvy and headed—south.

MY TROUBLE WITH MEN

Eulalia ("Sister") Bourne

EULALIA ("SISTER") BOURNE WAS BORN in West Texas, drifted to New Mexico with her parents, and eventually arrived in Arizona to become an extraordinarily effective teacher, rancher and writer. She finished her education at the University of Arizona and began her thirty-year career as a country schoolteacher, choosing schools as far from city streets as she could possibly manage. At the same time she homesteaded in Peppersauce Canyon in the Santa Catalina Mountains northeast of Tucson, eventually establishing a ranch in Copper Canyon in still wilder country on the other side of the San Pedro River. Her writing career began with newspaper columns describing her adventures as a ranch woman and, later on, resulted in such well loved books as *Woman in Levis* (1967) and *Ranch School-Teacher* (1971). She loved both her occupations, and her unquenchable sense of humor made even her hardships enjoyable to the reader.

The usual man-trouble that every woman is heir to has no place in this chronicle. My bill of particulars is here alleged against the sturdy male—age under-fifteen to over-fifty—who, out of pity, or for the mere pittance I can dig up to pay, or in response to the call of the vast outdoor romance of range country, has fallen by chance into the small world of my authority, *mi ranchito*.

Before making my complaint, let me express under solemn vow my sincere gratitude, and make a haphazardly hasty attempt to give the devil his due. That it is a man's world will be denied by no one but men, and even then *in sincerity* by only a handful of henpecked husbands. If it isn't a man's world, *Homo sapiens* does

From *Woman in Levi's*. Tucson: University of Arizona Press, 1967, pp. 37–50.

155

not have his just rights, for he is the most interesting, masterful, and in many ways the most admirable phenomenon of creation.

From the cradle he feels superior to all women. With reason. He has advantages that females can only envy. By nature, he is endowed with a power that makes clear to him, such incomprehensibles as mercury switches, up-draft carburetors, venturis, and torsion-bar suspension. Formulae, slide-rules, railroad timetables, ropes, shovels, axes, instructions that come with stationary engines— all make sense and become sufficient in his naturally competent hands. Instinctively, he can drive a nail without choking up on the hammer....

Of dozens of men, I can think of only two who have felt obliged to take orders and paychecks from the same source: Wilbur took pains to do things exactly as I directed, and the good Uncle often said, with obvious reservations of male opinion: "Well, if that's the way you want it, that's the way I'll do it."

But the Uncle was never a hired hand. It happened that out of mutual need and his chivalrous sympathy for underdogs and women in distress, he adopted me, and with the attitude of a partner, did his best for the place he picked out to be his home during the last eighteen years of his long life.

He drew no wages. Experienced by a half-century of working with cow outfits, he would hopefully ask when we shipped our calves: "Did we get enough to pay up?"

In a way, I inherited this good old man who was known to the countryside as "Uncle Jim," and he turned out to be a legacy more precious than gold. When the Cowboy moved from his homestead down the canyon up to headquarters as the Man-on-the-Place, he hired the Uncle—whom I did not know until then—for twenty dollars a month and "keep," to stay on the abandoned Windmill Ranch in his stead. "Keep" amounted to so little I was ashamed to be a party to it. Weekends I cooked a roast or a stew and a big pie and took them down to him with a few canned goods to pep up his regular diet of biscuits, beans, jerky, and syrup. I didn't suspect how much he appreciated it. When the Cowboy flew the coop and the Uncle went back to his old job as watchman for a little business (service station, commissary, and bar) in the village, he told Vi (the friendly young woman who worked there) when they were discussing me: "Talk about your good cooks, now there's a good cook!" I had guessed right; he *was* hungry.

And never did bread I cast upon the waters bring better return.

Left alone, I struggled beyond my capacity for three months. In November I was trying to brand the big spring calves. It was more than I could handle alone, and I didn't have money to hire help. One day I met Uncle Jim in the postoffice.

"How you gittin' along?" he asked so solicitously that I could not hold back the tears.

"Don't worry," he said. "I'm trying' to git me a little pension, and when I git it I'll go down and he'p you."

He was considered too old for work, long before I met him. Ten years later I saw him put in day after day of hard labor afoot and on horseback, and he wanted to do it. Soon after he was installed as my "pardner," The Old Cowman, chief adviser who was never around when real labor was taking place, counseled: "Git rid of that old feller. He'll git too old on you and git down and you'll have to take care of him."

"I only hope I get the chance!" I answered.

I did. He stayed with me until the last. The final three years he lived, he did not realize how dependent he had become, or that the man I hired for $100 a month (when I was working for $150 and love of my job) was there to take care of him. When he did understand that he could no longer do for himself, he died in spite of all I could do.

The fall he came to "he'p," he took over the chore routine when we got the calves branded and watched the outfit so that I could go back to school. He was the luckiest thing that ever happened to me as a ranch-keeper. His services were beyond the humiliation-tainted barter of human sweat for cash. His pension was small, but since the ranch furnished his livelihood and that of his beloved bay horse, his needs amounted to little more than pipe tobacco, a quart of whiskey a week, a Sunday hat every three or four years, and now and then some denim pants and jackets. Birthdays and Christmas took care of his shirts and small items. He never considered coins as being money. When we went to town and he came home with a pocket full of change, he'd put it away in tobacco cans to give to the schoolboys who came to stay with us in summertime. He was never broke—my usual condition. When I started out on a business trip, he would pull out his wallet and say: "Do you need any money?" The ranch dogies were his. They grew up to be mother cows, so he always had a few calves to sell.

The Uncle's greatest value to the little ranch was that he loved it. Its troubles were his troubles. He gave it the loyalty we save for the last things of earth we cling to. And always he was my friend. He never intruded in my personal life, or tried to take part in the things that interested me outside the ranch. We did not read the same books, or—except for newscasts—enjoy the same radio programs. Our relationship was that of two self-respecting people who respected each other and kept a decent reserve between them. It comforted me to know that whatever happened, however wrong I was, he was on my side. Nobody said anything against me in his presence. If I got into trouble, he, in his words, "takened it up."

Naturally he had the limitations arising from a long hard life. He was no good at any kind of night job because he couldn't see after dark. And he was seriously afflicted with "rheumatics." He did the best he could, and was always there tending to the place; nothing more was expected of him.

But at certain times of the year and in emergencies, it was necessary to hire a man or two. There began my trouble with men.

If you are a woman with an income of two or three thousand dollars a day from oil wells and are ranching just for romance, you can sit in luxury in your western low-roofed castle, call the bunkhouse by intercom system to give directions to the foreman, and spend a great deal of money hiring and firing men who jeer at you behind your back. (Such a woman was for a time my neighbor.)

On the other hand, if you are existing on a shoestring with little hope of gaining prosperity, and haven't sense enough to give up and quit, you'll have to solve manpower crises with something besides cash.

When the necessity arises, and you go looking for help from the stronger sex, you give yourself a talking-to. You will be tactful. You will keep to the sidelines and let him take over as much as possible. You will assert your checkbook-right with the utmost diplomacy and *never* say *frog* when you want him to jump.

If the available cowboy (or reasonable facsimile) is young, he will want to rip and snort. He will try to ride and rope in a dashing manner with little regard for the cattle on the other end of his jaunty action. Odds are, he will already have what knowledge he thinks he needs about the cow business; he has learned it from TV or at the big outfit he worked for (and was fired from), and they "done it this-a-way." He wants a free hand with plenty of horses and plenty of cattle, and a car to use after work.

"Look, cowboy," you say, "play it cool. We don't want to cripple the old horses or booger the cattle. I have to keep these old cows gentle so that I can work them alone. Take it easy. Don't crowd them. Talk to them, whistle at them. Don't run at them swinging your rope. Let's ease them up to the corrals and catch them on foot."

That loses you your man (right now or as soon as he has traveling money). You are the one who is going to get the job done, and it will gall him to poke along being flunky to a cranky old woman.

You let him rope the calves when you get to the corrals, and tie them down, and you keep your mouth shut when several of them get up. But when you insist on doing the branding yourself—because you use a really hot iron, smacking it down fast in the interest of mercy—and assign him the disagreeable task of keeping up the fire, your employee-management relations have "blowed up."

And do not imagine that the remedy is simply to find a not-young cowpuncher. The older ones, if any are available, *know* all right. They were born to work, and don't know there is any other way to live. But as long as they are able-bodied, in these times they have good steady jobs to pick and choose from. Those available to small-timers like me are broken-down old fellows who still want to do what they no longer can. You have to look out for them while they're doing the stock work. It is easy to get one hurt or killed.

Old Perry, when he voluntarily came to help me out while the Uncle was hospitalized from a malignant tumor, did not know that he was "riding the chuck line." He thought he was putting in time until his "very-coarse veins" cleared up so his legs would be well enough to permit him to get on the roster of some good outfit again. He had run several big ones in his day. Sadly I considered the fifty years and more he had devoted himself to making cattle pay for the big livestock companies. Now that he was deaf and crippled, he had been turned out to die like an old horse. I pitied him for being reduced to my size. But on his part, there was no question of gratitude. He thought he was doing me a real favor. In his heart he had only contempt for little outfits. His talk was big. He had dealt in steers by the thousands. So it didn't matter, I soon learned, if a few of them died every day or two.

He made fun of me for my lavish use of smears and sprays. Why, when he worked for the So-and-So's (in high-mountain country, I knew), they never doctored a case of worms in the fifteen years he was there. In nine days the "bugs" just fell out!

He was honest and brave and tried to help. It was my hard luck that he couldn't make a hand because he was infirm and would make no compromises with his infirmities.

One cold windy day we saddled up to drive a bunch of cows off several miles to where there was still some grass. He didn't know the country and took little notice of my efforts to brief him on the job. He knew how to drive cattle! Why, he was driving cattle before I was born!

I took the lead down a long winding canyon, and Perry kept them coming, hollering and singing and popping the end of his rope against his chaps to move the drags. I stopped at the point where we were to turn them up the ridge. That was his signal to come around the side to me and help push them out on the mesa. When he kept driving them into me, I yelled and waved and fought the astonished cows. He never looked up, but kept driving. I had to let the cattle go; climb around to him and plant myself in his face; and yell at the top of my voice that *THAT WAS THE PLACE.*

He couldn't hear it thunder, but he would not watch to see if I motioned to him. On rounds to gather the calves for branding, I tried to figure out some prearranged signals with my arms and hat. He was cold to such as that. He told me a story about a boss he had one time, who, when they went out together, would ride up on a high place and yell at Perry, then point down into a steep brushy draw. Perry would ride through the thorny bushes and over the steep rocky gullies and bring out the little bunch of cattle. The boss, still up there like a statue, would point over a steep ridge into another rough gulch, dark with spiny thickets. Perry would go in and dig out the cattle. One day Perry rode up on the high point where the boss was stationed, pulled him off his horse, and punched him in the nose.

A cousin offered to stay with old Perry when the Christmas holidays were over and I had to go back to school. The old fellow had plenty of fault to find with the way I ran cattle, and relieved his mind to the cousin, who had plenty of time to listen. Perry said that if I'd turn the ranch over to him, he'd make some money out of that little bunch of nellies. Only on condition—he wanted it understood—that I stay down at that school and leave him alone. The poor fellow was already moribund. Two years later I helped bury him.

Formal education helps smooth the male's problem of being "told" by a woman. Two young college graduates holding executive positions at a mine up the creek were visiting the ranch when someone dropped the top of a lotion bottle into the lavatory sink so that it exactly fit, and was too far down to be grasped by any tool. The young men were trying various methods of gouging when I came along. "I wonder if the plumber's friend would get it?" I suggested.

The suction worked. The boys exchanged amused secret-order glances and smiles and muttered something I didn't quite catch about "...trust a woman..."

If you do anything at all, you are bound to err—especially on rangeland. When you do succeed in an endeavor, you are fool enough to wish for credit but not fool enough to expect it from range men. Even if it's good, they resent it.

Late one day a man came in his truck, wanting to buy a two-year-old mule from me. I had got a broken arm teaching her to lead, and was not anxious to continue tutoring her. But I didn't think we could load her before dark, although she was already in the main corral. The cocky young cowboy who was with the buyer spoke up, declaring he would bet me $5.00 he could load her alone before dark. I said "all right," and the buyer and I climbed up on the corral fence to watch.

The cowboy put his rope on little Jessie and led her around and around. She was on to that. I watched with pride. But when he opened the little gate in the corner and tried to lead her into the small crowding chute, she quit him. He tried over and over. Nothing doing. It began to get dark. He began to get mad. He snubbed the long rope over a post in the chute wall, got behind her, and whipped her with the rope's doubled end. She humped up and took the whipping. He didn't kick her then, for she was in position to kick back. Finally he tightened the rope and choked her down. She lay broadside in the dusk, gasping loudly against strangulation, while he kicked her now—in the back, the belly, and the head. I jumped down and ran with a big bucket of water from the trough and dashed it on her head. She jumped up, and lunged into the chute and on up into the truck in one wild movement. The cowboy's only comment: "That's a goddam mule for you."

There must be some deeply buried reason why it annoys a man to see a woman show sympathy for a suffering animal. Maybe it's a throwback to the time when he was a cave-dweller, tooth and claw against an enemy varmint, and his contrary female bet against him. Range hands laugh at sentiment. If they weren't born sadistic barbarians, they have become so by contemptuous familiarity. The Cowboy hit a tied-down calf across the nose with a hot branding iron because he was irritated by my remarks about his unnecessary cruelty.

The first fall that I undertook to brand my own cattle, there was some big spring calves with three-inch horns, most of them bulls. To say I had a tough time is understatement. To say I did it alone is false. I had a wonderful horse—man-trained, of course—to help me. We would get a long-ear into the corral and I would make a fire to heat the irons. After running the calf down afoot, I would snare the loop over his head and tie him to the fence. When I got a second rope around his hind legs above the hocks, I'd get on my good bay pony, Buddy, who would back up until the calf was stretched out. He would hold the taut rope while I got off, tied its front legs to the fence and loosened the neck rope before the calf strangled. While the struggling beast squirmed and fought I would call upon heaven in various ways, choked with smoke from burning hair, splattered with blood, gobs of black smear and dehorning paint. It was not an operation to be recommended.

One day I was working the country around some good corrals

twelve miles from the nearest neighbor. Just as I arrived with a bunch of eight big unbranded calves, up rode three cowboys. I hailed them with joy. They were *puros vaqueros*, the McCoy of the craft. As one, the gallant three got off their horses and over the fence. Ropes swished and snapped home. In five minutes the eight calves were securely tied in the dust. But not even a fire built! As I scurried to rustle wood I thought of the tight tourniquets made by the thin *madrinas* (pigging strings) on all those legs, the circulation stopping, the crippling after effects! But I dared not open my mouth. They were experts; I was a woman.

One man started a blaze under the wood while the others took out their razor-sharp knives and went to work on the trussed-up animals. They got the squeezers and snipped off the horns. With no hot irons for cauterizing! Blood gushed and spouted and lay in thick puddles in the dirt.

I can never forget that hour of excessive, unusual, and—in truth—unnecessary gore. Left alone with the half-killed animals, I thought weakly: *"They meant to be kind. Kind to me."* Then I thought, with passionate fury, of how right was the literary wit who never wrote "mankind" but always "man-unkind."

Not counting experience and the printed word, the know-how (such as it is) that I have about maintaining life and passable solvency in rough desert canyons stocked with cows, has been learned from men. My teachers could never have qualified for medals for patience or for courtesy. That's all right. I'm glad I was taught the hard way and had my head chewed off when I dallied in the pinches. Thereafter, when it was up to me to make good, if I couldn't get the job done, as the old saying goes; "two good men better not try."

CITY STREETS

Of course Mother had boarders long before she had us children. In fact, the first ones she had she got soon after she was married, and she sneaked them into the house when Father wasn't looking.

CITY HUMOR IS THE SAME as country humor in one respect: it deals with peculiar people or with people in peculiar situations. The difference is that people in groups get into different circumstances and get out of line in different ways. Taking in boarders, as Rosemary Taylor's mother did, is by no means the same thing as managing a herd of mindless cows. And Dr. Lao could not have set up his circus tent in the country. His customers, however, show the same ignorance, pettiness, and provincialism which creates a sense of the ridiculous in every time and place.

FATHER SLEPT ON THE FLOOR

Rosemary Taylor

BORN IN PHOENIX IN 1889, Rosemary Drachman (known to her readers as Rosemary Taylor) moved with her parents to a precarious life in Tucson in 1904. The Drachmans were pioneer businessmen who left their mark on their home territory, but at the turn of the century they were struggling to survive. Mrs. Drachman operated a boarding house in Tucson, and her frustrations and her triumphs were chronicled by her daughter in her best-selling novel, *Chicken Every Sunday*. It was the basis for a play which ran for a year on Broadway and for a moving picture premiered in Tucson in 1949. The book was translated into at least four European languages and has continued to delight readers for half a century. Several humorous novels followed *Chicken*, but none had the impact or the success of that first book, probably because Rosemary wrote from her heart about people she loved.

Of course Mother had boarders long before she had us children. In fact, the first ones she had she got soon after she was married, and she sneaked them into the house when Father wasn't looking.

I've heard Father tease Mother with the story so often—usually at mealtime, with some later-day boarders as audience—that it almost seems as if I'd been there myself.

"Yes, sir," Father would say, "I left the house one morning, and when I came home there was this man and woman in our bedroom, and all she had for me to sleep on was a mattress down on the floor."

"Don't forget I was sleeping on it, too," Mother would put in, "and it was only for one night until I could get a bed."

From *Chicken Every Sunday* by Rosemary Taylor. Philadelphia: The Blakiston Co., 1945, pp. 18–32.

"Then I went away on a trip," Father continued, "and she got two more people and put them in that bed, and this time what she had for me to sleep on was a 5-foot cot (Father was 6 feet) in the dining room, and my feet could just hang over."

"They did not hang over," protested Mother. "I had that orange box at the end."

"That's right," said Father. "My bed was in two pieces, and one of the pieces was an orange box. It certainly was comfortable."

Whenever Mother was put out, her Virginia accent came in thick and strong. "Well, Ah got $30 each from those boarders. That was $120. And Ah reckon you liked that all right." And she would put her chin up in the air and pretend she was hurt. But actually she wasn't. I think she liked Father to tease her.

"You bet I liked it," said Father. "I still like it when you bring in money." And he'd lean back in his chair and grin at the boarders. "I never worry about going broke. I've got a smart wife. She can support herself, and the kids, and me, too."

"I should think you'd be ashamed," Mother would scold, "wanting a woman to support you."

"I don't want you to support me, but it's good to know you can if you have to." And Father would ask, "You wouldn't turn me out, would you?"

"No, I wouldn't turn you out, but I wouldn't have you sitting around the house doing nothing. You'd certainly have to help me with the work."

And then we children and the boarders would all laugh, for Father was one of those helpless men about the house, and the idea of his doing any domestic chores struck us as extremely funny.

But Father never quite went broke, although he teetered on the edge of it most of the time. So he never had to help Mother with the boarders.

Mother and Father were married in 1897. They lived in Phoenix first in a little brick house on Second Avenue, which they'd built with the money they'd saved before they were married. It was an unpretentious, little cracker box of a place—after all you can't save much on a schoolma'am's salary of $75 a month and a wholesale-house clerk's remuneration of $100. But it had a parlor, dining room, bedroom, kitchen, and two-thirds of a bathroom.

Since there were no sewer connections on Second Avenue, there was only the tub and basin inside—with the waste water flowing out on the trench where Mother had planted the roses. The other necessary one-third of the plumbing was taken care of by a little house in the rear.

Since the house had cost $1,500 to build instead of the $1,200 they'd planned, they had to skimp on furniture. They had a golden-oak dining-room set, a bed and a bureau, a kerosene stove and a table in the kitchen, and nothing at all in the parlor. They kept the parlor shades down and took any callers into the dining room.

Father was still at his job in the wholesale grocery and one day happened to tell Mother about a liquor salesman who had come into the office, a Stephen Kane.

"Seems like a nice fellow," said Father. "He's going to locate here and work out of Phoenix."

"Where is he staying?" asked Mother.

"At a hotel, but he has a wife and wants to find a room in a private home."

As soon as Father left Mother telephoned to the wholesale house and asked if Mr. Kane were there. He was, and Mother said to him, "Mr. Kane, my husband tells me you're looking for a room. I wish you'd come out and talk to me."

When Father came home that night and started up the walk, he saw sitting on the porch a shirt-sleeved man who looked vaguely familiar.

Father didn't go in the front door but went around to the back and into the kitchen.

Thundered Father, "Who's that man on the porch?"

"Shhh," cautioned Mother. "You know him; it's Mr. Kane."

Just then there bustled into the kitchen a plump little woman whom Mother introduced as Mrs. Kane. Mrs. Kane went over to a kerosene stove, a duplicate of Mother's, that Father hadn't seen before, and began dishing something out of a pot.

"We feel so grateful to you," Mrs. Kane beamed at Father, "for telling your wife about us."

Father gurgled something in his throat, and then in came Mr. Kane and thanked him again.

The Kanes sat down at the kitchen table and began to eat, and Father and Mother went into the dining room where the argument went on in whispers.

"Taking in roomers!" hissed Father. "People will think I can't support my wife."

"Who cares what they think?" soothed Mother. "We'll have $20 a month, won't we?"

"But how have you worked for it? That room had no furniture."

"Oh, I've given them our room," explained Mother.

"Our room!"

"Don't worry. I've got some furniture for us."

"No privacy," mourned Father, "strangers all over the house."

"They won't bother us. They'll stay in their own room and they'll eat in the kitchen. You won't even see them."

At this point Mrs. Kane came in and asked if she could have a little of Mother's mustard until she got some tomorrow.

"Certainly," said Mother. "Help yourself."

"Thank you," smiled Mrs. Kane, and then, putting her head round the door again, "I do think it's too mean to make your husband sleep on the floor. We should have stayed at the hotel tonight."

"Oh, he won't mind a bit," Mother assured her, trying not to see Father's expression.

"Well, anyway, it's awfully nice of him," and she withdrew her head.

Without saying a word Father rose to his feet and stalked over to the parlor and opened the door. Mother followed him.

There was nothing in the room but a mattress on the floor where Mother had made up the bed and, holding their clothes in place of a bureau, three orange boxes piled one on top of the other.

While Father stared in speechless fury, Mother babbled, "Tomorrow, the first thing, I'll go down and buy a bedstead and a bureau. I couldn't do it before; he didn't give me the $20 until tonight. It's a good mattress. I borrowed it from Mrs. Bennett. Mr. Kane carried it over. Well, you needn't look like that. I don't know any easier way of making $20 than sleeping on the floor for one night.

Still speechless, Father went back to the table and sat down, while Mother kept on talking.

"It's wicked to keep that room to ourselves when we don't need it and they do. You know there isn't a place to stay in town. If they lived at the hotel all he made would go for their room. And it's wicked not to get that money, when it won't inconvenience us at all, when we won't even *see* them...."

Mrs. Kane now appeared in the doorway with a platter in her hand.

"Won't you have some of our meat balls? I made too many and they're awfully good." She put some on Mother's plate, and despite Father's violent gesture of protest, on his plate, too.

"Thank you," said Mother, "and won't you have some of our salad?" She put in into the plate that had held the meat balls.

Mrs. Kane stood in the doorway tasting. "My, that's good. You'll have to give me the recipe for your dressing. Now I'll hurry and get my dishes out of the way before you come in."

Exploded Father, "This is the damnedest, silliest arrangement! Two women cooking on two stoves, eating at two tables, swapping food back and forth! Hell! If we're going to have them in the house, they might as well eat with us."

"I think so, too," agreed Mother.

So the next day they took the kerosene stove back, and Mother charged them $30 each for room and board. After a few days Father stopped sulking, for Mother fixed up the parlor very comfortably, and the Kanes were really awfully nice. And he could see the extra money was going to come in very handy.

In fact, because of it—and also because Steve Kane kept telling him he was being wasted in office work—Father gave up his job in the wholesale grocery store and took on the agency for Arbuckle's coffee for Arizona and New Mexico.

"I wouldn't have done it," Father told protesting and panicky Mother, "but you've got that board money and I know we won't starve. Now I've got a chance to get ahead. Look what Steve makes on his liquor sales. I can do the same with coffee."

So Father and Uncle Steve—was we children called him later— traveled about the territory and over into New Mexico getting orders for liquor and coffee, both happy that their wives had each other's company.

When Uncle Steve was away Mother deducted 50 cents for every day he was gone. But even so she made money on what the Kanes paid her. Food was very cheap in Phoenix then. A chicken cost 25 cents, eggs were never more than 15, and sometimes 10, cents a dozen. Vegetables were almost nothing, and besides Mother had a little garden of her own where she grew potatoes and beans and onions and carrots. An expensive item was ice. It was 3 cents a pound, and she got two 50-pound pieces a week. These she wrapped carefully in newspapers before putting them in the ice chest, and of course they were never chipped. For cool drinking water she depended on an earthen olla which swung on the porch. Kerosene was cheap, and, because of the Phoenix climate, she needed a fire in the dining-room stove for only about 4 months of the year, and then usually just in the morning and at night. The wood was brought in by Indians who drove along the streets in the creaking old wagons crying, *"Quiere leña?"* These wood sellers, and the occasional squaw who came to the door selling baskets, were about the only picturesque notes in Phoenix.

Phoenix, unlike Tucson, had no old Spanish background but was settled by Americans in the sixties, and, with its little brick houses and tree-lined streets, might have been any Midwestern town.

Right from the first Father did well with his coffee, selling worlds of it to the wholesale houses, and ranches, the mines, the Indian trading posts. But of course he didn't have a steady income. Some months his commissions were big; some months they were small. This worried Mother, who liked to know, as she put it, "where she was at."

Mother, having been born right after the Civil War, had gone through those poverty-stricken times of the ravaged South. She had been brought up on a war-ravaged plantation, with its trunkfuls of Confederate money and not one penny to buy anything. Mother had a terror of not having something laid by, of a precarious income. Whenever there was the possibility of making money, Mother felt she had to seize it, but it had to be a pretty certain possibility.

Father also had known poverty as a child. Mother might be an F.F.V., but Father was an F.F.A.—First Family of Arizona. His father had come west in '54. His mother was the second American woman to arrive in Tucson. Father was brought up in an adobe house with a dirt floor and no windows. At the age of six years Father was adding to the family income by selling newspapers on the street and sweeping out the saloons in the morning. Father didn't want to miss any opportunities for making money either. But unlike Mother he was after "killings." "I can't waste time on this penny-ante stuff," he'd tell Mother.

It happened once that when Father was away on an extended trip, Mother heard of another couple, the Sawyers, who were looking for a room. They were from Michigan, and Mrs. Sawyer had lost a child and was so melancholy about it that her husband had brought her out to Phoenix to see if she wouldn't pick up in the warmth and sunshine.

Mother couldn't resist this chance to make a few dollars. So she gave the Sawyers her and Father's room, and for herself rented at a dollar a week a couch which she put in the dining room. It was one of those contraptions that fold up into a bench in the daytime and then unfold into a bed at night.

She warned the Sawyers they could stay only by the week and that when Father came home they would have to go.

Since the only entrance into the bathroom was through one of the bedrooms, she brought her things out and washed at the sink.

"I don't know any easier way of earning $2 a day than washing at the sink," she told Auntie Rose, Uncle Steve's wife.

Father always let Mother know when he was coming home, and she thought she could get the Sawyers out before he appeared. But this time he walked in unexpectedly, just before dinner.

"Having someone in?" he asked, seeing the extra places at the table. And then, noticing the couch, "What in the name of God is that thing?"

"Well," said Mother, "it's this way. Mrs. Sawyer lost her baby, and Mr. Sawyer wanted to get her out in the sunshine...." And Mother hurried on with explanations.

Of course Father blew up. He raved, he stormed, he shouted so loud Mother dragged him into the kitchen where the Sawyers couldn't hear him.

"You ought to be ashamed of yourself," scolded Mother. "Here that poor woman's lost her child and you're carrying on like this."

"I'm sorry she's lost her baby," cried Father. "It's tough to lose a baby. But is that any reason for me to wash in the sink and sleep in a couch with my feet hanging over?"

"Why will your feet hang over?" demanded Mother.

"Because that couch is too damn short. I should think you could tell by looking at it. That's a child's bed!" And Father strode into the dining room and flung himself down on the couch. Mother saw it was true. There was a foot less of couch than there was of Father.

"I'll fix it," promised Mother. "I'll make it longer."

"How can you make it longer?" snorted Father. "Are you a magician?"

"I've got an orange box. I'll put it at the end. I'll put a pillow on the box. It'll be perfectly comfortable. It's just for three days. Their week is up Sunday."

But when Sunday came the Sawyers didn't want to leave. "Please let us stay on another week," Mrs. Sawyer begged Mother. "My wife is so much better. She's almost happy here. I know that couch isn't comfortable for your husband. I'll buy you another one. And come through our room to the bathroom. We won't mind."

"What can I do?" Mother said to Father. "We'll have to stand it one more week. And we're getting a present of a new couch."

But at the end of the week it was just the same. Mr. Sawyer pleaded, "My wife says she must stay here, she simply *must*. She says this is the place for her. . . . Well, this is the place for her to get well. I know it's lots of work for you. I want you to get yourself a maid, and I'll pay her wages."

"I can't put them out," Mother told Father, "and it will be fine having a maid."

"Well," moaned Father, "I'm away a lot. At least I can be comfortable away from home."

But he couldn't stay mad. Mrs. Sawyer was so pathetic, such a thin little thing. He joined with the others in trying to make her eat and in trying to amuse her. And Father couldn't be indifferent to all that money coming in. Sixty dollars from the Sawyers, besides the $3 they paid to the Indian maid, and from $45 to $50 from the Kanes, depending on how many days Uncle Steve was home.

They now had quite a little nest egg in the bank, over which Mother gloated proudly.

But then one time when Father was in Tucson a queer feeling came over Mother—she was always getting queer feelings of one kind and another, and usually they were right, too—that the nest egg was no longer in the nest. So persistent was this idea that she put on her hat and went down to the bank and asked for their balance. It was something under $9!

Yes, said the cashier, her husband had drawn out the money some time ago.

Mother was almost beside herself with anger and curiosity. Why had Father taken that money? What could he be going to do with it? She got him on the long-distance telephone—an unheard-of extravagance.

Father was soothing, but vague. Yes, he'd drawn out the money. Yes, he had a deal on. What was she worrying about? Didn't she have her boarder money coming in regularly? Yes, he'd be home in a week and tell her all about it.

The next day Mother got an envelope addressed to her in Father's handwriting and in it was a handbill:

Acreage to Be Cut Up

CHOICE LOTS

Will be Auctioned Off

TUESDAY

April 3

Follow the Brass Band

to the

UNIVERSITY

Join the Crowds

under the

BIG TENT

Bargains in Home Sites

LOTS OF LOTS FOR LOTS OF

PEOPLE

Free Transportation Free Lemonade

COME ONE COME ALL

And there wasn't another thing in the envelope.

Consumed by angry curiosity, Mother waited for Father to come home.

He arrived one night a little after dinner, looking as smug and complacent as the canary-eating cat. The Kanes and the Sawyers, sensing a domestic crisis, vanished into their rooms.

After listening to a furious lecture on the way he had treated her, taking "our" money out of the bank without consulting her, Father calmly announced that he'd bought a lot of land around the university, about 80 acres, in fact.

At that time Tucson's university consisted of one extremely ugly brick building and two stone dormitories, set down in the midst of the mesquite and cactus about two miles from the center of town.

"University!" wailed Mother. "Why would you buy land around the university, way out there in the country?"

"I got it cheap," explained Father, "around $4 an acre."

"Four dollars an acre!" gasped Mother, for that meant he'd spent the entire nest egg. "What will you do with that land?"

"Didn't you read the handbill I sent you?" demanded Father.

"Of course I read it, but I don't now what it means."

"Just what it says. I cut up those acres into lots. I rented a big circus tent and a brass band. I hired an auctioneer and a lot of carriages. I got the people out there and auctioned off the lots. Gave them free lemonade, too."

"Of all the crazy schemes! Spending our money on such foolishness!" As an afterthought, "Did you sell any lots?"

Father nodded casually. "A few." Then he got up and pulled down the shades, doing it slowly and carefully. Father knew a dramatic moment when he had one.

"Yes, I sold a few," repeated Father, standing before the table. Then before Mother's popping eyes he began to empty his pockets, pulling out roll after roll of bills until the table was covered with them. Last was a canvas sack of gold and silver coins.

"Want to count it?" asked Father. "I think it amounts to $1,827."

Father had made a "killing."

The handbills, the brass band, the free carriages, had drawn Tucsonans out to the university by the hundreds. Under the stimulus of the free lemonade and the auctioneer's gavel, they'd bought lots hand over fist, bidding $5, $10, even as high as $20 for some of the choice lots. When all expenses were paid Father had over $1,800.

"Well," gloated Father, "what do you think now?"

Mother was so excited she couldn't talk. "I think you're wonderful," she got out finally.

Father gathered up the money. "I guess we'd better sleep with this." He let down the couch and stuck the wads of bills and sack of coins under the covers.

"Here I am a rich man, and I've got to sleep on this damn couch. I tell you, if those Sawyers don't go soon, I'm going to build on another room. But what would be the use? I'd go away on a trip, and you'd have that rented, too. When *do* you suppose the Sawyers will go?'

"I don't know," said Mother, "but you know we could take part of the money and put on one or two more bedrooms and . . ."

"Nix," interrupted Father, "I've got a place for that money, and it's not in more bedrooms for more boarders."

"Now don't put it into anything foolish," begged Mother. "Another bedroom would be sensible; you wouldn't have to sleep on the couch."

"Why I don't mind the couch," said Father, "not with this wad of money in with me. And a pretty girl," he added gallantly. "Let the Sawyers stay on forever."

But then a few days later Mr. Sawyer came to Mother, his face beaming, and said they'd be leaving for Michigan the next day. And Mrs. Sawyer looked radiant, too, and for the first time gobbled up her dinner like a little pig.

Afterward she took Mother into her room for a long talk.

"What do you suppose struck them?" Father asked Mother when they went to bed. "All this time they couldn't leave, just *had* to stay here, and now they're off in this awful hurry. It sure is a mystery."

"No, it isn't," said Mother. "She told me why. She's going to have a baby."

"Oh, she is. Well, that's good. That'll cheer her up. But it's still no reason for this hasty exit."

"I think she's a little bit crazy," said Mother. "She told me she had to stay here until she got pregnant, that if she went away before, she knew she wouldn't get pregnant."

"Of all the loony ideas!" snorted Father. "Couldn't she get pregnant back in Michigan? Any particular magic in this house?"

"Maybe," said Mother.

Father pondered on that. "What do you mean 'maybe'?"

"Well . . . Rose Kane is going to have one."

"Oh! Well, that's fine."

"And," added Mother casually, "we are, too."

"Great jumping grasshoppers!" cried Father. "Why don't you tell a fellow?"

DR. LAO'S CIRCUS STOPS
AT ABALONE, ARIZONA

Charles G. Finney

CHARLES FINNEY, BORN AND EDUCATED in Missouri, spent his last fifty-four years working in various capacities for the Tucson *Arizona Daily Star*. The experience which gave him his best material as a writer, however, was an Army tour of duty from 1927 to 1929 in Tientsin, China. It gave him the perspective he needed and the character of Dr. Lao.

The Circus of Dr. Lao was published in 1935, five years after his arrival in Tucson, then a large village just about to become a small city. Dr. Lao's circus, with exhibits of monsters and marvels from classical and oriental mythology, is pretty much wasted on the citizens of Abalone (read Tucson), Arizona, and the discrepancy between their limited views and the truly miraculous circus is ironic in the extreme. "I was very critical of the human race as a whole," in those days, he told a reporter shortly before his death, "but I've warmed up since then."*

He wrote seven novels and articles by the dozen, but *Circus* is his ticket to posterity. It won the National Book Award in 1935, was made into a movie called *The Seven Faces of Dr. Lao*, and has gone through at least four editions and many reprints.

In the *Abalone* (Arizona) *Morning Tribune* for August third there appeared on page five an advertisement eight columns wide and twenty-one inches long. In type faces grading from small pica to ninety-six point the advertisement told of a circus to be held in

From, *The Circus of Dr. Lao.* New York: Viking, 1935, 1961, pp. 7–12, 30–40, 57–64.

*Kenneth LaFave, "Charles Finney's *Circus of Dr. Lao, Arizona Daily Star,* April 15, 1984.

Abalone that day, the tents to be spread upon a vacant field on the banks of the Santa Ana River, a bald spot in the city's growth surrounded by all manner of houses and habitations.

Floridly worded, the advertisement made claims which even Phineas Taylor Barnum might have hedged at advancing. It alleged for the show's female personnel a pulchritude impossible to equal in any golden age of beauty or physical culture. The mind of man could not conceive of women more beautiful than were the charmers of this circus. Though the whole race of man were bred for feminine beauty as the whole race of Jersey cattle is bred for butterfat, even then lovelier women could not be produced than the ones who graced this show. . . . Nay, these were the most beautiful women of the world; the whole world, not just the world of today, but the world since time began and the world as long as time shall run.

Nor were the wild animals on display at the circus any less sensational than were the girls. Not elephants or tigers or hyenas or monkeys or polar bears or hippopotami; anyone and everyone had seen such as those time after time. The sight of an African lion was as banal today as that of an airplane. But there were animals no man had ever seen before; beasts fierce beyond all dreams of ferocity; serpents cunning beyond all comprehension of guile; hybrids strange beyond all nightmares of fantasy.

Furthermore, the midway of the circus was replete with sideshows wherein were curious beings of the netherworld on display, macabre trophies of ancient conquests, resurrected supermen of antiquity. No glass-blowers, cigarette fiends, or frogboys, but real honest-to-goodness freaks that had been born of hysterical brains rather than diseased wombs.

Likewise, the midway would house a fortuneteller. Not an ungrammatical gypsy, not a fat blonde mumbling silly things about dark men in your life, not a turbaned mystic canting of the constellations; no, this fortuneteller would not even be visible to you, much less take your hand and voice generalities concerning your life lines. Anonymous behind the veil of his mystery he would speak to you and tell you of foreordained things which would come into your life as the years unfolded. And you were warned not to enter his tent unless you truly wanted to know the truth about your future, for never under any condition did he lie about what was going to happen; nor was it possible for you after learning your future to avert in any way its unpleasant features. He absolutely would not, however, forecast anything of an international or political nature. He was perfectly capable of so doing, of course, but the management had found that such prophecies, inasmuch as they were invariably true, had in the past been used to unfair and dishonorable advantage by unscrupulous financiers and politicians: that which had been meant for mankind had been converted to personal gain—which was not ethical.

And for men only there was a peepshow. It was educational rather than pornographic. It held no promise of hermaphroditic goats or randy pony stallions lusting after women. Nor any rubberstamp striptease act. But out of the erotic dramas and dreams of long-dead times had been culled a figure here, an episode there, a fugitive vision elsewhere, all of which in combination produced an effect that no ordinary man for a long series of days would forget or, for that matter, care to remember too vividly. Because of the unique character of this segment of the circus, attendance would be limited to men over twenty-one, married men preferred; and absolutely no admittance to any man under the influence of liquor.

In the main tent the circus performance proper, itself diverting beyond description with colorful acts and remarkable scenes, would end with a formidable spectacle. Before your eyes would be erected the long-dead city of Woldercan and the terrible temple of its fearful god Yottle. And before your eyes the ceremony of the living sacrifice to Yottle would be enacted: a virgin would be sanctified and slain to propitiate this deity who had endured before Bel-Marduk even, and was the first and mightiest and least forgiving of all the gods. Eleven thousand people would take part in the spectacle, all of them dressed in the garb of ancient Woldercan. Yottle himself would appear, while his worshippers sang the music of the spheres. Thunder and lightning would attend the ceremonies, and possibly a slight earthquake would be felt. All in all it was the most tremendous thing ever to be staged under canvas.

Admission 10c to the circus grounds proper. 24c admission to the big top; children in arms free. 10c admission to the sideshows. 50c admission to the peepshow. Parade at 11 a.m. Midway opens at 2 p.m. Main show starts at 2:45. Evening performance at 8. Come one, come all. The greatest show on earth.

The first person to notice anything queer about the ad, aside from its outrageous claims, was the proofreader of the *Tribune* checking it for typographical errata the night before it appeared in the paper. An ad was an ad to Mr. Etaoin, the proofreader, a mass of words to be examined for possible error both of omission and commission, manner and matter. And his meticulous, astigmatic, spectacle-bolstered eyes danced over the type of this full-page advertisement, stopping at the discovery of transposition or mis-spelling long enough for his pencil to indicate the trouble on the margin of the proof, then dancing on through the groups of words to the end. After he had read the ad through and corrected what needed correcting, he held it up at arm's length to read over the bigger type again and ascertain whether he had missed anything at the first perusal. And looking at the thing in perspective that way, he discovered that it was anonymous, that it carried on endlessly as to the wonders of the show but never said whose show it was, that never a name appeared anywhere in all that over-abundance of description.

"Something's screwy," reflected Mr. Etaoin. And he took the ad copy to the *Tribune* advertising manager for counsel and advice.

"Look here," he said to that gentleman, "here's a whole page of hooey about some circus and not a word as to whose circus it is. Is that O.K.? Is that the way it's supposed to run in the paper? Generally these circus impresarios are hell on having their names smeared all over the place."

"Let's see," said the ad manager, taking up the copy. "By God, that is funny. Who sold this ad, anyway?"

"Steele's name's on the ticket," offered the proofreader.

Advertising Solicitor Steele was summoned.

"Look here," said the ad manager, "there aint any name or nothing on this ad. What about that?"

"Well, sir, I don't know," said Steele vaguely. "A little old Chinaman brought the copy in to me this morning, paid cash for the ad, and said it was to run just exactly the way it was written. He said we could use our judgment about the type face and so on, but the words must be exactly the way he had 'em. I told him O.K.

and took the money and the ad, and that's all I know about it. I guess that's the way he wants it, though. He was so insistent we mustn't change anything."

"Yeah, but doesn't he want his name in there somewhere?" persisted the proofreader.

"Damn if I know," said Steele.

"Let it ride just the way it is," ruled the manager. "We got the money. That's the main thing in any business."

"Sure must be some show," said the proofreader. "Did you guys read this junk?"

"Nah, I didn't read it," said Steele.

"I aint read an ad in ten years," said the manager. "I just look at 'em kinda; I don't read 'em."

"O.K.," said Mr. Etaoin, "she goes as is then. You're the boss."

At a quarter past twelve, Mr. Etaoin, the *Tribune* proofreader, went around to the *Tribune* newsroom to see about getting a pass to the circus.

The city editor gave him one. "Old Chink brought 'em this morning. Funny old bird. Spoke good English. Didn't want any free publicity for his show or anything. Said he understood it was customary for newspaper men to get in at all the shows and entertainments for nothing anyway, so he was bringing around a few passes to save trouble out at the grounds. Oh, by the way, Etaoin, did you see the parade this morning? I missed it, but from what I've heard it was a kinda screwy thing."

"It was unusual rather than screwy," said Etaoin. "Did you hear anything about a bear that looked like a man?"

"No," said the editor, "but I did hear something about a man that looked like a bear."

"That's just as good," said the proofreader.

"Well, what about this unicorn stuff?" asked the editor.

"Yeah, they had a unicorn, too."

"Oh, yeah? Seems to me I heard something about a sphinx, also."

"There was a sphinx there, too."

"Oh, yeah?"

"Uh huh. And the golden ass of Apuleius was there and the sea serpent and Apollonius of Tyana and the hound of the hedges and a satyr."

"Quite a collection," said the editor. "You haven't forgotten any of them, have you?"

Etaoin thought awhile. "Oh, sure," he said; "I did forget. There was that Russian."

At a quarter of two Mr. Etaoin started for the circus grounds intent on viewing the sideshows first before the big top opened up for the main performance. He had a pass good for everything anyway; there was no profit in not using it to the uttermost; no sense in not squeezing from it everything gratis that could be squeezed. Money was made to buy things with, but passes were designed to take you places for nothing. The freedom of the press.

It was hot as he walked through the streets of Abalone. Etaoin reflected how much better it was to have it so hot rather than correspondingly cold—it would be way below zero. Overcoats. Mufflers. Overshoes. Eartabs. And every time he'd go in a door the lenses of his glasses would cloud over with opaque frostiness, and he would have to take them off and regard things with watery eyes while he wiped them dry again. A pox on wintertime. A curse on cold weather. An imprecation on snow. The only ice Mr. Etaoin ever wanted to see again was ice in little dices made in electric refrigerators. The only snow he ever wanted to see again was the snow in newsreels. He wiped the perspiration from his brow and crossed to the shady side of the street. On the telephone wires birds perched, their bills hanging open in the terrific heat. Heat waves like cellophane contours writhed from building roofs.

By the time he reached the circus grounds he had almost forgotten the circus; and, as he walked up to the tents, he was at a loss to think what he was doing there in that dusty field under the red-hot sun at that time of day. Then over the pathway between the rows of tents he saw a big red and black banner. It proclaimed:

THE CIRCUS OF DOCTOR LAO

"So that's the name of it," thought Mr. Etaoin.

The tents were all black and glossy and shaped not like tents but like hard-boiled eggs standing on end. They started at the sidewalk and stretched back the finite length of the field, little pennants of heat boiling off the top of each. No popstands were in sight. No balloon peddlers. No noisemakers. No hay. No smell of elephants. No roustabouts washing themselves in battered buckets. No faded women frying hot dogs in fly-blown eating stands. No tent pegs springing up under one's feet every ninth step.

A few people stood desultorily about; a few more wafted in and around the rows of tents. But the tent doors all were closed; cocoon-like they secreted their mysterious pupae; and the sun beat down on the circus grounds of Abalone, Arizona.

Then a gong clanged and brazenly shattered the hot silence. Its metallic screams rolled out in waves of irritating sound. Heat waves scorched the skin. Dust waves seared the eyes. Sound waves blasted the ears. The gong clanged and banged and rang; and one of the tents opened and a platform was thrust out and a Chinaman hopped on the platform and the gong's noise stopped and the man started to harangue the people; and the circus of Doctor Lao was on:

"This is the circus of Doctor Lao,
We show you things that you don't know.
We tell you of places you'll never go.
We've searched the world both high and low
To capture the beasts for this marvelous show
From mountains where maddened winds did blow
To islands where zephyrs breathed sweet and slow.
Oh, we've spared no pains and we've spared no dough;
And we've dug at the secrets of long ago;
And we've risen to Heaven and plunged Below,
For we wanted to make it one hell of a show.
And the things you'll see in your brains will glow
Long past the time when the winter snow
Has frozen the summer's furbelow.
For this is the circus of Doctor Lao.
And youth may come and age may go;
But no more circuses like this show!"

The little yellow wrinkled dancing man hopped about on the platform sing-songing his slipshod dactyls and iambics; and the crowd of black, red, and white men stared up at him and marveled at his ecstasy.

The ballyhoo ceased. The old Chinaman disappeared. From all the tents banners were flung advertising that which they concealed and would reveal for a price. The crowd lost its identity; the individual regained his, each seeking what he thought would please him most. Mr. Etaoin wondered just where to go first. Over him fluttered a pennant crying, FORTUNES TOLD. "I shall have my fortune told," Mr. Etaoin confided to himself; and he scuttled into the tent.

At about two-thirty two policemen arrived at the circus ground to look the show over and see that nothing inimical to the public interest took place. One of the cops was a big fat jolly ignorant-looking guy; the other was a tall thin ugly man. They wore uniforms, Sam Browne belts, sidearms and shiny, brassy badges. Doctor Lao spotted them from afar and slipped up behind them.

"Whatsah mattah? Chase crook? Somebody steal? Whatsah mattah cops come this Gloddam place? This my show, by Glod!"

"Now don't get all excited," said the fat cop. "We just come out to look around a little. Jest keep yer shirt on, slant-eye. We aint gonna arrest nobody unless they needs it. We're officers; how about us takin' in a few of these here sideshows?"

"Make yourselves at home, gentlemen," said Doctor Lao. "Go where you please when you please. I shall instruct the ticket-takers to let you in wherever you may choose to go."

"That's the way to talk," said the policeman. "Whatayah got that's hot right now?"

"The sideshows are all open. Go anywhere you please," said the doctor. "You must excuse me now; I must go and give my lecture on the medusa."

The cops wandered around a little, peering in tents and staring at people and nodding to their friends. They caught a little boy sneaking in under a tent, pulled him back, bawled him out, and sent him home in tears. Then they decided to see a sideshow or two.

"We'll jest go in one right after another so's not to miss anything," said the thin ugly cop.

"Right," said the fat ignorant-looking cop. "Ever see such a goofy circus?"

"Never," said his buddy. "Let's go in here."

They went in the medusa tent. The interior was tinted a creamy yellow, and pale silver stars spangled the yellowness. A big mirror hung on the far wall. Before the mirror was a canvas cubicle, the interior of which was reflected in the mirror. One could not see into the cubicle unless one looked in the mirror. Mirror and cubicle both were roped off so that no one could approach very near to either.

Sitting on a couch in the cubicle was the medusa paring her nails. Her youth was surprising. Her beauty was startling. The grace of her limbs was arousing. The scantiness of her clothing was embarrassing. A lizard ran up the canvas side of her enclosure. One of the snakes on her head struck like a whiplash and seized it. The other snaked fought with the captor for the lizard. That was bewildering.

"What in the devil kind of a woman is that?" demanded the big fat ignorant-looking cop.

"Ladies and gentlemen," said Doctor Lao, "this is the medusa. She is a Sonoran medusa from Northern Mexico. Like her Gorgon sisters, she has the power to turn you into stone if you look her in the eye. Hence, we have this mirror arrangement to safeguard our customers. Let me beg of you, good people, to be satisfied with a reflected vision of her and not to peeking around the edge of the canvas at her. If anybody does that, I forecast lamentable results.

"First of all, however, look at her snakes. You will notice that most of them are tantillas, those little brown fellows with black rings about their necks. Toward the rear of her head, though, you can see some grey snakes with black spots on them. Those are night snakes, Hypsiglena ochrorhyncus, as they are called in Latin. And her bangs are faded snakes, Arizona elegans, no less. One of the faded snakes just now caught a lizard which some of you may have seen. Her night snakes also eat small lizards, but the tantillas eat nothing but grubs and similar small worms; the feeding of them is sometimes difficult in colder climes.

"It was a doctor from Belvedere, I believe, who first pointed out that the snakes of a medusa were invariably the commoner snakes of the locality in which she was born; that they were never poisonous; that they embraced several different species; that they fed independent of the woman they adorned. This Belvederian doctor was interested primarily in the snakes and only secondarily in the medusa, so his observations, as far as sideshow purposes are concerned, leave much to be desired. However, I have made a study of this and several other medusas and, hence, am able to tell you a little about them.

"The origination of medusas is a puzzle to science. Their place in the evolutionary scale is a mystery. Their task in the great balance of life is a secret. For they belong to that weird nether-world of unbiological beings, salient members of which are the chimera, the unicorn, the sphinx, the werewolf, and the hound of the hedges and the sea serpent. An unbiological order, I call it, because it obeys none of the natural laws of hereditary and environmental change, pays no attention to the survival of the fittest, positively sneers at any attempt on the part of man to work out a rational life cycle, is possibly immortal, unquestionably immoral, evidences anabolism but not katabolism, ruts, spawns, and breeds but does not reproduce, lays no eggs, builds no nests, seeks but does not find, wanders but does not rest. Nor does it toil or spin. The members of this order are the animals the Lord of the Hebrews did not create to grace His Eden; they are not among the products of the six days' labor. These are the sports, the offthrows of the universe instead of the species; these are the weird children of the lust of the spheres.

"Mysticism explains them where science cannot. Listen: When the great mysterious fecundity that peopled the worlds at the command of the gods had done with its birth-giving, when the celestial midwives all had left, when life had begun in the universe, the primal womb-thing found itself still unexhausted, its loins still potent. So that awful fertility tossed on its couch in a final fierce outbreak of life-giving and gave birth to these night-mare beings, these abortions of the world. Ancient man feebly represented this first procreation with his figurine of the Ephesian Diana, who had strange animals wandering about her robe and sheath and over her shoulders, suckling at her numerous bosoms, quarreling among the locks of her hair. Nature herself probably was dreaming of that first maternity when she evolved the Surinam toad of the isthmian countries to the south of here, that fantastic toad which bears its babes through the skin of its back. Yes! Perhaps through the skin of the back of the mighty mother of life these antibiological beings came forth. I do not know.

"Now this medusa here is a young one. I should place her age at less than one hundred years. Judges of women have told me she is unusually attractive, that she possesses beauty far more lovely than that possessed by the average human girl. And I concede that in the litheness of her arms, the swelling of her breasts, the contours of her face, there is doubtless much that would appeal to the artistic in man. But she is a moody medusa. Sometimes I try to talk to her, to find out what she thinks about sitting there regarding all the world reflected in a mirror, potentially capable of depopulating a city merely by walking down the streets looking at the passers-by.

"But she will not talk to me. She only glances at me in the mirror with boredom—or is it pity or amusement?—on her face and fondles her snakes, dreaming, doubtless, of the last man she has slain.

"I recall an incident of some years ago when we were showing in the Chinese city of Shanhaikwan, which is situated at the northern extremity of the Great Wall. The medusa and some of the other exhibits in my circus were slightly ill from a long sea voyage, and the whole circus had a droopy air about it that was simply devastating to the business. Well, we put up our tents in Shanhaikwan and thought to stay there awhile until our animals had recovered. It was summer; the mountain breeze from Manchuria was re-freshing. There was no war in progress thereabouts for a wonder, for that is the most war-ridden spot in the whole world; and we decided to stay there awhile and try to regain our customary equanimity.

"Sailors were in the city, sailors from foreign countries who were off their warships on shore leave; and they came to see my circus. They were a gang of drunken swine, but they paid the money, and I let them in. They saw the medusa and, being asses, thought she was just a girl I had fitted out with a cap of snakes in order to fool people. As if one had to go to all that trouble to fool people! However, as I was saying, they thought the medusa was an imposture; but they were enamored of her beauty and, for a boyish lark, they planned among themselves to kidnap her one night, take her down on the beach, rape her, and then cast her aside.

"So one black night, when the moon was behind a cloudbank, these sailors came sneaking up to the circus grounds and with their knives sliced a hole in the medusa's tent and went in after her. The night being so dark that they could not see her face, they were safe enough for the time being, at least.

"Apollonius and I were returning from a wineshop and realized what they were doing as we came staggering and arguing to our tent. I was very angry and would have loosed the sea serpent upon the ravishers; but Apollonius said not to, that the moon would be out presently, and then matters would take care of themselves. So I quieted down, and we watched and waited.

"There were ten drunken sailors in the mob. Pale as ghost-flesh were their white uniforms in the black darkness. As I say, they split the tent with their knives, seized the medusa, gagged her, and carried her down to the beach. Just when they got her past the dunes, the moon came out from behind its veil. And I assume the sailors were standing in a semicircle about the medusa, for next morning, when Apollonius and I went down there, ten stone sailors were careening in the sand just as she had left them after looking at them; and the drunken leers were still on their silly, drunken faces. And still are for aught I know, for those leers were graved in the living stone.

"I tell you, it does not pay to fool with a medusa. Are there any questions anyone would like to ask? If not, I suggest we go and look at the sphinx."

A big fat woman in the crowd said: "Well, I don't believe a word you say. I never heard so much nonsense in all my living days. Turning people to stone! The idee!"

A little man beside her said: "Now, Kate, don't go sounding off that way in front of all these people."

Kate said: "You shut up, Luther; I'll say what I darn good and well please!"

Doctor Lao said: "Madam, the rôle of the skeptic becomes you not; there are things in the world not even the experience of a whole life spent in Abalone, Arizona, could conceive of."

Kate said: "Well, I'll show you! I'll make a liar out of you in front of all these people, I will!"

And Kate shouldered her way through the onlookers to the roped-in canvas cubicle where lounged the medusa.

"In the name of the Buddha, stop her!" screamed Doctor Lao.

But Kate bent under the guard rope and stuck her face around the edge of the cubicle. "Hussy," she started to say. And before she could utter a third syllable, she was frozen into stone.

Later on, while everybody was stewing around wondering what to do about it, a geologist from the university examined Kate. "Solid chalcedony," he said. "Never saw a prettier variegation of color in all my life. Carnelian chalcedony. Makes mighty fine building stone."

COCKTAIL PARTY

Glendon Swarthout

GLENDON SWARTHOUT, WHO HAS SETTLED in Scottsdale, Arizona, has earned a PhD and has done time as an English professor at Michigan State and Arizona State Universities, but he left the profession to become a successful novelist. *They Came to Cordura* set mostly in Mexico during the 1916 campaign against Pancho Villa, gained him a reputation, and a series of novels followed, the best known being *The Shootist*, based on the life of John Wesley Hardin. Both novels were made into highly successful movies. *The Cadillac Cowboys* is set in suburban Scottsdale, where Eddie Bud Boyd has built an expensive house and wants to break into local society. Eddie Boyd is perfectly at home on the range, and he has become rich as a high-pressure cattle buyer. The narrator meets him at a cocktail party, described with malicious humor, and undertakes to initiate Eddie Boyd into the tribal rites of suburbia.

The most fortuitous event of my life, with the exception of marriage to Reba, transpired last night. We attended a cocktail party at a showplace on Lame Quail Run. The invitation read 7:30 to 9:30, which we learned means here 8:30 to staggering; while these hours also implied, we were informed, a buffet of heavy hors d'oeuvres, enough that is for one to make out his evening meal, as opposed to light hors d'oeuvres; insufficient, in other words, to sober one up after he has been rendered hors de combat. Drinking is more fun in Arizona. Thanks to the aridity of the climate, a dry martini is really dry. The standard joke in this connection is that after a cocktail party one requires not a urinal but a dustpan.

Our hostesses are like airline stewardesses, their parties first-class flights organized to perfection yet at the same time mechanical and dehumanized. The Cadells were greeted at the top of the

From *The Cadillac Cowboys*. New York: Random House, 1964, pp. 15–22.

ramp with a public-relations smile, briefed on the oxygen equipment, and were presently airborne. The soiree itself was a rather conventional bacchanal. Perhaps two hundred nouveaux riches and a scatter of oldveaux conversed fiercely and trivially. There were bars in the house and in the extensive patio near the illuminated pool. In the patio, too, was stationed a troupe of *mariachis* in gay caballero costume whose entire repertoire seemed to consist of a listless "Jalisco" and "Guadalajara." Like saboteurs, waiters slunk in and out of the shrubbery. So many torches lit the scene that one sprightly dame, bound unsteadily for the sauce, set her wig afire and had to be doused with gin and tonic. I became separated from Reba, and being a stranger to these social parts, felt it incumbent upon me to widen my acquaintance. This was the ideal occasion as well on which to commence my search for a living, breathing embodiment of the Old West. Hand outstretched, I plunged into the field, as it were, and in the course of the next hour classified a number of readily recognizable denizens of the New West.

My heart leaped at the first introduction, to a bona fide native of the state, an octogenary bewhiskered desert-billy who happened to be squatting before the land boom on some worthless acreage for which he eventually got millions. I attempted to question him about territorial days, but for my pains got only a suggestion that I join the John Birch Society. It is discomposing to come west and find the conservative's arrogance as insufferable as the Eastern liberal's hauteur. Neither accords one a middle ground, a saving grace of moderation, a sweet tincturing of doubt. Each has all the answers. Disagree with the liberal and he calls you a stupid son-of-a-bitch; with the conservative and he calls you a Communist. The one impugns your mother, the other your patriotism. Meekness they knew not, hence they cannot possibly, thank God, inherit so much as a midgeon of the earth. And besides, since both sincerely believe politics to be more interesting than men, both are crashing bores.

I chatted with several "jack" Mormons, pleasant people so called because, although they eschew polygamy, they do smoke and drink.

An imperious matron sighted on me through her lorgnette and hove to, flying her jewels. She monologued about horse-breeding until, overcome by the redolence of the stable, like the Arabians I folded my tent and stole silently away.

I was besieged for a time by desperate refugees from Social Security City, a local community designed for the elderly. Their existence, they said, was miserable. Their friends' only interests were surgery and funerals, and they had come to the party, they admitted frankly, to seek youth through alcohol.

At this point a dozen or two of the guests were bowled over by a gigantic poodle named Tiki which, on command of his owner, our hostess, ran through the patio, into the house, bounded upon a bench, and proceeded to induce with his paws thunderous open diapasons from an electric organ.

After the ovation I turned to recoil from a retired Marine officer so decorated and ramrod that I would have saluted had I known how. This was the fabulous General W.G.D. "What'll God Do" (when he gets there) Howlett, who had slaughtered thousands of his troops on almost every Pacific beach and thereby earned the undying gratitude of his country.

Wondering it had never struck anyone he might not, after all, get there, I chukkered with a hyperthyroid heiress who left a Madison Avenue penthouse to vanish forever among the Hopis and adopt their customs but who had now sublimated herself in her third husband's hobby, polo.

Next came a farmer-magnate from Kansas whose land holdings were so immense that the government, terrified he would grow wheat on them, paid him yearly, so he was candid enough to state, close to $300,000 to let them lie fallow and to hunt doves instead.

I genuflected before the Marchioness of Pontifex, an English-woman who was extremely gigged and a real fakeroo, I was convinced. They strain their sacroiliacs over nobility in Arizona, especially if it is fraudulent.

Just then Tiki, returning elated from his recital, burrowed between our legs, the Marchioness's and mine, and I fetched him a secret, stunning kick in his organs.

Not the least interesting of my encounters was that with one of the state's pride of young, self-made millionaires, in this instance a construction tycoon, thirtyish, and a compulsive fingernail nibbler, who had finished sixth grade, carried a hod, and later mass-built thousands of "tract homes." These are small, slapped-on-concrete-slab anonymities placed so close together that when a vulgar neighbor breaks wind, every house on the block sways as though in a gale. Phoenix is the only city in America building new slums; the others are content with their old.

Conversation with a Middle Western industrialist elicited his principle claim to fame, and something else. A few years back, he related, President Eisenhower had passed through town and shot a round of golf at Camino d'Oro. While he had not been lucky enough to play with the presidential party, he had been the first one permitted by the Secret Service into the locker room after Ike had showered—see his prize! From an inner pocket he brought forth a pair of mildewed disposable paper sandals, the very ones worn by our last Republican chief executive on that memorable day. Friends had offered as much as five hundred dollars for them. He let me look, but not touch, when suddenly he brushed away a tear. Oh, he mourned, if only they had been Bob Taft's!

Then the moment. All began. Drama, drama. Even now the pen trembles in my hand.

To recover from the effects of the human smörgasbord I had just sampled, I stepped biliously into a corner of the patio. Upon another guest, who likewise stood alone, my eye fell, focused, fixed, widened, glazed. He was a man of medium height. He was powerfully handsome. From his face, tanned saddle dark, there was absent any corrosion, either of care or weather, which would place his age within ten years of mine. His eyes were blue and placid as a Teton tarn. He wore a ranch suit of the best gray whipcord, with narrow trousers and pleated back, obviously tailor-made, the coat open the better to display a wide belt buckled with hand-hammered bronze, a canary yellow shirt, and a string tie tipped with agate. He was shod in black sharp-toed, high-heeled, custom-made boots patterned in silver thread. His head served as base for the most splendiferous Stetson I had ever beheld, at least a twelve-gallon. Taken in composite, except for an infelicitous heft of hip and the morning of a belly, he was a superb figure of a man's man. Touching my bald spot to be sure I was not dreaming him, I dared to approach.

"H. Carleton Cadell, sir."

"Howdy."

I gasped. Howdy!

"Boyd's the handle."

I had gone rigid. Lines from the Western reading I had gluttonized in the New York Public Library began to billboard themselves upon the screen of my brain as though it were a microfilm enlarger.

"Enjoying yourself, Mr. Boyd?"

"Quite a hoe-dig."

Hoe-dig! Frederic Remington: "Cowboys possess minds which, though lacking of embellishment, are chaste and simple, and utterly devoid of a certain flippancy which passes for smartness in situations where life is not so real."

"Are you in business for yourself, Mr. Boyd?"

"Thet's right. Cut mah own string."

Joseph G. McCoy: "Cowboys are a hardy, self-reliant, free and independent class, acknowledging no superior or master in the wide universe."

"I don't mean to be personal, sir, but do you mind my asking what you do?"

"Cattle."

It was too good to be true! A whole herd of questions milled to my mind, but before I could sort them they were stampeded by another extraordinary incident. Men exclaimed, women screamed, pandemonium reigned in the patio as something, I could not immediately see what, dispersed the guests in all directions. My first, wishful hunch was an Apache raid, but the locus of attention was the swimming pool and I knew the savages had been more interested in crime than recreation. Boyd strode toward it. Hesitantly I followed. People ran back and forth, toppling torches, pointing helplessly. Finally we could see. In the floodlit blue water splashed an animal, a young mule deer. Hunted down the mountain probably by dogs, it had leaped the patio wall, and blinded by the lights and the glitter of this assemblage had fallen into the pool. Now it thrashed in panic from one side to the other, churning waves, unable to clamber out for the human hullabaloo. Gradually the deer's exertions fatigued it, and the despairing creature might have drowned before our eyes had not a nonfictional Deersaver, a true champion, come to its rescue. Ordering the morbid throng away, Boyd knelt on the coping, waited motionless, and as the deer swam near, reached underwater and with both arms like a lariat looped its legs and lifted it bodily out of the water, binding it inexorably to him. It was an act of gallantry to cast shame into every pithless Eastern breast. Paul Horgan: "The cowboy triumphed at a lonely work in a beautiful and dangerous land. Those of his qualities that did the job were the good ones—courage, strength, devotion to duty." The crowd gasped and parted as he carried it toward a door in the wall. In awe I opened it for him as might a faithful Sancho for his knight, and made bold to accompany him out into the desert. He walked some hundred yards from the house, then stood patiently as the youngling, which must have weighed at least seventy pounds, ceased to struggle, seemed, indeed, to rest, to renew its strength from that muscular bassinet of gentleness and constancy which surrounded it. There we were together, outdoorsman and wild animal and city dweller. In ourselves we three were time's relentless trinity, past, present, and future. I listened to the doe's trustful breathing. I felt the granite presence of the man just met, stranger from an age more rudimentary. I sensed the desert about us, old and wise and weird, the towering cacti with their spiny arms uplifted. With all this I now seemed one, an integral part, a link of The Great Chain of Being. I was at last alive. Too soon, back in the patio, the *mariachis* resumed, wafting lament commercial on the dry night air.

"That was a brave thing to do, Mr. Boyd."

"Ride down the road." He was embarrassed. "Too much paw an' beller back theah for this youngster 'n me. Reckon he's 'bout got 'is wind again, so le's turn 'im out."

He set the deer tenderly on its legs. It paused, unafraid, then clicked gracefully from sight.

"How long have you lived in Arizona, Mr. Boyd?"

"Born heah."

"You don't say? I presume there are few natives extant any more."

"Ex-tant?"

"Living."

"Nope. Mostly pilgrims now'days."

"Pilgrims?"

"Dudes."

From his breast pocket he drew a cloth sack of tobacco, from another a packet of papers, and began, actually, to my delight and disbelief, to create out of them a cigarette! I watched the process much as Adam must have watched the creation of Eve from his rib by the Almighty. Theodore Roosevelt: "Brave, hardy, and adventurous, the cowboy is the grim pioneer of our race; he prepares the way for the civilization from whose face he must himself disappear." And when he actually wet down, lit up, and actually smoked, I could no longer contain myself.

"Mr. Boyd," quixotically I burst out, "I'd like very much to know you better!"

"Thet's right nice of you," he said. He hesitated shyly before letting out of the chute the longest speech I had yet heard him make. "We're strangers heah, me 'n the missus, an' we know 'bout city livin' like a screwworm knows 'bout axle grease. We're scairt we'll let our calves suck the wrong cows, so we're jes' settin' on our shirttail 'til we get us some savvy. Bought us a house is all, on Fas' Draw Drive—ain't thet a hell of a name, though, for a street?"

"Why, that's near us!"

"Powerful glad t' hear it, Mister C'dell."

"Please call me Carleton, Mr. Boyd."

"An' you jes' call me Eddie Bud."

ARIZONA POLS: FASTEST WITS IN THE WEST

Most of them spent their time oscillating between these two points.

A SUCCESSFUL POLITICIAN is usually a great humorist. The job demands it. In the give-and-take of campaigning the ability to find chinks in an opponent's armor and turn the laugh on him is a formidable weapon, and in defeat a sense of humor eases the pain. Arizona politicians have been especially gifted as wielders of the quip and spur. Before the turn of the century Marcus Aurelius Smith, perennial fighter for statehood, was famous locally and in Congress for his droll repartee, and in later times Barry Goldwater, Sam Steiger and Morris K. Udall have dominated the hustings. Erma Bombeck calls Mo Udall "The fastest wit in the West." In *Too Funny to Be President*, which is really a handbook of political humor, Mo talks with wry amusement about his unsuccessful candidacy for the presidential nomination in 1976 and draws conclusions from it. Every budding pol should read it.

THE UNITED STATES OF LAUGHTER

Morris K. Udall

MORRIS K. UDALL WAS BORN into a pioneer Mormon clan at St. John's, Arizona, earned a law degree at the University of Arizona, and embarked on a career in public service. A Democrat in a predominantly Republican state, he was unbeatable at the polls and continued in service until 1976, when he sought the Democratic nomination for the presidency. Jimmy Carter outmaneuvered him, however, and Mo went back to Congress. In 1984 the full membership voted him the most respected and effective member of the house.

From the beginning of his political career he was known for his ability to charm an audience with humorous commentary. In 1986 he published *Too Funny to Be President*, an account of his campaign together with a discussion of political humor which may be the best thing in the field.

I'm not sure most Americans realize how lucky they are to live in one of precious few nations on earth where laughter of, by, and for the people is not regarded as a dangerous and subversive force. In my view, what's most remarkable about America is not that any child can grow up to be president, but rather that any child or adult can safely make jokes *about* the president—and not just in the privacy of his or her home. Try that in Chile, Iran, or pre-glasnost Russia.

Ronald Reagan is the maximum leader of the free world, the Supremely Addled Commander, some would say, of a military force on which we lavish $300 billion per year. And yet, if you wake up one morning with the urge, you can, in complete safety,

From *Too Funny to Be President*, by Morris K. Udall. New York: Henry Holt, 1988, pp. 1–12.

place a full-page ad in your local paper saying, "IMPEACH BONZO!" Alternatively, you can go down to your neighborhood shopping mall and don a signboard stating, "REAGAN HAS QUAKER OATS FOR BRAINS." If this entails some risk, it's because you're maligning a brand-name product, not the president.

Not only can Americas freely poke fun at the president (it goes without saying that such piddling potentates as congressmen, governors, et cetera are fair game, too), more than a few humorists have become rich and famous for doing so. Think of Johnny Carson, Art Buchwald, Russell Baker, Garry Trudeau, and Pat Oliphant as just a few examples. Of course, bumbling statesmen aren't their only targets, but when all else fails, well, the foibles and follies of politicians are always good for a few laughs. Easy targets, no doubt about it.

For more than two hundred years our robust tradition of political humor has been a reflection of our occasionally robust democracy. "Democracy," one philosopher said, "is like sex. When it is good, it is very, very good. And when it is bad, it is still pretty good." So is much of our humorous political folklore. Throughout our history political jokes have served to humanize our democratic process and to reaffirm our common heritage. The schoolchild who is taught all about American history, names and dates and places, but who does not learn that the founding fathers were gifted with humor as well as wisdom, has been done a disservice. Humor is one form of history, and helps bring it alive.

One of our first political humorists was Ben Franklin. Picture him hunched over a desk, chuckling to himself while writing a tongue-in-cheek article about the marvels of America for the unwitting readers of a London newspaper: "The grand leap of the whale up the Fall of Niagara is esteemed, by all who have seen it, as one of the finest spectacles in nature."

In the first years after America won her independence, she was regarded as a brash newcomer abroad, and her envoys were held in the lowest possible esteem. At one diplomatic affair in Versailles, a group of dignitaries were offering toasts to their respective sovereigns. The British ambassador toasted King George III and likened him to the sun. The French foreign minister then proposed a toast to King Louis XVI and compared him to the moon. One-upping them, Franklin raised his glass and proposed a toast to "George Washington, commander of the American armies, who, like Joshua of old, commanded the sun and the moon to stand still, and they obeyed him."

Franklin's wit spanned the spectrum from lighthearted jests— "The noble turkey rather than the thievish bald eagle should be our national bird"—to pithy aphorisms, such as his remark to John Hancock at the signing of the Declaration of Independence: "We must indeed all hang together, or, most assuredly, we shall all hang separately." Franklin even found time, amid his other duties, to write a tract enumerating reasons for selecting an elderly mistress, which concluded: "Eighth and lastly, they are so grateful."

An examination of quips from the eighteenth and nineteenth centuries reveals that the basic themes of political humor—politicians, Congress, presidents, Democrats, Republicans, controversial issues, scandals—have remained the same. These are rich veins, and although they have been mined by a long line of political humorists for more than two centuries, they show no sign of depletion.

More than two hundred years ago, Franklin drew laughs when he said of one bombastic politician: "Here comes the orator, with his flood of words and his drop of wisdom." A few decades later, Ralph Waldo Emerson mocked another sententious politician, saying, "The louder he talked of his honor, the faster we counted our spoons." Abraham Lincoln shook his head over another long-winded orator and remarked, "He can compress the most words into the smallest idea of any man I ever met."

Presidents always make jokes about Congress but it's hard to beat Lincoln's jest: "I have been told I was on the road to hell, but I had no idea it was just a mile down the road with a Dome on it." The real essence of the institution may have been captured by a baffled foreign observer, Boris Marshalov, who reported: "Congress is so strange. A man gets up to speak and says nothing. Nobody listens—and then everybody disagrees."

One famous humorist who lived during Lincoln's day was Charles Farrar Browne, who wrote political satire under the pseudonym Artemus Ward. Ward was one of the first to discover that a man could make a good living by roasting politicians. "I am not a politician," Ward once said, "and my other habits are good also." Ward typically looked at government with a twinkle in his eye—while writing in a tortured vernacular meant to represent the common man. "My pollertics," Ward exclaimed, "like my religion, is of an exceedin' accommodatin' character." Surveying the political scene, Ward found that "The prevailin' weakness of most public men is to slop over"; they would do better to follow the example of "G. Washington, who never slopt over."

Either by coincidence or reincarnation, in 1867, the same year that Browne died, Finley Peter Dunne was born. Speaking through a character he created, an Irish bartender named Mr. Dooley, Dunne was to become the most popular political humorist of the late nineteenth century. Of American justice and corrupt politicians Dooley said, "This is the home iv opporchunity where ivry man is th' equal iv ivry other man befure th' law if he isn't careful." The best political humor packs a hidden punch—you couldn't find a more apt moral for Watergate.

Mr. Dooley had a good grasp of the role of the vice president: "It is his jooty to rigorously enforce th' rules iv th' Sinit. There ar-re none. Th' Sinit is ruled by courtesy, like th' Longshoreman's Union."

Dooley was not the first or last to discover that "Th' dimmycratic party ain't on speaking terms with itself." Of political idealists, Dooley remarked, "A man that'd expict to thrain lobsters to fly in a year is called a loonytic; but a man that thinks men can be tu-rrned into angels by an iliction is called a rayformer an' remains at large."

As our political parties evolved—if that's the right word—into their current forms during the second half of the last century and the first half of this one, political humorists, led by Will Rogers, began to take aim at Republicans and Democrats.

"The 1928 Republican convention opened with a prayer," Rogers reported. "If the Lord can see his way clear to bless the Republican Party the way it's been carrying on, then the rest of us ought to get it without even asking." Rogers was a populist and his aim was completely bipartisan: no politician was safe from his zingers. "I generally give the Party in Power, whether Republican or Democrat, the more digs because they are generally doing the Country the most damage, and besides I don't think it is fair to jump too much on the fellow who is down. He is not working, he is only living in hopes of getting back on the graft in another four years."

Clare Boothe Luce, the sharp-tongued former congresswoman and widow of *Time* magazine publisher Henry R. Luce, said of the Democratic party: "Its leaders are always troubadours of trouble; crooners of catastrophe.... A Democratic president is doomed to proceed to his goals like a squid, squirting darkness all around him." Is *that* why we've only had one Democratic president in the last twenty years?

Come presidential election time, Democrats, like so many blind pigs looking for acorns, begin snuffling about the political landscape vainly searching for unity. Inspired by some convention donnybrook, one reporter quipped, "When Democrats form a firing squad they probably arrange themselves in a circle."

Of course, these intraparty feuds never prevent Democrats from sniping at Republicans. Adlai Stevenson proposed a ceasefire: "If the Republicans will stop telling lies about Democrats, we'll stop telling the truth about them." Harry Truman had a slightly different formulation: "I don't give 'em [Republicans] hell; I just tell the truth and they think it's hell."

Political humor is also spawned by controversial social issues. During the great debate over repealing Prohibition, one wit criticized the Prohibitionists for advocating "the reckless use of water," W.C. Fields, renowned for his fondness for spirits, complained that Prohibition had forced him to live "for days on nothing but food and water." As the debate raged, and state after state voted on the issue, Will Rogers predicted, "Oklahoma will remain a dry state as long as the voters can stagger to the polls." In 1928, the Democrats straddled the fence by nominating Governor Alfred Smith, who favored repeal, for president, and Senator Joseph Robinson, who favored Prohibition, for vice president. Will thought they should reverse the ticket: "They got a wet head and a dry tail. It's better to have your feet wet than your head."

Taxes are a perennial target, proof again that laughter can triumph over any adversity. "If Patrick Henry thought taxation without representation was bad," an anonymous wit once said, "he should see it *with* representation."

Political scandals, too, are guaranteed to tickle the national funny bone. Meg Greenfield, editorial page editor of the *Washington Post*, likes to tell this story: The late Joe Staszek was a Baltimore tavern owner and state senator who worked tirelessly for legislation that would help his own liquor business. When asked whether such efforts did not constitute a conflict of interest, Staszek replied in wonderment: "How does this conflict with my 'interest'?"

During the Iran-contra scandal, when it was first revealed that National Security Council "cowboys" working out of the basement of the White House had run amok, trading a cake, Bible, and one thousand TOW antitank missiles to "Iranian moderates" in return for kidnapped American hostages, one wag asked, "How does the NSC staff differ from kids in a day-care center?" The answer: "The kids have adult supervision."

"What's the definition of an Iranian moderate?" comic Mark Shields was soon asking. Answer: "A graduate student who's run out of ammunition." "Husbands don't listen to their wives enough," gag writer Bob Orben wrote. "All this could have been avoided if Ronnie had cleaned out the basement like Nancy kept telling him to." As the White House kept insisting that the whole idea had been Oliver North's, somebody quipped, "Oliver North. The first lieutenant colonel in the history of the Marine Corps who believed that the chain of command started at the bottom." Asked if we were contemplating making more shipments to Iran, President Reagan answered, "We were considering one final shipment, but no one could figure out how to get Sam Donaldson in a crate."

Although such jokes offer a cutting commentary on current events, it would be wrong to conclude that our rich tradition of political humor demeans the political institutions or politicians. Of course, humor can be, and from time to time has been, used for this purpose. But the motives behind it are usually transparent and the "jokes" fall with a dull thud. Political humorists always walk a fine line—and even the best of them sometimes fall off.

For example, Mark Twain seemed to become less and less funny to the people of his time as he grew older and more irascible, railing against all institutions, politicians, and religions. "Reader," began one article, "suppose you were an idiot. And suppose you were a member of Congress. But I repeat myself." That's a funny gibe, and one can momentarily enjoy the play on words, yet it ultimately fails to illuminate or persuade. "Wit has truth in it," said *The New Yorker*'s Dorothy Parker, drawing a crucial distinction.

Wisecracking is simply calisthenics with words." In his later years, many of Twain's fulminations were seen as dyspeptic rather than humorous. Even his classic zinger—"A dead politician is the noblest work of God"—was about as unfunny as saying, "The only good Indian is a dead Indian." I think you'll find that most politicians and Indians concur.

Don't get me wrong—I don't believe that politicians or any other area of political life should be off limits. But in my opinion, the best political humor, however sharp or pointed, has a little love behind it. It's the spirit of the humor that counts, and that's why Will Rogers was the best and most popular political humorist this country has ever produced.

Will loved America, was a friend of many politicians, and, of course, "never met a man I didn't like." People always understood this—which is why politicians found it easy to forgive him when they were the butt of one of his jokes. Rogers was a prolific gag writer, but as he once remarked, "There's no trick to being a humorist when you have the whole government working for you." One of his favorite targets was Congress: "When the Congress makes a law, it's a joke; and when the Congress makes a joke, it's the law."

Presidents, of course, have never been spared as objects of humor, with the exception of George Washington, probably because he never "slopt over." In fact, some presidents have been closet humorists themselves. Why, even Gerald Ford told jokes. I mean, *on purpose.* Asked by reporters to comment on the earthshaking controversy raging a few years ago as to whether Ronald Reagan dyed his hair, Ford replied that he didn't think he did. "It's just prematurely orange."

Calvin Coolidge, President Reagan's favorite president (he said it, I didn't), was a man of few words and even fewer actions. Coolidge explained his terseness, "If you don't say anything, you won't be called on to repeat it." Years earlier at a dinner party in Boston a woman gushed, "Oh, Mr. Coolidge, what do you do?" "I'm the Lieutenant Governor," he replied. "How interesting, you must tell me all about it." Said Coolidge, "I just did." He later remarked, "I should like to be known as a former President who minded his own business." Asked once what direction the economy was headed, he boldly predicted, "Business will be better or worse." On hearing that "Silent Cal" had died, Dorothy Parker asked, "How could they tell?"

Although Coolidge was taciturn in public, around the White House he was an inveterate practical joker. One night a group of guests arrived for dinner. Inquiring about the proper table manners in such an elegant setting, they were advised to simply do whatever the president did. After sitting down, Coolidge called for a glass of milk. All the guests did the same. When his milk arrived, Coolidge poured some of it in a saucer. The guests did likewise. Then, without a word, Coolidge put his saucer down on the floor for the cat. The embarrassed guests, not knowing what else to do, followed suit. On Coolidge's sealed lips there was just a faint flicker of a smile as he continued eating.

On another occasion a woman accosted the president and gushed that she had bet a friend that she could get him to say more than two words. "You lose," Coolidge replied.

Another low-profile chief executive was Millard Fillmore. Fillmore was acutely self-conscious about his impoverished background and borderline literacy. After leaving the White House, Fillmore toured Europe. Offered an honorary degree by Oxford University, he declined to accept, for fear that students would make fun of him: "They would probably ask, 'Who's Fillmore? What's he done? Where did he come from?' My name would, I fear, give them an excellent opportunity to make jokes at my expense." Besides, he added, "no man should, in my judgment, accept a degree he cannot read."

President Herbert Hoover was a dour man, not much given to mirth. But he did have the capacity for an occasional wry observation. In retirement he said, "Once upon a time my political opponents honored me as possessing the fabulous intellectual and economic power by which I created a worldwide depression all by myself." Hoover also said something that is becoming more apropos all the time: "Blessed are the young, for they shall inherit the national debt." Sounds like David Stockman.

Lyndon Johnson was a humorous braggart in the swaggering Texas style. When West German chancellor Ludwig Erhard met LBJ for the first time, he said, "I understand you were born in a log cabin, Mr. President." Johnson replied, "No, Mr. Chancellor, I was born in a manger."

On another occasion, as a fleet of helicopters sat waiting at an air base in Vietnam to whisk the presidential party away, LBJ got out of his limousine and began walking toward one of the helicopters. A young military attaché ran up and tried to redirect the president. "Sir, your helicopter is over there." LBJ fixed him with a baleful eye and drawled, "Son, they're all my helicopters."

The types of jokes a president tells offers insights into his personality. LBJ liked to tell the story of a boy who showed up late for work one day. When his boss asked why, the boy explained, "Well, I listened to a United States senator make a speech." The boss said, "Well, the senator didn't speak all day, did he?" The boy said, "Mighty near, mighty near." The boss then asked, "Who was the senator and what did he speak about?" "Well," said the boy, "boss, his name was Senator Joseph Weldon Bailey from Texas, and I don't recall all the senator talked about, but the general impression I got was that he was recommending himself most highly." After telling the story, LBJ would purr, "It is naturally to be assumed that I would recommend myself most highly."

American government offers a wide playing field for the political comedian. One can make jokes about politicians running for office, politicians *in* office, presidential appointees, even bureaucrats. Asked to define a bureaucrat, the late vice president Alben Barkley replied, "A bureaucrat is a Democrat who had a job some Republican wants."

There's another joke that is applicable to any administration simply by inserting the correct names. As the story goes, the president is deeply troubled by the difficulty he is having with leaks to the press and constant squabbling among the cabinet members. Sound familiar? Seeking relief, the president evades his Secret Service at Camp David and walks deep into the woods. As dusk falls, the president notices a small cave. On coming closer, he sees a white-bearded man dressed in robes huddled in the cave's entrance. There is an aura of mysticism about the old fellow.

"I need a sign," the president says. "Can you give me your wise counsel?"

"Ask me a question," the old man replies, "and by my answer you will have your sign."

"I need to know if my secretary of state, secretary of defense, and secretary of the treasury all climbed to the top of the

Washington Monument and jumped at the same instant, which would land first?"

The sage bows his head in contemplation. When he finally looks up, he says, "That is not important. What is important is that they should jump."

But of course it is when election time draws near that our body politic is most likely to break out in a rash of jests, gibes, and tales. That is when the fur and words fly. The rash can appear in a lot of different places, from comic strips like *Doonesbury* to campaign buttons. (When Barry Goldwater declared at the 1964 GOP convention that "extremism in the defense of liberty is no vice and moderation in the pursuit of justice is no virtue," buttons immediately appeared that said, "I'm a moderate extremist.") Oftentimes, the humor that endures is not that manufactured by the gag writers and clever columnists; instead, it is the humor that springs from the people themselves that proves to be the wisest and wittiest.

During the 1976 Wisconsin presidential primary campaign I found myself talking to a bright-eyed seventy-year-old farmer in a small upstate town.

"Where you from, son?" he asked.

"Washington, D.C.," I replied.

"You've got some pretty smart fellas back there, ain't ya?" he asked.

"Yes, sir, I guess we do."

"Got some that ain't so smart, too, ain't ya?" he said.

"Well," I replied, "I guess that's true too."

"Damn hard to tell the difference, ain't it," the old-timer concluded with a chuckle.

In a democracy, you see, the people always have the last laugh.

A Loose Herd of Arizona Pols

Don Dedera

DON DEDERA OF PHOENIX and Payson, long-time Arizona journalist, collected several varieties of Arizona humor in his 1986 volume *The Cactus Sandwich*. The vagaries and idiosyncracies of Arizona politicians have long been dear to his heart and he displays a few of them here.

"Facts are like cattle," Charlie Pickrell often said. "You can't judge a herd until the last cow is in the pen." We never seem capable of rounding up every last political cow, and lacking all the facts, we are left with legends, as this one, delivered without notes by Senator Henry Fountain Ashurst:

> The glorious character of the Thirteenth Legislature was Mickey Stewart of Flagstaff.... He was in court one day defending a man accused of shooting three times at another man. He said, "Gentlemen of the jury, do you blame my client? This man was advancing upon him, hurling vile EPITAPHS at him as he came."
>
> The District Attorney interrupted, "I'm sure, Mr. Stewart, you mean vile EPITHETS, not EPITAPHS."
>
> "No," said Counselor Stewart, "I don't mean epithets. I know what I mean. I mean epitaphs. The law does not permit you to strike or shoot a man when he hurls epithets at you, but in our western life, in our pioneer world, when a man comes at you hurling EPITAPHS, then it's time for you to finish him."

Ashurst likewise is the source of a biographical peek at his colleague, Senator Ralph H. Cameron:

From *The Cactus Sandwich*. Flagstaff: Northland Press, 1986, pp. 27–29.

He didn't waste time in words. He said I wasted time in words. One morning he received a letter from a constituent when he was a delegate to Congress. It said, "Dear Cameron, now that you're in Congress and we're from Christian homes, we want you to get us an appropriation for a church." Cameron wired back, "I can't get you an appropriation for a church. You can't dip into public funds for church matters. Besides, Congress doesn't know anything about religion. And secondly, what you need there is not a church. What you need there is a jail. I'll get you a jail."

A public official continuing the good humor of Ashurst is Arizona's veteran Congressman Morris (call me Mo) Udall, who may gain more attention with his book *Just Laughing About It This Morning* than he ever did with his tries at the presidency. The title of the book of twelve hundred funnies, gassers, and anecdotes comes from his 1976 experience in the New Hampshire primaries. He walked into a barbershop and gushed, "Hi, I'm Mo Udall. I have just announced that I am running for president." The barber replied, "Yep. We were just laughing about it this morning."

Depending upon one's political loyalties, Congressman Sam Steiger served through the 1960s and 1970s either as the rankest of Republican reactionaries or the ablest of Constitutional fundamentalists. But love him or leave him, Sam was never dull. He relished telling how, late in a tough election, carburetor ice forced down his light airplane in a cold, remote, barren, and radio-blind Arizona canyon. To keep from freezing, Sam and his pilot were obliged to burn bales of his campaign literature. No loss, probably, because as Sam told it, he eventually flew on to Clifton, a mining town ninety-nine percent Democrat. Sam quoted a Mexican miner: "I sure am mad at my brother because of you." Why? Steiger wondered—"Your brother has been dead for twenty years!" "That is true, Mr. Steiger," the man answered, "but the last time you ran for Congress, he came back to life and voted for your opponent seven times, and my brother, he never dropped by the house once to say hello."

Another Arizona politician with a quick wit: Barry Goldwater.

Once an editor suggested that the most famous native son of Arizona likely was not Goldwater but Geronimo. A strained look crossed the features of Senator Goldwater, also Arizona-born and the state's only candidate for the presidency. "Well," the editor hurried on, "all over the world did you ever hear of somebody bailing out of an airplane, pulling the parachute ripcord, and yelling, GOLDWATER?" The senator mulled that over, and conceded. "You're right. Geronimo is the most famous Arizonan—ever."

When he finally was allowed in 1969 to go to Vietnam—having been denied permission for years by the Democratic administration— Goldwater rattled the nerves of his security-conscious aides by pooh-poohing dangers. Mortared at Da Nang, Goldwater slept through it. Cautioned about appearing unguarded in an ordinary sedan in riot-torn Saigon, Goldwater quipped, "You forget, in Washington every day I go to work in an unsecured government village." And deep in the jungles of the Central Highlands during a lull in combat, a cavalry sergeant rose from his muddy foxhole to shout down the barbed wire, "Barry, I voted for you in '64, and I'd vote for you again!" Goldwater turned to a companion and muttered, "Hell, obviously, I was running in the wrong precinct...." But the man who was rejected 49 to 1 by the United States (Goldwater DID carry his home state) must have derived some gratification when, after the election, an old Arizona rancher moseyed up to him and confided, "Barry, they said if I voted for you in 1964, we'd be in a land war in Asia within six months. So, I voted for you, and SURE ENOUGH...."

When Burton Barr gave up his powerful post of house majority leader to run for governor, he claimed, tongue-in-cheek, that he had to hire a lunatic to telephone his house two or three times a night and cuss him out just so he could get some sleep. Having made his political decision, Barr now may mull over that mother's apocryphal lament, "Once I had three sons. And they have all disappeared. One joined a cloistered order. Another was lost at sea. And the third ran for governor of Arizona, and won."

Let us reserve a warm spot for Arizona legislator Patrick W. O'Reilly who justified for all time the high salaries of professors. Most of the Arizona legislators that year were ranchers, who could not understand why anyone should be paid handsomely, fulltime, for teaching only a few hours a day. "A professor is much like a bull," O'Reilly explained. "We must not consider the amount of time he spends, but the importance of what he does."

Mark Smith of Tombstone

C. L. Sonnichsen

WILLIAM AURELIUS KING LEFT his native Louisiana in 1870 at the age of 14 to become a Texas cowboy. Always restless, he migrated to Tombstone, Arizona, in 1882, where he worked as a ranch manager, peace officer, and bartender. Eventually he became a professional gambler and saloonkeeper. When the mines failed, he operated in a number of boom camps, but finally settled in El Paso, Texas. He died there in his late eighties.

His memory was good and he was full of stories about Tombstone in its great days. In 1941 he collected some of them in *Billy King's Tombstone*. In a chapter called "Rotten Row" he recorded his memories of some notable Tombstone lawyers, beginning with Marcus Aurelius Smith. "Mark" Smith was, of course, a great Arizonan who spent many years as Arizona's delegate in Congress, always fighting valiantly for statehood. King's view probably exaggerates Mark's bibulous propensities.

One street in Tombstone was known as Rotten Row. The reason was that all the lawyers had their offices on it. To be precise, Rotten Row was the portion of Fourth Street which lay between Tough Nut and Allen Streets; no doubt it first attracted the learned and the eloquent because it was only two jumps from the courthouse and less than that from the nearest saloon. Most of them spent their time oscillating rapidly between these two points. If any street in Tombstone is haunted, it would be Rotten Row, for some of the most remarkable personalities did a good part of their living there.

The buildings in which the Tombstone bar did its scheming,

From *Billy King's Tombstone*. Caldwell, Idaho: Caxton Printers, 1941, pp. 161-165.

studying, and sobering up are still to be seen—a long row of one-story adobes with peeling window and door frames and mud bricks showing through the cracked and broken plaster. It is quiet enough now, but fifty years ago, when Tombstone was a metropolis and the county seat, it overflowed with whiskey and oratory, especially when court was in a session.

It wouldn't be safe to say that all the early-day Tombstone lawyers were pickled in alcohol. Ben Goodrich wasn't. He stayed in his office, attended to business, and never amused the town with original antics when in his cups. But this respectable and orderly conduct was so remarkable, considering where and what he was, that Tombstone hardly knew what to make of him.

He did not drink, he did not gamble, he never turned up in the red-light district. He didn't even go to church. In fact, he had no small vices.

The community was tolerant, however. It was a place where everyone was expected to be himself as long as his strength held out, so Ben Goodrich was allowed his peculiarities along with the others.

The rest of the legal talent of Tombstone did what it could to live down Ben Goodrich's bad example, and his partner held a leading position in the campaign. This partner was the famous Marcus Aurelius Smith, whose name is still glorious in Arizona. "Mark," as he was called, was a large, handsome, luxuriantly mustached Kentuckian who took to the free-and-easy frontier life like a prohibitionist to water. Everybody knew him. Everybody liked him. Everybody called him by his first name. And everybody voted for him. For years he represented the Territory of Arizona at Washington and sent back gossipy personalities to the boys at Tombstone—about visiting his old home at Cynthiana, Kentucky; about his misadventures in the Legislature. In 1887 the *Epitaph* got hold of this one from "Our Mark":

Mark Smith writes from Washington that he never was considered good at draw, but his late luck beats all. In drawing for seats Mark's was next to the last name to come out. He was compelled to take a back seat on the Republican side.

It was one of the few occasions on which Mark is known to have taken a back seat.

Even in the East, Mark was recognized as a colorful personality;

and when he had a chance he enjoyed playing his role of frontier legislator for the Eastern audience. Sometimes an echo of his fame was heard faintly in his home town, to the great delight of his friends. They rejoiced especially over a clipping from the New York *Graphic*, in July of 1888, describing Mark's effect on the New York eye:

He is over six feet high and built in proportion. Hair a little unkempt, a moustache running down over his chin and collar, unique if not careless in his dress, and with the general appearance of a far Western rustler from away back. One funny thing about Marcus Aurelius is that he did not want to go to congress, but was elected almost in spite of himself.

The fact that Mark probably sent this story back to the *Epitaph* himself didn't make it any the less pleasing.

Back in Arizona, after his trips East, Mark stayed in character. He was not too proud to drink or gamble with anybody, and that was sound morality in Tombstone.

His game was faro bank, and to it he gave an almost religious devotion. The best story ever told about him goes back to a time when he was in a high and alcoholic good humor and decided he wanted to buck a game of bank. He went to the Crystal Palace. Back jack and poker—nothing else. He stepped across to the Oriental. Two Jewish drummers playing Coeur d'Alene. He finally found what he wanted at the Pony Saloon, where a couple of transients had set up a table "dealing brace" with a crooked box.

Word went out at once that Mark was bucking a sure thing. The boys fidgeted and decided it was Mark's business and they had no call to interfere as long as their own money was safe.

At last the rumor reached King's Saloon, where Mark's best friends hung out.

"Hell, we can't stand by and see him robbed!" said Billy King, to Allen English, Mark's law partner (Ben Goodrich had gone to California by this time). "You're right, we can't" agreed English.

Billy sent Butch, his bouncer, to see what could be done; English went along.

"Come out of it," they advised Mark. "Don't you know they're dealing the best of it? You haven't got a chance to win."

"What of it?" he inquired with a contented hiccup. "It's the only game in town, ain't it?"

This story has been told of greater gamblers than he, but it was never more appropriately applied than to Marcus Aurelius Smith.

The whole town was sad when he moved to Tucson, and local sports used to quote with a regretful shake of the head the epitaph he devised for his tombstone (long before an epitaph was called for): "Here lies a good man—a lover of fast horses, pretty women, and good whiskey."

The memory of Mark Smith brings a happy quirk to the lips of all who knew him.

TALL-TALE ARIZONA

Nothing I could do but turn him around and come back.

THE ULTIMATE EXPRESSION of country humor in Arizona is the tall tale, the whopper, the big, straight-faced lie.

Specialists in humor think of it as an art form—an expression of the creative spirit. It can also be looked at as a favorite indoor and outdoor sport—mostly outdoor—featuring a group of cowboys around the campfire describing weird and unbelievable situations and adventures, sometimes their own, with straight faces. Etiquette demanded that each story be accepted as truth and topped by the next man, if he had the imagination to do so. This epic lying, however, did not have to be organized. John Hance, early-day guide in the Grand Canyon, was at his best when innocent tourists asked a simple-minded question. Hance always rose to the occasion and every old timer knew some Hance stories. Frank C. Lockwood of the University of Arizona came along too late to know Hance himself, but he assembled a group of friends who did, and he got many of the stories out of them. Not all, however! Noone mentioned the time Hance told about going over the edge riding his mule and falling all the way to the bottom. "And how did you survive?" "Why, just before we hit bottom, I stepped off the mule and I never got a scratch." Half a dozen aficionados, beginning with Dick Wick Hall of Salome, made up more than they collected. Later specialists like Ruffner and Dedera put them together in books.

FORT YUMA

J. Ross Browne

JOHN ROSS BROWNE, IRISH BORN, came to San Francisco in 1849 as a government agent after spending several unhappy years as a Washington bureaucrat. He did voluminous reports on western mines and on government agents and agencies to support his family, but his real passion was for the open road and the far horizons. Much of his life was spent in visiting and writing about interesting places and people. He was also a talented artist and illustrated his books and articles. In 1864 he made a tour through Arizona and northern Mexico and published his observations, first as magazine articles and then as a book which has been many times reprinted. He wrote easily, was a good observer, and often took the humorist's stance. He loved a tall tale and was capable of humorous exaggeration himself. Charles Henry Dana's *Two Years before the Mast* and Mark Twain's *Roughing It* may have been influenced by Browne.

In half an hour more we reached Fort Yuma, where we were received with great kindness and hospitality by Colonel Bennet, the commanding officer, who provided us with excellent quarters. Twelve days had passed since our departure from Los Angeles; and we were not slow to enjoy the luxury of a bath and a change of raiment. Captain Gorham and his command, a cavalry company of volunteers, had preceded us from Camp Drum, and were encamped near the fort. This command was destined for the protection of Arizona, and would probably soon be stationed at Tucson.

As soon as we had refreshed ourselves with the customary appliances of civilization at frontier posts—lemonade, if you please—we

From *Adventures in the Apache Country*. New York: Harper & Brothers, 1869, pp. 55–57.

sallied forth to enjoy a view of the fort and surrounding country from the opposite side of the river.

I was not disappointed in my first impressions of Fort Yuma. Weird and barren as the adjacent country is, it is not destitute of compensating beauties. The banks of the river for many miles below are fringed with groves of mesquit and cotton-wood; above the junction of the Gila and the Colorado an extensive alluvial valley, clothed with willow, cotton-wood, mesquit, and arrow-weed, stretches far off to the foot-hills of Castle Dome; and toward the great desert a rugged range of mountains, over which rises in solitary majesty the "Chimney Peak," forms the background. An atmosphere of wonderful richness and brilliancy covers the scene like a gorgeous canopy of prismatic colors, and the vision is lost in the immensity of the distances. The fort stands on an elevated bluff, commanding the adjacent country for many miles around, and presents an exceedingly picturesque view with its neat quarters, store-houses, and winding roads. It was with emotions of national pride that we gazed upon the glorious flag of our Union as it swelled out to the evening breeze from the flag-staff that towered above the bluff; and we felt that, so long as that emblem of our liberty floated, there was hope for the future of Colorado and Arizona.

The climate in winter is finer than that of Italy. It would scarcely be possible to suggest an improvement. I never experienced such exquisite Christmas weather as we enjoyed during our sojourn. Perhaps fastidious people might object to the temperature in summer, when the rays of the sun attain their maximum force, and the hot winds sweep in from the desert. It is said that a wicked soldier died here, and was consigned to the fiery regions below for his manifold sins; but unable to stand the rigors of the climate, sent back for his blankets. I have even heard complaint made that the thermometer failed to show the true heat because the mercury dried up. Everything dries; wagons dry; men dry; chickens dry; there is no juice left in any thing, living or dead, by the close of summer. Officers and soldiers are supposed to walk about creaking; mules, it is said, can only bray at midnight; and I have heard it hinted that the carcasses of cattle rattle inside their hides, and that snakes find a difficulty in bending their bodies, and horned frogs die of apoplexy. Chickens hatched at this season, as old Fort Yumers say; come out of the shell ready cooked; bacon is eaten with a spoon; and butter must stand an hour in the sun before the flies become dry enough for use. The Indians sit in the river with fresh mud on their heads, and by dint of constant dipping and sprinkling manage to keep from roasting, though they usually come out parboiled. Strangers coming suddenly upon a group squatted in water up to their necks, with their mud-covered heads glistening in the sun, frequently mistake them for seals. Their usual mode of travelling down the river is astride of a log—their heads only being visible. It is enough to make a man stare with amazement to see a group of mud-balls floating on the current of a hot day, laughing and talking to each other as if it were the finest fun in the world. I have never tried this mode of locomotion; have an idea it must be delightful in such a glowing summer climate.

The Colorado was lower than any of the residents at Fort Yuma had ever before known it. It could scarcely fall any lower without going entirely through its own bottom. A more capricious river does not exist. Formerly it ran through the desert to the northwest, but for some reason or other it changed its course, and now it runs about three feet above the level of the desert. As a navigable stream it possesses some advantages during the dry season; boats can seldom sink in it; and for the matter of channels it has an unusual variety. The main channel shifts so often that the most skillful pilot always knows where it is not be found by pursuing the course of his last trip. The little steamer which plies between the fort and the mouth of the river, distant one hundred miles, could not make the round trip in less than two weeks, owing to shoals and shifting bars. Up to La Paz and Fort Mojave the navigation was still worse. Twenty or thirty days up and down was considered a fair trip. The miners in that region were suffering for supplies, although six hundred tons of freight lay at the embarcadera awaiting transportation. I mention this as a hint to the delegate soon to be elected to Congress from Arizona. If he can prevail upon that liberal body to grant half a million of dollars toward plugging up or calking the bottom of the river so that it won't leak, or procuring rain by joint resolution, he will forever after merit the suffrages of his fellow-citizens.

JOHN HANCE—CHAMPION LIAR

Wallace E. Clayton

WALLACE E. CLAYTON, a retired Detroit advertising executive, came
to the southwest with two associates in 1966 looking for investment opportunities. They found what they were looking for in
Tombstone and optioned several historic properties, including the
venerable *Tombstone Epitaph*, founded in 1880. Clayton now edits
and publishes a national edition of the paper once a month,
helping "to keep the Old West alive." He does some of the writing
himself. His article on Captain John Hance puts together most of
what is known about a master of the tall tale.

Incredible was the career of John Hance, the first man to break
a trail down into the Grand Canyon, the first to guide tourists
below the rim, and a man paid—and praised—for being the most
interesting liar on the Southwestern Frontier.

As the first white man to live in the Canyon, one who discovered
eleven ways to get from the rim to the Colorado River some 3,500
feet below, and the first to establish a camp for Grand Canyon
visitors, he would rate at least an asterisk in Arizona history.

But he is best remembered for the tall tales he told everyone
from a President of the United States to resort hotel guests
entranced by the frontiersman's wonderous stories.

Little is known of Hance's background; he is believed to have
been born in Tennessee, fought in the Civil War and then, it was
said, drifted to Texas. When asked about his past, he would end
the conversation with a curt, "I don't like ancient history."

However, when pressed as to why and how he came to Arizona,
he would say he grew tired of Texas when all of a sudden he saw

From the *Tombstone Epitaph*, July, 1989, pp. 1, 11–12.

a huge herd of buffalo migrating north toward the Arizona Territory.

"I climbed a mesquite tree," he said, "And as the herd passed by underneath, I waited for a big bull, then dropped down on his back. Took us two weeks to reach Arizona."

Sometimes came the logical question, "How did you eat, riding that long atop a buffalo?" Explained Hance, "I just cut chunks off the buffalo's rump—that's the tastiest spot."

Hickock's Brother

It is known that Hance came West from Fort Leavenworth, Kansas, working with a mule train owned by the younger brother of "Wild Bill" Hickock. He spent some time at the settlement of Camp Verde, near present-day Prescott, then moved to Williams, about forty miles south of the south rim of the Canyon. "Odd jobs" seems to be the best way to describe his activities until about 1883, when he went down into Grand Canyon for the first time.

He recalled that the trip down and up the cliffs where there was no trail took three days round-trip. He said he joyfully bathed in the Colorado River and (strangely) having no knife, picked up a piece of granite and scratched his name on some sandstone rock. It was prophetic.

Hance's first and subsequent trips down into the Canyon were for the same reasons a few other daring men were descending the cliffs—to prospect and hunt. However, with increasing popular interest in the natural wonderland, first completely and intensely explored by John Wesley Powell in 1869, Hance sensed people would be wanting to sightsee in the Canyon.

For many months he worked to clear a trail down the seven miles from the south rim to the Colorado River. Just when he took the first visitors down is not known for certain; some sources say 1884, some a couple of years later. But Hance was right about people wanting to visit the Canyon; and soon built a camp for tourists just east of Grandview Point.

There was a log cabin headquarters/storeroom, surrounded by tents where sightseers would spend the night before starting a pre-dawn descent. Newspaper and magazine writers making the trip on assignments invariably would note the cleanliness of the accommodations. The tents had wooden floors, iron beds with mattresses and Navajo blankets. Trips were two days: a day going down, and one coming back. On both legs there were stops at a rock cabin Hance had half-way down the trail. Here his guests had dinner (lunch) and rested before resuming the journeys.

Faced Starvation

For several winters Hance lived in this cabin, packing down enough supplies to sustain him as he spent the time prospecting. Once, he often told visitors, he ran out of supplies just as a heavy storm started. He made snowshoes from a couple of pine boards, and, when the storm stopped, headed for civilization. But he fell, hurt his ankle, and painfully had to return to the cabin.

"I found there was nothing left but half a jar of sorghum molasses and a box of Babbitt's Best Soap. I made of mixture of soap and molasses in a skillet, slicing the soap into flakes, and adding a few shavings from an old boot to make it as tasty as possible. That's all I had to eat for a week, until the snow melted.

"I tell you frankly, I have never liked the taste of soap from that day to this."

At the headquarters cabin, Hance kept guest books. As tourists were leaving he would ask them to note their reactions to the Canyon and their visit. Some 2,000 did.

Buckey O'Neil, a Prescott newspaperman who would be killed as a Rough Rider in the Spanish-American War wrote, "God made the Canyon, John Hance the trails. Without the other, neither would be complete." A lady from Boston, after noting that the Canyon was "the most beautiful sight in the world added, "Capt. John Hance is here, too. He will interest you if the Canyon doesn't." And another wrote, "To see the Canyon only and not see Captain Hance is to miss one-half the show."

And early on Hance was being called "Captain," reason unknown. Perhaps it was because he was such a dominant figure in Canyon affairs. A stagecoach driver took a magazine writer aside at the end of the trip to Hance's camp and said, "He has no right to 'Captain,' but if it pleases him, we let it pass." It obviously pleased him, since that's how he referred to himself.

Early Ladies' Slacks

Although Hance's Trail was the only passable one for several years, it was not an easy descent. The (Prescott) *Arizona Enterprise* had an article on June 9, 1892 which said "the last mile and a half is so steep, rope ladders are needed in places to overcome perpendicular cliffs." It reported that many women had gone down, noting that "very often they discard their skirts and wear a bloomer-style of trousers."

The same paper reported on October 6 that "only by descending the Hance Trail can one arrive at anything like a comprehension of the proportion of the Canyon, and the descent cannot be too urgently recommended to every visitor who possesses a stout heart and capacious lungs." The article added that "Hance's service as a guide is invaluable, and if the entire trip down is planned, almost indispensable."

Because his first trail was so rugged, Hance kept exploring other possibilities, finally developing one—"Hance's New Trail"—in which pack animals could go all the way down to the river. (On the original trail, Hance himself would have to pack the supplies over the last mile and a half. He said he would carry the grub, but the visitors had to tote their own blankets.)

While Hance was exploring ways to get down the Canyon, he also was trying ways to get across it. He would tell visitors of the time he had a really fast horse, and he was sure, with the proper start, he could ride that horse across the Canyon from south rim to north. He went back three miles from the rim, and spurred the horse into a wild gallop to the edge, where he took off.

"But I wasn't half-way across when I saw he couldn't make it," Hance would say. "We hadn't taken enough of a start."

Then he would pause for the inevitable question of, "What happened?"

"Nothing I could do but turn him around and come back."

A version of this was Hance's accounting of the time his horse was spooked by some mountain sheep and ran out-of-control over the Canyon's rim. Horse and rider were plummeting to the earth 3,500 feet below.

Someone would break in saying something to the effect that this was nonsense. . . . how could he have lived to tell about it?

"Well, I just stuck to the saddle, riding that horse down. . . . and when we got a few feet from the ground, I just jumped off."

Of course, said Hance, he had walked over. . . . whenever there was a heavy fog he would put on a pair of fine snowshoes he had bought and could go right across on the fog. But one had to be careful, he warned.

"Once the fog went out real fast and left me on the other side without food or drink," he complained. "I had been marooned about four days when it returned, but not as thick. I'd grown lighter by this time, and got across all right.

But the fog was so thin in spots that several times I was afraid I'd break through and go to the bottom."

Man of Fame

Hance's tall tales.... his well-known knowledge of the Canyon and reputation as the Canyon's most competent guide.... made him known throughout the Southwest. In 1896, a writer for *Leslie's Popular Monthly*, Edith Sessions Tupper, came to Arizona to take his Canyon tour. She wrote that all the way from Albuquerque you hear of "Hance's Trail," "Hance's New Trail," "Hance's Old Trail," "Hance's cabins."

"You begin to wonder if Captain John Hance owns the Grand Canyon," she wrote, noting that in Flagstaff the name was heard even oftener. "Now you wonder if you've come to see the Grand Canyon or Hance," she commented.

This feeling was reflected by another writer, Maurice Salzman, who accompanied President Theodore Roosevelt's party on the tour of the Canyon via Hance's New Trail, by far the most commonly used.

"From Hance's Old Trail to Lee's Ferry and on down to Yuma in one direction, and beyond the Grande in the other, the Captain knows his home. Every nook, pinnacle, every waterfall and stream calls him by name. He is truly the monarch of all he surveys."

Mind Wanders

Early in the trip, the President and Hance were talking about the problems of the large trade rats around camps, getting into food supplies and frightening lady visitors. Hance seemed to wander off the subject, commenting that he always liked to smoke his pipe just before he went to sleep, recalling a time on a camping trip when he finished his smoke and put the pipe beside him on the ground.

To the puzzled question of what this had to do with trade rats, Hance replied, "Well, one morning my pipe was gone. And no one else was with me. Real puzzled, I went hunting for it, and there on a hummock was the biggest, fattest, sassiest trade rat I ever saw, just sitting and smoking my pipe."

Angry Bear

Trees, Hance added, were very valuable things.... made good scenery, provided wood and were places of refuge. To the expected question of what he meant by that, he delightedly would tell the story of the time he was being chased by an angry bear.

"Every minute I thought he'd get me by the pants. I sighted a big pine tree ahead with a limb about 30 feet up, and I concluded I would have to get that, or the bear would get me. So I made a big jump for that limb, the biggest jump I ever made in my life. I missed it entirely!

"That is, I missed it going up, but I caught it coming down."

With Hance's flourishing tourist business in the summer, and his winter-time months living in the Canyon and prospecting, there is only one time when he was known to have gone far from his land where he was "monarch of all he surveys." This trip was brief.... and was the result of his prospecting. In 1898, he sold one of his claims for $10,000 and went to San Francisco.

He was quoted in Frank D. Lockwood's article in the July, 1940 issue of *Desert* magazine as having said, "We had a pretty good time; but I tell you that although I spent $1,000 a day each day I was there, thousands of people in San Francisco didn't even know there was such a person as John Hance.

"Sometime I'm going to get up about $50,000 and wake that town up."

Just who he meant by "we" is unknown—perhaps it was just the editorial usage of the word. He was a bachelor all his years in Arizona, although sometimes he would acknowledge having had a wife when questioned by prying tourists.

Old Wives Tales

Once he said he had had a wife, "but she must be far gone now." When asked what he meant, he said he used to have a farm along the one good road in the county, but he and his wife didn't get along.

"So I kept the farm and gave her the road," he said.

Another time he told an insistent questioner that yes, he had been married once. When prodded to tell what happened, he said during the slack season he and his wife would ride their horses down into the canyon. One time, he said, she was thrown and broke her leg. In the excitement, the horses ran away and he was helpless to get her out of the Canyon.

"What could I do but shoot her?" His question ended the conversation.

By the mid-1890s, a hotel had been built just north of Hance's camp, and most visitors chose to stay in rooms instead of tents. Hance continued to guide tourists down his New Trail—and would stop by the hotel in the evenings to entertain his competitor's guests with his stories of Grand Canyon life.

He would caution them not to get too close to the very rim of the Canyon when looking down into it, illustrating his warning with an account of one tourist who leaned too far over and fell, but managed to get into an upright position as he went down.

"He was wearing new rubber boots," Hance said, "So naturally every time he struck bottom he'd bounce up again. This happened several times, but he never could catch hold of the rim, and we couldn't grab him.

"Finally we had to shoot him to keep him from starving to death."

Hance soon sold his land to a friend, operator of a stage line from Flagstaff to the rim, who let him continue to live in a small cabin about a mile from his camp, where he had lived in the summers. But in 1906, the land again was sold, and Hance was told he had to leave.

By this time there was another hotel on the south rim, the Bright Angel, operated by the Fred Harvey Company, known for its innovations. Company officials offered Hance room and board, and a pittance, to be sort of a Grand Canyon host to their guests, giving them trail advice, telling about the Canyon, and—most of all—to entertain them with his stories.

Stories such as the time he was stranded in a small canyon without supplies when the Colorado River flooded. But, he said, he didn't go hungry. He cut his chewing tobacco into little pieces, and threw them into the river.

"When the fish came up to spit, I'd club them with a heavy mesquite branch."

He once boasted to a friend that he could make the tourists believe that frogs ate hard boiled eggs and carried them a mile to find a hot rock to cook them on.

For six years, the lean, neat symbol of the Grand Canyon made thousands of passing-through friends with his tall tales. But in the latter part of 1918 he became too ill to make his lobby and rim visits. The people at the Harvey hotel cared for him until it closed for the season, then provided for him at a Flagstaff hotel; soon he became so ill he had to be taken to the county hospital.

On January 6, 1919, the man who said he and a Scotsman had dug the Grand Canyon looking for his companion's lost dime, found his Last Trail.

An epitaph might be President Roosevelt's farewell to him some years before:

"I shall be pleased to say I have seen God's greatest and most stupendous natural wonder—the Grand Canyon. But the greatest satisfaction of all will be the remembrance of having shaken hands with the greatest liar on earth."

THE HONK HONK BREED

Stewart Edward White

MICHIGAN-BORN STEWART EDWARD WHITE became a professional writer early in the present century. He set his stories in many places —Alaska, the Dakotas, California, Kentucky, Africa—where he would get his characters out of doors. His Arizona stories stem from several visits to Colonel Henry C. Hooker's ranches in the Sulphur Springs Valley north of Willcox. *Arizona Nights* was one of his favorite books and has pleased critics and anthologists since its publication in 1907. Of it Lawrence Clark Powell says, "...this small book bids fair to outlast the rest and be discovered anew by each generation of readers."* No truer or funnier story about the West has ever been written.

It was Sunday at the ranch. For a wonder the weather had been favourable; the windmills were all working, the bogs had dried up, the beef had lasted over, the remuda had not strayed—in short, there was nothing to do. Sang had given us a baked bread-pudding with raisins in it. We filled it in—a wash basin full of it—on top of a few incidental pounds of *chile con*, baked beans, soda biscuits, "air tights," and other delicacies. Then we adjourned with our pipes to the shady side of the blacksmith's shop where we could watch the ravens on top the adobe wall of the corral. Somebody told a story about ravens. This led to road-runners. This suggested rattlesnakes. They started Windy Bill.

"Speakin' of snakes," said Windy, "I mind when they catched the great-grandaddy of all the bullsnakes up at Lead in the Black Hills. I was only a kid then. This wasn't no such tur'ble long a snake, but

From *Arizona Nights*. New York: McClure, 1907, pp. 219–237.

*Lawrence Clark Powell, *Southwest Classics* (Los Angeles: Ward Ritchie Press, 1974), p. 192.

he was more'n a foot thick. Looked just like a sahuaro stalk. Man name of Terwilliger Smith catched it. He named this yere bull-snake Clarence, and got it so plumb gentle it followed him every-where. One day old P.T. Barnum come along and wanted to buy this Clarence snake—offered Terwilliger a thousand cold—but Smith wouldn't part with the snake nohow. So finally they fixed up a deal so Smith could go along with the show. They shoved Clarence in a box in the baggage car, but after a while Mr. Snake gets so lonesome he gnaws out and starts to crawl back to find his master. Just as he is half-way between the baggage car and the smoker, the couplin' give way—right on that heavy grade between Custer and Rocky Point. Well, sir, Clarence wound his head 'round one brake wheel and his tail around the other, and held that train together to the bottom of the grade. But it stretched him twenty-eight feet and they had to advertise him as a boa-constrictor."

Windy Bill's history of the faithful bullsnake aroused to remi-niscence the grizzled stranger, who thereupon held forth as follows:

Wall, I've see things and I've heerd things, some of them ornery, and some you'd love to believe, they was that gorgeous and improbable. Nat'ral history was always my hobby and sportin' events my special pleasure—and this yarn of Windy's reminds me of the only chanst I ever had to ring in business and pleasure and hobby all in one grand merry-go-round of joy. It come about like this:

One day, a few year back, I was sittin' on the beach at Santa Barbara watchin' the sky stay up, and wonderin' what to do with my year's wages, when a little squinch-eye round-face with big bow spectacles came and plumped down beside me.

"Did you ever stop to think," says he, shovin' back his hat, "that if the horse-power delivered by them waves on this beach in one single hour could be concentrated behind washin' machines, it would be enough to wash all the shirts for a city of four hundred and fifty-one thousand one hundred and thirty-six people?"

"Can't say I ever did," says I, squintin' at him sideways.

"Fact," says he, "and did it ever occur to you that if all the food a man eats in the course of a natural life could be gathered together at one time, it would fill a wagon-train twelve miles long?"

"You make me hungry," says I.

"And ain't it interestin' to reflect," he goes on, "that if all the finger-nail parin's of the human race for one year was to be collected and subjected to hydraulic pressure it would equal in size the pyramid of Cheops?"

"Look yere," says I, sittin' up, "did *you* ever pause to excogitate that if all the hot air you is dispensin' was to be collected together it would fill a balloon big enough to waft you and me over that Bullyvard of Palms to yonder gin mill on the corner?"

He didn't say nothin' to that—just yanked me to my feet, faced me towards the gin mill above mentioned, and exerted considerable pressure on my arm in urgin' of me forward.

"You ain't so much of a dreamer, after all," thinks I. "In important matters you are plumb decisive."

We sat down at little tables, and my friend ordered a beer and a chicken sandwich.

"Chickens," says he, gazin' at the sandwich, "is a dollar apiece in this country, and plumb scarce. Did you ever pause to ponder over the returns chickens would give on a small investment? Say you start with ten hens. Each hatches out thirteen aigs, of which allow a loss of say six for childish accidents. At the end of the year you has eighty chickens. At the end of two years that flock has increased to six hundred and twenty. At the end of the third year—"

He had the medicine tongue! Ten days later him and me was occupyin' of an old ranch fifty mile from anywhere. When they run stage-coaches this joint used to be a road-house. The outlook was on about a thousand little brown foothills. A road two miles four rods two foot eleven inches in sight run by in front of us. It come over one foothill and disappeared over another. I know just how long it was, for later in the game I measured it.

Out back was about a hundred little wire chicken corrals filled with chickens. We had two kinds. That was the doin's of Tuscarora. My pardner called himself Tuscarora Maxillary. I asked him once if that was his real name.

"It's the realest little old name you ever heerd tell of," says he. "I know, for I made it myself—liked the sound of her. Parents ain't got no rights to name their children. Parents don't have to be called them names."

Well, these chickens, as I said, was of two kinds. The first was these low-set, heavy-weight propositions with feathers on their laigs, and not much laigs at that, called Cochin Chinys. The other was a tall ridiculous outfit made up entire of bulgin' breast and gangle laigs. They stood about two foot and a half tall, and when they went to peck the ground their tail feathers stuck straight up to the sky. Tusky called 'em Japanese Games.

"Which the chief advantage of them chickens is," says he, "that in weight about ninety per cent. of 'em is breast meat. Now my idee is, that if we can cross 'em with these Cochin Chiny fowls we'll have a low-hung, heavy-weight chicken runnin' strong on breast meat. These Jap Games is too small, but if we can bring 'em up in size and shorten their laigs, we'll shore have a winner."

That looked good to me, so we started in on that idee. The theery was bully, but she didn't work out. The first broods we hatched growed up with big husky Cochin Chiny bodies and little short necks, perched up on laigs three foot long. Them chickens couldn't reach ground nohow. We had to build a table for 'em to eat off, and when they went out rustlin' for themselves they had to confine themselves to sidehills or flyin' insects. Their breasts was all right, though—"And think of them drumsticks for the boardin'-house trade!" says Tusky.

So far things wasn't so bad. We had a good grubstake. Tusky and me used to feed them chickens twict a day, and then used to set around watchin' the playful critters chase grasshoppers up an' down the wire corrals, while Tusky figgered out what'd happen if somebody was dumfool enough to gather up somethin' and fix it in baskets or wagons or such. That was where we showed our ignorance of chickens.

One day in the spring I hitched up, rustled a dozen of the youngsters into coops, and druv over to the railroad to make our first sale. I couldn't fold them chickens up into them coops at first, but then I stuck the coops up on aidge and they worked all right, though I will admit they was a comical sight. At the railroad one of them towerist trains had just slowed down to a halt as I come up, and the towerists was paradin' up and down allowin' they was particular enjoyin' of the warm Californy sunshine. One old terrapin, with grey chin whiskers, projected over, with his wife, and took a peek through the slats of my coop. He straightened up like someone had touched him off with a red-hot poker.

"Stranger," said he, in a scared kind of whisper, "what's them?"

"Them's chickens," says I.

He took another long look.

"Marthy," says he to the old woman, "this will be about all! We come out from Ioway to see the Wonders of Californy, but I can't go nothin' stronger than this. If these is chickens, I don't want to see no Big Trees."

Well, I sold them chickens all right for a dollar and two bits, which was better than I expected, and got an order for more. About ten days later I got a letter from the commission house.

"We are returnin' a sample of your Arts and Crafts chickens with the lovin' marks of the teeth still onto him," says they. "Don't send any more till they stops pursuin' of the nimble grasshopper. Dentist bill will foller."

With the letter came the remains of one of the chickens. Tusky and I, very indignant, cooker her for supper. She was tough, all right. We thought she might do better biled, so we put her in the pot over night. Nary bit. Well, then we got interested. Tusky kep' the fire goin' and I rustled greasewood. We cooked her three days and three nights. At the end of that time she was sort of pale and frazzled, but still givin' points to three-year-old jerky on cohesion and other uncompromisin' forces of Nature. We buried her then, and went out back to recuperate.

There we could gaze on the smilin' landscape, dotted by about four hundred long-laigged chickens swoopin' here and there after grasshoppers.

"We got to stop that," says I.

"We can't," murmured Tusky, inspired. "We can't. It's born in 'em; it's a primal instinct, like the love of a mother for her young, and it can't be eradicated! Them chickens is constructed by a divine providence for the express purpose of chasin' grasshoppers, jest as the beaver is made for buildin' dams, and the cow-puncher is made for whisky and faro-games. We can't keep 'em from it. If we was to shut 'em in a dark cellar, they'd flop after imaginary grasshoppers in their dreams, and die emaciated in the midst of plenty. Jimmy, we're up agin the Cosmos, the oversoul—" Oh, he had the medicine tongue, Tusky had, and risin' on the wings of eloquence that way, he had me faded in ten minutes. In fifteen I was wedded solid to the notion that the bottom had dropped out the chicken business. I think now that if we'd shut them hens up, we might have—still, I don't know; they was a good deal in what Tusky said.

"Tuscarora Maxillary," says I, "did you ever stop to entertain that beautiful thought that if all the dumfoolishness possessed now by the human race could be gathered together, and lined up alongside of us, the first feller to come along would say to it 'Why, hello, Solomon!'"

We quit the notion of chickens for profit right then and there, but we couldn't quit the place. We hadn't much money, for one thing, and then we kind of liked loafin' around and raisin' a little garden truck, and—oh, well, I might as well say so, we had a notion about placers in the dry wash back of the house—you know how it is. So we stayed on, and kept a-raisin' these long-laigs for the fun of it. I used to like to watch 'em projectin' around, and I fed 'em twict a day about as usual.

So Tusky and I lived alone there together, happy as ducks in Arizona. About onc't in a month somebody'd pike along the road. She wasn't much of a road, generally more chuck-holes than bumps, though sometimes it was the other way around. Unless it happened to be a man horseback or maybe a freighter without the fear of God in his soul, we didn't have no words with them; they was too busy cussin' the highways and generally too mad for social discourses.

One day early in the year, when the 'dobe mud made ruts to add to the bumps, one of these automobeels went past. It was the first Tusky and me had seen in them parts, so we run out to view her. Owin' to the high spots on the road, she looked like one of these movin' picters, as to blur and wobble; sounded like a cyclone mingled with cuss-words, and smelt like hell on housecleanin' day.

"Which them folks don't seem to be enjoyin' of the scenery," sais I to Tusky. "Do you reckon that there blue trail is smoke from the machine or remarks from the inhabitants thereof?"

Tusky raised his head and sniffed long and inquirin'.

"It's langwidge," says he. "Did you ever stop to think that all the words in the dictionary hitched end to end would reach—"

But at that minute I catched sight of somethin' brass lyin' in the road. It proved to be a curled-up sort of horn with a rubber bulb on the end. I squoze the bulb and jumped twenty foot over the remark she made.

"Jarred off the machine," says Tusky.

"Oh, did it?" says I, my nerves still wrong. "I thought maybe it had growed up from the soil like a toadstool."

About this time we abolished the wire chicken corrals, because we needed some of the wire. Them long-laigs thereupon scattered all over the flat searchin' out their prey. When feed time come I had to screech my lungs out gettin' of 'em in, and then sometimes they didn't all hear. It was plumb discouragin', and I mighty nigh made up my mind to quit 'em, but they had come to be sort of pets, and I hated to turn 'em down. It used to tickle Tusky almost to death to see me out there hollerin' away like an old bull-frog. He used to come out reg'lar with his pipe lit, just to enjoy me. Finally I got mad and opened up on him.

"Oh," he explains, "it just plumb amuses me to see the dumfool at his childish work. Why don't you teach 'em to come to that brass horn, and save your voice?"

"Tusky," says I, with feelin', "sometimes you do seem to get a glimmer of real sense."

Well, first off them chickens used to throw backsommersets over that horn. You have no idee how slow chickens is to learn things. I could tell you things about chickens—say, this yere bluff about roosters bein' gallant is all wrong. I've watched 'em. When one finds a nice feed he gobbles it so fast that the pieces foller down his throat like yearlin's through a hole in the fence. It's only when he scratches up a measly one-grain quick-lunch that he calls up the hens and stands noble and self-sacrificin' to one side. That ain't the point, which is that after two months I had them long-laigs so they'd drop everythin' and come kitin' at the *honk-honk* of that horn. It was a purty sight to see 'em sailin' in from all directions twenty foot at a stride. I was proud of 'em, and named 'em the Honk-honk Breed. We didn't have no others, for by now the coyotes and bob-cats had nailed the straight-breds. There wasn't no wild cat or coyote could catch one of my Honk-honks, no, sir!

We made a little on our placer—just enough to keep interested. Then the supervisors decided to fix our road, and what's more, *they done it!* That's the only part in this yarn that's hard to believe, but, boys, you'll have to take it on faith. They ploughed her, and crowned her, and scraped her, and rolled her, and when they moved on we had the fanciest highway in the State of Californy.

That noon—the day they called her a job—Tusky and I sat smokin' our pipes as per usual, when way over the foothills we seen a cloud of dust and faint to our ears was bore a whizzin' sound. The chickens was gathered under the cottonwood for the heat of the day, but they didn't pay no attention. Then faint, but clear, we heard another of them brass horns:

"Honk! honk!" says it, and every one of them chickens woke up, and stood at attention.

"Honk! honk!" it hollered clearer and nearer. Then over the hill come an automobeel, blowin' vigorous at every jump.

"My God!" I yells to Tusky, kickin' over my chair, as I springs to my feet. "Stop 'em! Stop 'em!"

But it was too late. Out the gate sprinted them poor devoted chickens, and up the road they trailed in vain pursuit. The last we seen of 'em was a minglin' of dust and dim figgers goin' thirty mile an hour after a disappearin' automobeel.

That was all we seen for the moment. About three o'clock the first straggler came limpin' in, his wings hangin', his mouth open, his eyes glazed with the heat. By sundown fourteen had returned. All the rest had disappeared utter; we never seen 'em again. I reckon they just naturally run themselves into a sunstroke and died on the road.

It takes a long time to learn a chicken a thing, but a heap longer to unlearn him. After that two or three of these yere automobeels went by every day, all a-blowin' of their horns, all kickin' up a hell of a dust. And every time them fourteen Honk-honks of mine took along after 'em, just as I'd taught 'em to do, layin' to get to their corn when they caught up. No more of 'em died, but that fourteen did get into elegant trainin'. After a while they got plumb to enjoyin' it. When you come right down to it, a chicken don't have many amusements and relaxations in this life. Searchin' for worms, chasin' grasshoppers, and wallerin' in the dust is about the limits of joys for chickens.

It was sure a fine sight to see 'em after they got well into the game. About nine o'clock every mornin' they would saunter down to the rise of the road where they would wait patient until a machine came along. Then it would warm your heart to see the enthusiasm of them. With exultant cackles of joy they'd trail in, reachin' out like quarter-horses, their wings half spread out, their eyes beamin' with delight. At the lower turn they'd quit. Then, after talkin' it over excited-like for a few minutes, they'd calm down and wait for another.

After a few months of this sort of trainin' they got purty good at it. I had one two-year-old rooster that made fifty-four mile an hour behind one of those sixty-horsepower Panhandles. When cars didn't come along often enough, they'd all turn out and chase jack-rabbits. They wasn't much fun at that. After a short, brief sprint the rabbit would crouch down plumb terrified, while the Honk-honks pulled off triumphal dances around his shrinkin' form.

Our ranch got to be purty well known them days among automobeelists. The strength of their cars was horse-power, of course, but the speed of them they got to ratin' by chicken-power. Some of them used to come way up from Los Angeles just to try out a new car along our road with the Honk-honks for pace-makers. We charged them a little somethin' and then, too, we opened up the road-house and the bar, so we did purty well. It wasn't necessary to work any longer at that bogus placer. Evenin's we sat around outside and swapped yarns, and I bragged on my chickens. The chickens would gather round close to listen. They liked to hear their praises sung, all right. You bet they *sabe!* The only reason a chicken, or any other critter, isn't intelligent is because he hasn't no chance to expand.

Why, we used to run races with 'em. Some of us would hold two or more chickens back of a chalk line, and the starter'd blow the horn from a hundred yards to a mile away, dependin' on whether it was a sprint or for distance. We had pools on the results, gave odds, made books, and kept records. After the thing got knowed we made money hand over fist.

The stranger broke off abruptly and began to roll a cigarette.

"What did you quit it for, then?" ventured Charley, out of the hushed silence.

"Pride," replied the stranger solemnly. "Haughtiness of spirit."

"How so?" urged Charley, after a pause.

"Them chickens," continued the stranger, after a moment,

"stood around listenin' to me a-braggin' of what superior fowls they was until they got all puffed up. They wouldn't have nothin' whatever to do with the ordinary chickens we brought in for eatin' purposes, but stood around lookin' bored when there wasn't no sport doin'. They got to be just like that Four Hundred you read about in the papers. It was one continual round of grasshopper balls, race meets, and afternoon hen-parties. They got idle and haughty, just like folks. Then come race suicide. They got to feelin' so aristocratic the hens wouldn't have no eggs."

Nobody dared say a word.

"Windy Bill's snake——" began the narrator genially.

"Stranger," broke in Windy Bill, with great emphasis, "as to that snake, I want you to understand this: yereafter in my estimation that snake is nothin' but an ornery angle-worm!"

THE RESCUE OF LEO THE LION

Frank V. Gillette

NOT ALL TALL TALES are lies. Some of the tallest are true. Frank V. Gillette, a lifelong resident of the rugged cattle country north of Globe, tells one of the best in his book *Pleasant Valley*, the story of "Leo the Lion."

The 1920s, Frank reminisces, were exciting times. Roads were opening up. A telephone line had been strung across the mountains to Payson by the Forest Service. People were hearing about a thing called "radio", and moving pictures were visible in Globe. The chatter of the Model T was heard in the land and "now they were making flying machines". Frank saw his first one fly over when he was seven, and not long after that Leo arrived.

Leo was the African lion used by Metro-Goldwyn-Mayer as its symbol and trademark. He lived at peace until someone conceived the idea of sending him to various centers of population in an airplane as an advertising venture. This his troubles began. Martin Jensen flew him safely in a small plane as far as Phoenix, but when he took off for Albuquerque, he chose the route across the mountains around Pleasant Valley and crashed near a place called appropriately, Hell's Gate. Neither man nor beast was badly hurt but it took Jensen three days walking before he encountered other human beings. In response to his anguished pleas, the local ranchers agreed to attempt a rescue. Four days after the crash they skidded Leo, still in his cage, down off the mountain, "doctored" him for screw worms, and sent him on his way back to Hollywood. The episode had its humorous aspects, though there was no fun in it for poor old Leo. We pick up the action as the ranchers prepare to set forth.

From *Pleasant Valley*. Privately printed, 1986, pp. 10–16.

Jensen hadn't been at Grady's garage long before Dave Martin drove up in his Model T.

"Now here's the man you want to see," Grady said. "He's a brother-in-law to Sam Haught."

Dave listened with interest as Jensen told his story. "I'm sure the Company would pay well to have Leo brought out," Jensen repeated. "He's really a very valuable lion."

"Load in and we'll see what Sam thinks," Dave said. They stopped first at Boy's place. Boy Hought was a powerful man, narrow of hip and wide of shoulder. To a sheltered city feller like Jensen he made a fearsome impression. Of course Jensen had no way of knowing that Boy was a good solid person with a heart of gold, who wouldn't hurt a flea! And Boy had a sense of humor and enjoyed a good laugh as well as the next man. Jensen was apologetic as he told his story . . . of being unable to gain elevation, of flying into the box canyon and then crashing and of his harrowing experience walking out. Boy listened with ill concealed amusement.

"We could probably get the lion out of there," he nodded. "We'll go over to Sam's place and see what he's doing. You fellers go ahead and I'll bring the team over."

The road from Boy's place on over to Bear Flat was narrow and it wound precariously down from a mountain into Tonto Creek. Jensen could look over the bank in places where, if the car went over the edge, it would roll hundreds of feet down. Dave didn't pay any attention to the steep grade. He just pulled the ears back on that Model T and let 'er go. He actually half-slid around some of the curves. By the time they reached the bottom, Jensen was visibly shaken.

Bear Flat was a lush green oasis on the bank of Tonto Creek, encompassing eight to ten acres. Sam and Mae Haught and their five kids lived there. It was a beautiful spot and the Haughts lived much the same as the pioneers had when they first moved into the country.

"Yeh, we can bring that lion out of there," Sam said when he heard the story.

"Boy's bringing the team over," Dave told him.

"Yeh, we'll need a team," Sam agreed. "We'll just cut a fork and put the cage on it and pull him out with a team. Shouldn't be too much of a job."

The rest of the evening was spent in preparation for the trip.

Boy brought the team over, and Louie Pyle, Ernie Sweet and Henry Steel had also come along. Word had spread quickly from Grady Harrison's garage.

Jensen was awed by the rugged country and by the rugged men who occupied it. What a waste, he thought, as he stood quietly on the sidelines and watched them work. These men would be "naturals" in western movies. Boy Haught could play the part of an outlaw. He wouldn't have to put on makeup or change clothes or anything. And Green Valley Sam would make a "natural" western Marshall.

After a breakfast of beef steak and biscuits, 'taters and gravy, they mounted up and rode away in the half-light of morning. Martin Jensen stayed at Beare Flat with Mae and the kids.

The mules had been standing motionless while the preparations had been underway. A bad sign, if any of the men had paid attention to it . . . it was as though they were building up a head of steam and getting all set to explode. For, when they were untied from the trees, they fairly well threw a wall-eyed fit, rearing high into the air and whirling till the man holding onto the end of the rope was flung about like a slingshot. It took two men to a mule to get them partly calmed down. None of the men were exceptionally hot-tempered, but by the time they got the mules back under some control again, they were breathing between clenched teeth. But, try as they may, they couldn't get the mules within twenty feet of the sled. Lesser men might have given up, but it would take tougher mules than these to get the best of these men!

Old Leo was pretty well beat by the time the cowmen found the plane wreck. They knew before they reached it that they were getting close by the way the horses and mules were acting. The breeze was coming from out of the south, and they knew their animals were scenting the lion. It was necessary to snub all the horses and mules to trees when they arrived at the plane. The days had been warm, and Old Leo was plumb hurting for water. The men were able to get a pan in between the bars of the cage and then pour water into it. Leo lapped up the water like a hound dog. It seemed like he would never get enough. He must have drunk three or four gallons. After drinking his fill he lay down in the cage, growling menacingly, as the men worked the cage around and got it out of the plane and onto the ground. They then took a couple of measurements and began to search for a suitable tree which they could cut down for a sled. Soon locating a workable forked oak, they chopped it down, then cut the two side branches off to the right length. Cutting the butt off just in front of the fork shaped the "sled" like the letter "V". After rounding the front off some with an axe, they drilled a hole through. Putting a pin through the hole they then attached the double trees, and the sled was ready to hook up to the team.

"Better lash the cage onto the sled," Sam said. "I'm thinking we're going to have Bear Cat hell getting that team hooked up." He knew the team well. They were young mules and not too well broken. They were hard to keep under control and would pull a runaway if given half a chance. And either one of them could kick a chew of tobacco out of a man's mouth.

The cage was lashed securely to the sled. The double trees were in place, and Sam had dropped a canvas over the cage to keep Leo out of sight of the half-wild mules. It would be almost impossible to turn the "V" sled over, whatever happened.

"Old Leo will probably think that aeroplane pilot is on a drunk once these mules take off with that sled," Boy grinned. "All right boys, let's hook 'em up!" A statement that was much easier said than done!

"Blind 'em!" Sam shouted, pulling off his denim jumper. Moving along the rope, hand over hand, he was finally able to get an arm around one of the mules' neck. The mule reared and plunged. But Green Valley Sam had his hold, and he was there to stay. "Now hand me the jumper!" Putting the jumper around the mule's head, he tied the sleeves under its throat. A mule is an extremely smart animal. Once he sees that he's fouled, he'll stop his fighting. So when Sam got the jumper in place and the mule was blinded, it stood still. After both mules were blindfolded, the men began working them slowly backward toward the cage. After much pulling and pushing and kicking and swearing, they had the mules in place to be hooked to the doubletrees. But every time a man would try to ease one of the tugs down from where it was hooked on the britchen, the mule would let fly with a kick that would have torn a man's head off had it connected.

"I'll put a stop to that," Henry Steel said, taking a pigging string out of his pocket. With the axe he cut a limb about a foot and a half long and about as big around as a man's wrist. Cutting the shot rope in two, he took one piece and made a twitch. That was just a small loop which he tied to the end of the stick. A cowman could put the loop around a mule's upper lip and begin to twist. When this painful process began on a blindfolded mule, the mule would at once freeze up and not move a muscle. So with a twitch on each mule's upper lip, they now stood quiet, ready to be hooked to the sled.

Getting on his horse, Sam took the tie ropes and dallied to the saddle horn. All right, let 'em go!" he shouted.

Of course, the mules had on blind bridles so they couldn't see directly behind them. But when the men jerked the jumpers off of their heads, the action started. Sam was an excellent horseman so the mules didn't get too far with their runaway. He just went with them and pointed them in the right direction. He could keep them from going too fast. He knew they would slow down after a while, when they began to tire. Meanwhile, he just trotted along beside them and kept them in check. The sled was bouncing roughly over the rocks. Leo was having an extremely rough ride!

For the first couple of miles, they worked their way up the big ridge, heading canyons and taking advantage of the swales and ridges. But by the time they reached the cross trails, the picture was beginning to change. There was a pretty good trail running east and west from Bear Flat across to Gorden Canyon. It was a plain, well beaten horse trail that was plenty wide for a horse and rider, and the packs on pack mules, if a man happened to be leading a pack train. The trail went east to Gorden Canyon where it joined the trail running north and south from the ranches in Gorden Canyon area to Pleasant Valley. Once they hit the main east-west trail, they turned left toward Hole in the Rock. The trail led straight off of a steep mountain. There were several switchbacks before they hit the bottom. The grade was about forty percent. The team was now beginning to show the rigors of the hard pull they had already made. They were acting docile, like any well-broken team, but Green Valley Sam hadn't forgotten the way they had acted earlier when they were trying to hook them to the sled. Several times he made them stop and breathe for a few minutes when they were strained and breathing heavily from a hard pull. By the way the crow flies, it probably wasn't over six miles from Bear Flat to the plane wreck. But the way they would have to go, it was probably ten or twelve. Slide off the mountain to

the bottom of the Canyon at the Hole in the Rock. Let the men
and animals take on a good cool drink of spring water, rest a little
while and it was time to move out. The trail leading out from the
Hole in the Rock was precarious and winding, narrow in places and
skirting bluffs with ten to twenty foot drop. If the sled went over the
edge and jerked the team over with it, it would be one of the gol
darndest mix-ups a man ever laid eyes on. Sam could envision a
tanglement of squealing, kicking mules and a snarling lion, all tied
together by cage and chain. They were part way up the mountain
when the sled became wedged against a rock. The mules made a
couple of feeble pulls, and let up as though they were all in.

"Come on you bastards," Sam shouted, swatting them across the
rumps with a rope. "You was acting awful damn tough this
morning. Where's all that toughness now?"

The men had pried the sled partly loose with a pole. The mules
made a half-hearted pull and gave up. The tarp was still around
Leo's cage, shielding him from view. Sam raised the tarp. The
mules turned their heads and saw the lion! Snorting shrilly they
lunged in terror, loosening the sled and plunging wildly up the
hill. If Sam hadn't had hold of the neck ropes, they would have no
doubt pulled a runaway. So, all the rest of the trip, when the
mules began having difficulty pulling the sled through a rough
place, all Sam had to do was raise the curtain!

It had been a hard ride, all right, all agreed, but they were
nearly home now. They had rimmed out from the Hole in the
Rock, crossed Boscoe Flat, and skirted the side of Bull Tank
Canyon. One more steep hill to go off and they would be home.
They made it without incident down the last hill and through the
back gate onto the meadow.

Sam drove the team across the meadow and up to the house
and unhooked the tired mules. Word had spread fast in Payson.
There was a sizable crowd there, all anxious to see the lion.

Martin Jensen had gone out into the meadow. Walking as fast as
he could to match the long strides of Green Valley Sam, he was
talking excitedly. "How is he?" he asked anxiously.

"Ornery as a damned lion." Sam said with a dry smile.

Old Leo wasn't in too frisky a mood. He hadn't had anything to
eat in four or five days, and he had a couple of ugly-looking sores,

one on his shoulder and the other on his side. Watery-looking blood was oozing from both sores.

Sam and the rest of the crew had spotted the sores right away when they first walked up to the cage.

"He's got screwworms." Boy had said.

"Don't do anything," Sam replied. "We'll doctor 'em when we get him home."

The first order of business was to feed Leo. But what does a lion eat? Sam had a quarter of beef hanging in the smokehouse, but damned if he could see feeding it to a damned lion.

"Feed him a chicken," someone suggested. So they caught a chicken and wrung its neck and pitched it in to Leo. Leo was half-starved. He leaped onto the chicken and, holding it between his great paws, began licking fiercely. He soon had all the feathers licked off. Then he ate it in two big bites. After about five more chickens he took a drink of water and then lay down, sighing contentedly.

Leo Kratzberg was a sort of trouble-shooter for MGM. He was tall and slim, and an immaculate dresser. His thin straight mouth was bridged with a small, neatly-clipped moustache, and his lean jaw jutted forward. He was energetic, demanding, and abrasive in manner. And he was a very efficient person, especially if there was a serious problem that needed quick attention in the movie business.

"Take a couple of men and get out to Payson, Arizona," his boss had said. "Pick up our lion. Rent a truck or something and haul him to Phoenix. We can put him on the train there and have him shipped back here."

The trip from Los Angeles to Phoenix was no picnic in those days. Part of the road had been paved, but there were stretches of dirt, too—deep, soft powdery dust would better describe it. By the time he reached Phoenix, the big "Moon" car they were driving wasn't shiny anymore, and Lee Kratzberg was far from immaculate. After sleeping a few fretful hours in the Adams Hotel, they asked directions on how to get to Payson. Roads weren't very well marked, and the few road maps that were available didn't show little two-rut dirt roads like the one that led to Payson. A driver just about had to stay in the ruts most of the time because if he got out of them he'd probably ruin a tire on a rock.

Kratzberg set out for Payson. Traveling at five to ten miles an hour, they drove for half a day without any particular difficulty. It wasn't until they started up Screw Tailed Hill that the big Moon car began to boil. They had put a five-gallon can of water in the trunk when they left Los Angeles, but when they now opened the trunk to get it, they found that it had turned over and most of the water had leaked out. The better part of an hour was killed in letting the car cool off. And from there on, the road became progressively worse. The grades were narrow and steep. Going down Slate Creek Canyon was a harrowing experience. Clear of the ridge, they were starting down the grade toward Gold Creek when they heard the ominous hissing sound. A tire was going flat. Nothing to do but dig out the tools, jack the car up and put on the spare. The two hired hands did the work while Kratzberg paced back and forth in the road, kicking little rocks and wringing his hands. He had been holding his temper in check since one of the workmen had told him in no uncertain terms that if he valued his face he'd better keep his mouth shut when things went wrong.

They made their way to Rye Creek, crossed on the bridge and continued on to Polly Brown's Store at the foot of Oxbow. There they filled their gas tank and bought cheese and crackers and canned meat. Polly had sized up the men, especially Kratzberg, the fancy new car and the California license plates, and had formed an immediate dislike for them. They were nothing but city slickers, and it was pretty sure they were up to no good. Of course, it was during prohibition, but Kratzberg hadn't had trouble so far in getting a drink whenever he wanted one.

"Any chance of getting a bottle of beer?" he asked casually.

"I'd just as soon sell a horse piss." Polly retorted. "Besides, it's against the law. What are you, a damned revenuer or something, trying to get me to do something so you can arrest me? Better get to hell out of here before I fill ya with buckshot!"

The road up Oxbow was steep and narrow. About half-way up, they heard the ominous hissing sound again. Another tire was going flat! This time they had to pry the tire from the wheel, take out the innertube and find the leak, then scrape the hole with the rough place on the top of the little can that held the glue and patches, then spread the glue, put on the patch and let it dry for a few minutes before stuffing the tube back inside the tire and mounting it back on the rim. After mounting the tire, they had to pump it up with the hand pump and hope the patch would hold.

It was getting nigh onto sundown when a tired, dusty, sweaty, disheveled and thoroughly angry Kratzberg drove into the little village of Payson, turned onto the dusty main street and stopped in front of the Hilligas Boarding House and Hotel. The accommodations were good by Payson standards. The food was good, and was served family style. The rooms were clean. A wash basin and pitcher of water were in each room. Kratzberg was no longer concerned with his appearance. His grey slacks were wrinkled and smeared with grime. His once shiny shoes had lost their luster. A stubble of beard showed on the jutting jaw and little whiskers seemed to be competing with the thin moustache for a place on his upper lip.

It was early the next morning when Kratzberg walked next door to the Payson Commercial. "Oh, you're the feller that owns the lion that was in the aeroplane that wrecked the other day, over by Hells Gate?" Mart McDonald was speaking. "I hear Sam and Boy and some fellers pulled him out on a "V" sled and have him over at Bear Flat. Better not try going into Bear Flat in that Moon of yours. Might get in there all right, but you might have hell getting out."

"I don't own the damned lion," Kratzberg said curtly. "If I did, I'd shoot the SOB. My company has hired me to take him back to Hollywood and, by grab, that is what I'm going to do." The lean jaw jutted out determinedly.

"Reese Powers has a Model T with a Ruxel gear and Grady Harrison has a Dodge with a compound gear," said McDonald. "Either one of those fellers could bring that lion, cage and all, right up out of Bear Flat."

"Where can I find one of those men?"

"Grady owns that garage right over there." Mart pointed across the street to the tin building that stood on the corner. "Reese will be downtown after a while."

Grady Harrison had a truck that would haul a ton and a half, and it had a compound gear. He was the logical one to bring the lion out from Bear Flat, Kratzberg decided.

"Yeh, I guess I could do it," Grady said. "Fact is, I'm going to Phoenix on Thursday, so I could haul him all the way to Phoenix for you."

It was midmorning when Grady Harrison worked his way down the steep grade, crossed Tonto Creek and drove up to the house at Bear Flat. Several people were standing around in the yard. They looked curiously at the truck as it drove up. Sam and Boy Haught and their families, Pappy Haught, the fellers who had helped bring the lion out the day before, and Martin Jensen were all there.

Kratzberg was no longer the suave, debonair gentleman who walked the streets of Hollywood. His clothes were wrinkled, dirty and sweat-stained; his eyes were bloodshot and his hair mussed. The long jaw snapped shut like a steel trap. He hurried out of the truck and walked with long determined steps to the lion cage.

"Thought you said he wasn't hurt," he said accusingly when he saw the bloody spot on Leo's side. He glared belligerently at Martin Jensen. "He has a bad wound!"

"Ain't nothin' to get excited about," Green Valley Sam said. "Just a case of screwworms."

"Screwworms?" Kratzberg repeated sharply. "And what, pray tell, is that?"

"Ain't nothin' to worry about. We doctor 'em all the time." Sam said. "You see, when an animal gets some kind of wound, the fresh blood will attract the blowflies. I guess they smell the blood or something; anyway, they settle on the wound and lay their eggs. These eggs turn to maggots; the maggots burrow into the flesh. The flies lay more eggs, and they hatch more maggots, till finally there's a whole lot of maggots burrowing into the flesh. If they're not killed out, they would eventually kill the animal. Just eat him up."

Kratzberg listened in silence, then looked again at the lion. His jaw went slack. Then he turned and glared again at Martin Jensen. "Then we'll have to get a veterinarian. Those worms must be killed immediately!" His voice had the ring of authority.

"Don't know that feller, Veterinarian." Pappy Haught was speaking. "But any damned thing that wears hair and walks on four legs that these here Haughts can't doctor, ain't no use sending for that feller."

"Would it be possible for you men to doctor him?" Kratzberg turned imploringly to Green Valley Sam.

"Hell, yes, we can doctor him! If you'd have been here an hour later, we'd have already had him doctored," Sam replied.

"Then go ahead," Kratzberg said with the air of a man defeated.

Sam and Boy and Henry Steel had already saddled up. The horses stood in the corral ready to go. The men mounted up and rode toward the lion cage.

"Let them smell of him," Sam said. It was with some difficulty that they got the horses close to the cage, but those fellers were excellent horsemen and they could make a horse do just about anything they wanted him to. After the first shock of the lion scent had worn off, they were able to ride the horses around in circles, right up close to the lion cage.

Leo sensed that something was about to happen. He bristled his big mane, got up onto his feet and stood peering out with his little yellow eyes. It wasn't easy to get the rope around his neck. One man had to ease a little loop through the bars and try to get it around past those jaws that were already biting at it. Leo had been raised in a zoo, but he had never had close physical contact with man. His natural instincts told him they were going to do something that he didn't like. He was growling deep down in his throat.

Finally they got the rope around Leo's neck. They threaded the long end out over the top of the gate and handed the rope to Green Valley Sam. Sam tied hard and fast to the saddle horn.

"Open the gate!" he shouted.

Someone worked the latch loose and swung the gate wide, opening the whole front of the cage. But Leo wouldn't come out. Instead, he crouched, as if to spring, the tip of his tail twitching nervously. Sam put the spurs to his horse and yanked Leo out; the lion came out of the cage with a mighty bound. When the rope went taut, Leo leaped high in the air and began fighting the rope. This was the end as far as the great lion was concerned. It was to be a fight to the death. His eyes had turned green; he was leaping high in the air and then rolling on the ground as he clawed and bit at the rope. The tranquil valley echoed and reverberated with the roars of the African lion.

Boy had made a loop in his rope. He spurred his old flea-bit grey. He rode forward, swinging the rope round and round his head. As Leo came past him on one of his charges, Boy threw the loop and roped him by both hind feet. Boy went one way and Sam the other, between them, stretching the lion out to his full length. Leo was trying to bite the rope, but they had him stretched out so tight he couldn't get a hold of it. But he was clawing fiercely with his powerful front feet.

"Get a rope on those front feet!" Sam shouted. Henry Steel ran forward with a rope, got it on one front foot, then got a half-hitch on the other, then bound them tightly together. Sam gave a little slack so Leo could get a breath, then tightened up again. Henry tied the two hind feet just below Boy's rope.

"Now get a stick in his mouth!" Sam yelled. A stick of oak, cookstove wood, about fifteen inches long was just right. Henry tied a half-hitch on one end of it, then when Leo opened his mouth to bite, rammed it in the big cat's mouth cross-ways, locking the powerful jaws open. He then brought the rope over back of Leo's head and tied it to the other end of the stick. Sam gave a little more slack to let the lion get a breath, then tightened up again. Henry put a loop around the front feet; Boy gave some slack on the hind feet. Pulling hard, he pulled the hind feet up over the front ones and took a turn. All he had to do then was take a few more turns and tie the rope, and Leo was tied down, totally helpless. All Leo could do was strain on the ropes and growl.

Once Leo was immobilized, the men could work on him. Sam raised the lion's lip and looked at the powerful teeth. Expertly he examined the wounds. "Yep, pretty bad case of worms in this one," he said. Picking up a small stick, he dug out some of the yellow wriggling worms. He pulled his knife and cut the entry wound a little bigger. "Easier to get to the worms this way," he said casually.

The men collected the medicine and went to work. They squirted Peerless Screw-Worm Medicine into the wound. It would kill the worms on contact. Took the little stick and dug out the dead ones, then squirted in some more medicine. Once the worms were all killed and there was nothing but puss and bloody water coming out of the wound, Sam saturated a piece of cotton in pine tar and stuffed it into the wound with a little stick. Then he brushed pine tar around the wound for a space as big as a man's hand.

"All done," Sam said. "The Peerless kills the worms and the pine tar will keep the flies away. Might tell that feller, Veterinarian, to smear some more pine tar on it in a week or so."

Sam and Boy, Lou Pyle, Henry Steel and Ernie Sweat were all seasoned cowhands. From the time they were small boys they had ridden half-wild horses, went plunging off of mountain sides and down the brushy canyons in pursuit of wild cattle. By the time they were teenagers, they were masters of their trade. They had doctored wild range bulls that were probably more dangerous than any African lion. They had trapped and gathered wild horses and castrated the stallions. These fellers could hold their own in any cow outfit, and could ride just about any man's horse! But in doctoring Leo, they set a record. Their record still stands: they are the only cowboys in the U.S.A. who ever roped an African lion by neck and hind feet, then tied him down and doctored him for screwworms.

After having doctored the worms, there was still the job of getting Leo back into the cage and taking the ropes off him. However, that was just a minor job for Green Valley Sam. He put the rope around his neck, then threaded it out through the back of the cage, then mounted up, took his dallies, and gave his horse the spurs. He drug the lion like dragging a dead cow, right up into the back of the cage. Someone closed the gate. When tying the knots, Henry had known that they would have to be untied, so he had left a loop in each one. All a man had to do was put his arm through the bars on the cage and pull the loops. The ropes would work themselves loose.

Leo was mad as a wet hen. He was turning round and round in his cage and acting like he was going to try to break out. He was probably physically able to tear the bars apart with his powerful claws if he actually tried.

"Better go over to the house and leave him to cool off for a while," Sam said.

Kratzberg looked at the formidable mountains looming up in every direction. "Heavens, if he got loose in *this* country we'd never catch him," he shuddered.

"Be no problem," Sam said confidently. "We have some hounds that would hold him at bay."

Kratzberg was awed at the confidence of these rugged, self-reliant men. Of course, the country was wild and rugged. So it stood to reason that the men in it would also have to be rugged to survive.

After retreating to the shade of the porch, the men sat around and whittled, and drank coffee and talked. Grady and Sam were doing most of the talking, and the other fellows just sat there and listened. They were reminiscing about their fishing trips off in Tonto above Hells Gate. They would ride across, through the Green Valley Hills, and work their way off into Tonto. There were swarms of trout down there, some of them big ones. No one had ever thrown a line in those big blue holes and the fish were gullible and unafraid of the sight of a man standing on the bank. The cowmen would carry a roll of fish line and a few hooks, and then they got down to where they were going to fish, they'd cut a willow pole and tie on hook and line, then catch some grasshoppers for bait. A man could just let a grasshopper float through a little swift water to where it emptied into a pool and he'd usually catch a fish. They didn't have to settle for little ones, so they would throw all the little ones back and keep the big ones. Then when they would come out of there with a half gunny sack full of big ones, they would have their fun by telling people that all the fish in the creek were that size. They spoke of the time they'd been fishing in a box canyon a ways up from Hells Gate. It was a nice day and the sun was shining bright. They hadn't paid any attention to the black clouds that were laced with lightning, up next to the Mogollon Rim. They were obsessed with their fishing, oblivious of time and place, when they looked up and saw a ten-foot wall of water rushing down upon them. They were barely able to scramble up a crevass to higher ground before the wall of water arrived. They were on the opposite side of the creek from their horses so they had to wait the rest of the day and part of the night before the water subsided enough for them to wade across. The talk went on.

After a couple of hours, Leo had calmed down enough that Sam figured it was safe to go ahead and load the cage onto Grady's truck.

Leo was a sensation in Payson. The people didn't know who Metro-Goldwyn-Meyer was, or Jensen or Kratzberg, for that matter. But old Leo was an immediate hit. They ganged around his cage, trying to feed him various things, with Kratzberg flitting about trying to keep them from it.

And so was the saga of Leo the Lion. When you see the trademark of MGM, and Leo turns his head with his mouth half-open, look closely at his pock-marked face and his scarred ear. They are not just make-believe. Old Leo has weathered some pretty tough storms.

HOW TO STOP A RATTLESNAKE'S RATTLE

Don Dedera

DON DEDERA SPENT PART of his boyhood at Sacaton on the Pima Reservation, where his father was doing scientific research, and went to high school in Casa Grande. He graduated from Arizona State University with a major in journalism and spent the next thirty years as a newsman, rising to become a columnist of the *Arizona Republic*. In 1983 he became editor of *Arizona Highways*, leaving to become a freelance writer. He has produced eight books and over two hundred major magazine articles, his favorite subjects being Arizona history, folklore and humor which he collects and retails with great gusto and enjoyment.

CHAMPIE RANCH–It is not every day that a man has to soak the tail of a rattlesnake, and to this fact Francis D. Hyde attributed his cheerful nature.

"Once was enough," said Frank.

He used to be a broker with a seat on the New York Stock Exchange. In the '30s he took his biggest flier. He closed his business and came to Arizona to find and mine metal. The sledge coarsened his hands, and the weather tanned his face, but he kept his Northeastern twang. He established main diggin's about 6 miles from the Champie dude ranch.

"We had killed a rattlesnake on the morning we were visited by a doctor from the American Museum of Natural History of New York," said Frank. "He was collecting specimens.

"We showed him around the mine. He was a pleasant sort until he saw the dead rattlesnake.

"'You fools!' he shouted. 'Why did you kill that snake?'

From *A Mile in His Moccasins*. Phoenix: McGrew Printing and Lithographing Co. 1960, pp. 151–152.

" 'Because we didn't want to be bitten,' we told him.

" 'Well, that is a very rare kind of black-tail rattlesnake, and I want to find its mate for the museum.' "

The second snake was cornered, and according to Frank, the doctor pinned the snake with a stubby, rotten stick.

"Hold that ore sack," commanded the doctor.

Frank reluctantly obeyed. The doctor swept the writhing reptile into the poke.

Frank said he thought that would be the end of it, "but I was the only one in the party with saddlebags. The doctor put the sacked snake into my pack, and I got up on my horse, a skittish roan mare.

"The snake buzzed, and the horse broke into full gallop.

"I couldn't stop her. She came down the canyon faster than she ever ran before, down that canyon that drops 700 feet in the course of a few miles. Thirst, I guess, finally stopped her at a little spring. It must have been a half-hour before the doctor caught up."

The naturalist was angry. "That was a terrible way to treat a rare museum specimen," he shot at Frank. Then the doctor removed the groggy snake from the saddle bags, revived it, and held its tail in the spring water.

"You know," said Frank, "those rattles became soft in the water, and no matter how fast that snake wriggled its tail, the rattles would make no noise. We brought in the snake without further trouble, by stopping to soak the snake's tail in every water hole along the way."

If anybody doubts this story, said Frank, he can prove it by showing them the water holes.

THE WAY WE LIVE NOW

There was a lady named Jessie with wild white hair and floppy rainboots who would dash into restaurants and scrounge the leftover fruit and melon rinds.

Novelist Barbara Kingsolver brings us up to date with pictures of the people we know and the things we live with. It all seems familiar—sometimes painfully familiar, and we realize, if we stop to think about it, that when we laugh, we are laughing at ourselves.

TAYLOR AND TURTLE FIND A HOME

Barbara Kingsolver

WE WERE IN TROUBLE. I lasted six days at the Burger Derby before I got in a fight with the manager and threw my red so-called jockey cap in the trash compactor and walked out. I would have thrown the whole uniform in there, but I didn't feel like giving him a free show.

I won't say that working there didn't have its moments. When Sandi and I worked the morning shift together we'd have a ball. I would tell her all kinds of stories I'd heard about horse farms, such as the fact that the really high-strung horses had TVs in their stalls. It was supposed to lower their blood pressure.

"Their favorite show is old reruns of Mr. Ed," I would tell her with a poker face.

"No! You're kidding. Are you kidding me?"

"And they *hate* the commercials for Knox gelatin."

She was easy to tease, but I had to give her credit, considering that life had delivered Sandi a truckload of manure with no return address. The father of her baby had told everyone that Sandi was an admitted schizophrenic and had picked his name out of the high school yearbook when she found out she was pregnant. Soon afterward the boy's father got transferred from Tucson and the whole family moved to Oakland, California. Sandi's mother had made her move out, and she lived with her older sister Aimee, who was born again and made her pay rent. In Aimee's opinion it would have been condoning sin to let Sandi and her illegitimate son stay there for free.

But nothing really seemed to throw Sandi. She knew all about things like how to rub an ice cube on kids' gums when they were

From *The Bean Trees*, by Barbara Kingsolver. New York: HarperCollins Publishers, 1988, pp. 66–76.

teething, and where to get secondhand baby clothes for practically nothing. We would take turns checking on Turtle and Seattle, and at the end of our shift we'd go over to the mall together to pick them up. "I don't know," she'd say real loud, hamming it up while we waited in line at Kid Central Station. "I can't decide if I want that Lazyboy recliner in the genuine leather or the green plaid with the stainproof finish." "Take your time deciding," I'd say. "Sleep on it and come back tomorrow."

Turtle would be sitting wherever I had set her down that morning, with each hand locked onto some ratty, punked-out stuffed dog or a torn book or another kid's jacket and her eyes fixed on some empty point in the air, just the way a cat will do. It's as though they live in a separate universe that takes up the same space as ours, but is full of fascinating things like mice or sparrows or special TV programs that we can't see.

Kid Central Station was not doing Turtle any good. I knew that.

After six days the Burger Derby manager Jerry Speller, this little twerp who believed that the responsibility of running a burger joint put you a heartbeat away from Emperor of the Universe, said I didn't have the right attitude, and I told him he was exactly right. I said I had to confess I didn't have the proper reverence for the Burger Derby institution, and to prove it I threw my hat into the Mighty Miser and turned it on. Sandi was so impressed she burned the french fries twice in a row.

The fight had been about the Burger Derby uniform. The shorts weren't actually plastic, it turned out, but cotton-polyester with some kind of shiny finish that had to be dry-cleaned. Three twenty-five an hour plus celery and you're supposed to pay for dry-cleaning your own shorts.

My one regret was that I didn't see much of Sandi anymore. Naturally I had to find a new place to eat breakfast. There were half a dozen coffeeshops in the area, and although I didn't really feel at home in any of them I discovered a new resource: newspapers. On the tables, along with their gritty coffee cups and orange rinds and croissant crumbs, people often left behind the same day's paper.

There was a lady named Jessie with wild white hair and floppy rainboots who would dash into the restaurants and scrounge the leftover fruit and melon rinds. "It's not to eat," she would explain to any-and everybody as she clumped along the sidewalk pushing an interesting-smelling shopping cart that had at some point in history belonged to Safeway. "It's for still-lifes." She told me she painted nothing but madonnas: Orange-peel madonna. Madonna and child with strawberries. Together we made a sort of mop-up team. I nabbed the newspapers, and she took the rest.

Looking through the want ads every day gave new meaning to my life. The For Rents, on the other hand, were a joke as far as I was concerned, but often there would be ads looking for room-mates, a possibility I hadn't considered. I would circle anything that looked promising, although people seemed unbelievably picky about who they intended to live with:

"Mature, responsible artist or grad student wanted for co-operative household; responsibilities shared, sensitivity a must."

"Female vegetarian nonsmoker to share harmonious space with insightful Virgo and cat."

I began to suspect that sharing harmonious space with an insightful Virgo might require even greater credentials than being a licensed phlebotomist in the state of Arizona.

The main consideration, though, was whether or not I could locate the address on my Sun-Tran maps of all the various bus routes. At the end of the week I made up my mind to check out a couple of possibilities. One ad said, among other things, "Must be open to new ideas." The other said, "New mom needs company. Own room, low rent, promise I won't bother you. Kids ok." The first sounded like an adventure, and the second sounded like I wouldn't have to pass a test. I put on a pair of stiff, clean jeans and braided my hair and gave Turtle a bath in the sink. She had acquired clothes of her own by now, but just for old time's sake I put her in my DAMN I'M GOOD T-shirt from Kentucky Lake. Just for luck.

Both places were near downtown. The first was a big old ramshackle house with about twelve kinds of wind chimes hanging on the front porch. One was made from the silver keys of some kind of musical instrument like a flute or clarinet, and even Turtle seemed interested in it. A woman came to the door before I even knocked.

She let me inside and called out, "The prospective's here." Three silver earrings–a half moon, a star, and a grinning sun–

dangled from holes in her left ear so that she clinked when she walked like some human form of wind chime. She was barefoot and had on a skirt that reminded me of the curtains in my room at the Republic. There was no actual furniture in the room, only a colorful rug and piles of pillows here and there, so I waited to see what she would do. She nested herself into one of the piles, flouncing her skirt out over her knees. I noticed that she had thin silver rings on four of her toes.

Another woman came out of the kitchen door, through which I was relieved to see a table and chairs. A tall, thin guy with a hairless chest hunkered in another doorway for a minute, rubbing a head of orange hair that looked like a wet cat. He had on only those beachcomber-type pants held up by a fake rope. I really couldn't tell how old these people were. I kept expecting a parent to show up in another doorway and tell Beach Blanket Bingo to put on his shirt, but then they could have been older than me. We all settled down on the pillows.

"I'm Fay," the toe-ring woman said, "spelled F-E-I, and this is La-Isha and that's Timothy. You'll have to excuse Timothy; he used caffeine yesterday and now his homeostasis is out of balance." I presumed they were talking about his car, although I was not aware of any automotive uses for caffeine.

"That's too bad," I said. "I wouldn't do anything with caffeine but drink it."

They all stared at me for a while.

"Oh. I'm Taylor. This is Turtle."

"Turtle. Is that a spirit name?" La-Isha asked.

"Sure," I said.

La-Isha was thick-bodied, with broad bare feet and round calves. Her dress was a sort of sarong, printed all over with black and orange elephants and giraffes, and she had a jungly-looking scarf wrapped around her head. And to think they used to stare at me for wearing red and turquoise together. Drop these three in Pittman County and people would run for cover.

F-E-I took charge of the investigation. "Would the child be living here too?"

"Right. We're a set."

"That's cool, I have no problem with small people," she said. "La-Isha, Timothy?"

"It's not really what I was thinking in terms of, but I can see it happening. I'm flex on children," La-Isha said, after giving it some thought. Timothy said he thought the baby was cute, asked if it was a boy or a girl.

"A girl," I said, but I was drowned out by Fei saying, "Timothy, I *really* don't see that that's an issue here." She said to me, "Gender is not an issue in this house."

"Oh,"I said. "Whatever."

"What does she eat?" La-Isha wanted to know.

"Mainly whatever she can get her hands on. She had half a hot dog with mustard for breakfast."

There was another one of those blank spells in the conversation. Turtle was grumpily yanking at a jingle bell on the corner of a pillow, and I was beginning to feel edgy myself. All those knees and chins at the same level. It reminded me of an extremely long movie I had once seen about an Arabian sheik. Maybe La-Isha is Arabian, I thought, though she looked very white, with blond hair on her arms and pink rims around her eyes. Possibly an albino Arabian. I realized she was giving a lecture of some kind.

"At least four different kinds of toxins," she was saying, more to the room in general than to me. Her pink-rimmed eyes were starting to look inflamed. "In a hot dog." Now she was definitely talking to me. "Were you aware of that?"

"I would have guessed seven or eight," I said.

"Nitrites," said Timothy. He was gripping his head between his palms, one on the chin and one on top, and bending it from side to side until you could hear a little pop. I began to understand about the unbalanced homeostasis.

"We eat mainly soybean products here," Fei said. "We're just starting a soy-milk collective. A house requirement is that each person spend at least seven hours a week straining curd."

"Straining curd," I said. I wanted to say, Flaming nurd. Raining turds. It isn't raining turds, you know, it's raining violets.

"Yes," Fei went on in this abnormally calm voice that made me want to throw a pillow at her. "I guess the child..."

"Turtle," I said.

"I guess Turtle would be exempt. But we have to make adjustments for that in the kitchen quota...."

I had trouble concentrating. La-Isha kept narrowing her eyes and trying to get Fei's attention. I remembered Mrs. Hoge with her shakes, always looking like she was secretly saying, "Don't do it" to somebody behind you.

"So tell us about you," Fei said eventually. I snapped out of my daydreams, feeling like a kid in school that's just been called on. "What kind of a space are you envisioning for yourself?" she wanted to know. Those were her actual words.

"Oh, Turtle and I are flex," I said. "Right now we're staying downtown at the Republic. I jockeyed fried food at the Burger Derby for a while, but I got fired."

La-Isha went kind of stiff on that one. I imagined all the little elephants on her shift getting stung through the heart with a tiny stun gun. Timothy was trying to get Turtle's attention by making faces, so far with no luck.

"Usually little kids are into faces," he informed me. "She seems kind of spaced out."

"She makes up her own mind about what she's into."

"She sure has a lot of hair," he said. "How old is she?"

"Eighteen months," I said. It was a wild guess.

"She looks very Indian."

"Native American," Fei corrected him. "She does. Is her father Native American?"

"Her great-great-grandpa was full-blooded Cherokee," I said. "On my side. Cherokee skips a generation, like red hair. Didn't you know that?"

The second house on my agenda turned out to be right across the park from Jesus is Lord's. It belonged to Lou Ann Ruiz. Within ten minutes Lou Ann and I were in the kitchen drinking diet Pepsi and splitting our gussets laughing about homeostasis and bean turds. We had already established that our hometowns in Kentucky were separated by only two counties, and that we had both been to the exact same Bob Seger concert at the Kentucky State Fair my senior year.

"So then what happened?" Lou Ann had tears in her eyes. I hadn't really meant to put them down, they seemed like basically good kids, but it just got funnier as it went along.

"Nothing happened. In their own way, they were so polite it was pathetic. I mean, it was plain as day they thought Turtle was a dimwit and I was from some part of Mars where they don't have indoor bathrooms, but they just kept on asking things like would I like some alfalfa tea?" I had finally told them no thanks, that we'd just run along and envision ourselves in some other space.

Lou Ann showed me the rest of the house except for her room, where the baby was asleep. Turtle and I would have our own room, plus the screened-in back porch if we wanted it. She said it was great to sleep out there in the summer. We had to whisper around the house so we wouldn't wake the baby.

"He was just born in January," Lou Ann said when we were back in the kitchen. "How old's yours?"

"To tell you the truth, I don't even know. She's adopted."

"Well, didn't they tell you all that stuff when you adopted her? Didn't she come with a birth certificate or something?"

"It wasn't an official adoption. Somebody just kind of gave her to me."

"You mean like she was left on your doorstep in a basket?"

"Exactly. Except it was in my car, and there wasn't any basket. Now that I think about it, there should have at least been a basket. Indians made good baskets. She's Indian."

"Wasn't there even a note? How do you know her name's Turtle?"

"I don't. I named her that. It's just temporary until I can figure out what her real name is. I figure I'll hit on it sooner or later."

Turtle was in a high chair of Lou Ann's that must have been way too big for a kid born in January. On the tray there were decals of Kermit the Frog and Miss Piggy, which Turtle was slapping with her hands. There was nothing there for her to grab. I picked her up out of the chair and hefted her onto my shoulder, where she could reach my braid. She didn't pull it, she just held on to it like a lifeline. This was one of our normal positions.

"I can't get over it." Lou Ann said, "that somebody would just dump her like an extra puppy."

"Yeah, I know. I think it was somebody that cared for her, though, if you can believe it. Turtle was having a real rough time. I don't know if she would have made it where she was." A fat gray cat with white feet was sleeping on the windowsill over the sink. Or so I thought, until all of a sudden it jumped down and streaked out of the kitchen. Lou Ann had her back to the door, but I could see the cat in the next room. It was walking around in circles on the living-room rug, kicking its feet behind it again and again, throwing invisible sand over invisible cat poop.

"You wouldn't believe what your cat is doing," I said.

"Oh yes, I would," Lou Ann said. "He's acting like he just went potty, right?"

"Right. But he didn't, as far as I can see."

"Oh, no, he never does. I think he has a split personality. The good cat wakes up and thinks the bad cat has just pooped on the rug. See, we got him as a kitty and I named him Snowboots but Angel thought that was a stupid name so he always called him Pachuco instead. Then a while back, before Dwayne Ray was born, he started acting that way. Angel's my ex-husband, by the way."

It took some effort here to keep straight who was cats and who was husbands.

Lou Ann went on. "So just the other day I read in a magazine that a major cause of split personality is if two parents treat a kid in real different ways, like one all the time tells the kid it's good and the other one says it's bad. It gives them this idea they have to be both ways at once."

"That's amazing," I said. "Your cat ought to be in *Ripley's Believe It or Not*. Or one of those magazine columns where people write in and tell what cute things their pets do, like parakeets that whistle Dixie or cats that will only sleep on a certain towel with pictures of goldfish on it."

"Oh, I wouldn't want anyone to know about Snowboots, it's too embarrassing. It's just about proof-positive that he's from a broken home, don't you think?"

"What does Pachuco mean?"

"It means like a bad Mexican boy. One that would go around spray-painting walls and join a gang."

Pachuco alias Snowboots was still going at it in the living room. "Seriously," I said, "you should send it in. They'd probably pay good money—it's unbelievable what kinds of things you can get paid for. Or at the very least they'd send you a free case of cat chow."

"I almost won a year of free diapers for Dwayne Ray. Dwayne Ray's my son."

"Oh. What does he do?"

Lou Ann laughed. "Oh, he's normal. The only one in the house, I guess. Do you want some more Pepsi?" She got up to refill our glasses. "So did you drive out here, or fly, or what?"

I told her that driving across the Indian reservation was how I'd ended up with Turtle. "Our paths would never have crossed if it weren't for a bent rocker arm."

"Well, if something had to go wrong, at least you can thank your stars you were in a car and not an airplane," she said, whacking an ice-cube tray on the counter. I felt Turtle flinch on my shoulder.

"I never thought of it that way," I said.

"I could never fly in an airplane. Oh Lord, never! Remember that one winter when a plane went right smack dab into that frozen river in Washington, D.C.? On TV I saw them pulling the bodies out frozen stiff with their knees and arms bent like those little plastic cowboys that are supposed to be riding horses, but then when you lose the horse they're useless. Oh, God, that was so pathetic. I can just hear the stewardess saying, 'Fasten your seat belts, folks,' calm as you please, like 'Don't worry, we just have to say this,' and then next thing you know you're a hunk of ice. Oh, shoot, there's Dwayne Ray just woke up from his nap. Let me go get him."

I did remember that airplane crash. On TV they showed the rescue helicopter dropping down a rope to save the only surviving stewardess from an icy river full of dead people. I remember just how she looked hanging on to that rope. Like Turtle.

In a minute Lou Ann came back with the baby. "Dwayne Ray, here's some nice people I want you to meet. Say hi."

He was teeny, with skin you could practically see through. It reminded me of the Visible Man we'd had in Hughes Walter's biology class. "He's adorable," I said.

"Do you think so, really? I mean, I love him to death of course, but I keep thinking his head's flat."

"They all are. They start out that way, and then after a while their foreheads kind of pop out."

"Really? I never knew that. They never told me that."

"Sure. I used to work in a hospital. I saw a lot of newborns coming and going, and every one of them's head was flat as a shovel."

She made a serious face and fussed with the baby for a while without saying anything.

"So what do you think?" I finally said. "Is it okay if we move in?"

"Sure!" Her wide eyes and the way she held her baby reminded me for a minute of Sandi. The lady downtown could paint either one of them: "Bewildered Madonna with Sunflower Eyes." "Of course you can move in," she said. "I'd love it. I wasn't sure if you'd want to."

"Why wouldn't I want to?"

"Well, my gosh, I mean, here you are, so skinny and smart and cute and everything, and me and Dwayne Ray, well, we're just lumping along here trying to get by. When I put that ad in the paper, I thought, Well, this is sure four dollars down the toilet; who in the world would want to move in here with us?"

"Stop it, would you? Quit making everybody out to be better than you are. I'm just plain hillbilly from East Jesus Nowhere with this adopted child that everybody keeps on telling me is dumb as a box of rocks. I've got nothing on you, girl. I mean it."

Lou Ann hid her mouth with her hand.

"What?" I said.

"Nothing." I could see perfectly well that she was smiling.

"Come on, what is it?"

"It's been so long," she said. "You talk just like me."